The Handbook for Museums

The Handbook for Museums provides essential ba   ..... .u. people working in the museum world. It presents theory and practice to emphasize the responsibilities of the museum worker and the public service role prescribed by the museum community. The book offers general instruction in the standards and ethics of the community.

The contents of The Handbook for Museums are formed around a commitment to professionalism in museum practice. The sections provide basic information on management security, care of collections, conservation, and education, and each section includes technical notes, questions from the field, and an international further reading list. The book is intended as a manual for creating and managing training courses, and for experienced museum practitioners in service who wish to upgrade their skills in marketing or management. It provides a definitive guide to "best practice" at a time in which museums require even more innovative solutions to processes of interpreting the world's cultural and scientific heritage.

The authors have extensive experience of day-to-day museum practice in the USA, and teach one of the most highly regarded Museum Studies courses in North America. They have also taught museum professionals in Latin America and the Far East.

The Handbook for Museums will be of great interest to students of Museum Studies and professionals in the museum world.

The Heritage: Care–Preservation–Management programme has been designed to serve the needs of the museum and heritage community worldwide. It publishes books and information services for professional museum and heritage workers, and for all the organizations that service the museum community.

Editor-in-chief: Andrew Wheatcroft

Architecture in Conservation: *Managing developments at historic sites*
James Strike

The Development of Costume
Naomi Tarrant

Forward Planning: *A handbook of business, corporate and development planning for museums and galleries*
Edited by Timothy Ambrose and Sue Runyard

Heritage Gardens: *Care, conservation and management*
Sheena Mackellar Goulty

Heritage and Tourism: *in the 'global village'*
Priscilla Boniface and Peter J. Fowler

The Industrial Heritage: *Managing resources and uses*
Judith Alfrey and Tim Putnam

Managing Quality Cultural Tourism
Priscilla Boniface

Museum Basics
Timothy Ambrose and Crispin Paine

Museum Exhibition: *Theory and practice*
David Dean

Museum, Media, Message
Edited by Eilean Hooper-Greenhill

Museum Security and Protection: *A handbook for cultural heritage institutions*
ICOM and ICMS

Museums: *A place to work – planning museum careers*
Jane R. Glaserjv with Artemis A. Zenetou

Museums 2000: *Politics, people, professionals and profit*
Edited by Patrick J. Boylan

Museums and the Shaping of Knowledge
Eilean Hooper-Greenhill

Museums and their Visitors
Eilean Hooper-Greenhill

Museums without Barriers: *A new deal for disabled people*
Fondation de France and ICOM

The Past in Contemporary Society: *Then/Now*
Peter J. Fowler

The Representation of the Past: *Museums and heritage in the post-modern world*
Kevin Walsh

Towards the Museum of the Future: *New European perspectives*
Edited by Roger Miles and Lauro Zavala

The Handbook for Museums

Gary Edson and David Dean

London and New York

First published 1994
by Routledge
11 New Fetter Lane, London EC4P 4EE

Simultaneously published in the USA and Canada
by Routledge
29 West 35th Street, New York, NY 10001

Reprinted 1996

First published in paperback 1996

Reprinted 2000

Routledge is an imprint of the Taylor & Francis Group

Typeset by Florencetype Ltd, Stoodleigh, Devon

Printed and bound in Great Britain by
Butler & Tanner Ltd, Frome, Somerset

British Library Cataloguing in Publication Data
A catalogue record for this book is available from the British Library

Library of Congress Cataloguing in Publication Data
Edson, Gary
The handbook for museums / Gary Edson and David Dean.
p. cm. – (The Heritage)
Includes bibliographical references and index.
1. Museums – Handbooks, manuals, etc. I. Dean, David. II. Title.
III. Series.
AM5.E37 1994
069'.5 – dc20   93–3881

ISBN 0–415–09952–8 (hbk)
ISBN 0–415–09953–6 (pbk)

This book is
para aquellos que vienen mas tarde.

Contents

Figures

Foreword

The publication of this handbook is without a question a major milestone in the history of museum management. For in spite of the large amount of literature covering virtually every aspect of the subject, there has not been, until now, one single volume which summarized basic principles, analyzed the reasons for their existence and provided guidelines for implementation.

It is, as well, a textbook for instruction and will be especially useful to those institutions that have courses in museum management. It strongly expresses dos and don'ts and in some of its chapters it may seem uncompromising in allowing for few exceptions. That is the nature of such an instructional work. It establishes a structure and defines hierarchies while inviting each institution and reader to consider the given imperatives within the framework of their own needs and the requirements dictated by local law and custom.

The publication of such a volume marks a new stage in the maturity of a profession which for decades has not attempted to define itself, let alone formally recognize that within its collective activities it did constitute a profession within which there were a large number of individual, but interrelated, disciplines.

There is no doubt, had such a volume been in existence a few decades ago, that practices currently in place in many institutions whether in the United States, Europe or other parts of the world, might be very different. The safety of collections, respect for their care, legality of their growth and their effectiveness as instruments of learning and social betterment, and the day-to-day handling of the myriad of aspects of museum administration, would all be more refined than they are now. Perhaps more important, we would be closer to having parity among institutions, across geographic, linguistic and political boundaries.

I commend this volume to a careful reading. It is replete with strong dos and uncompromising don'ts. This aspect should be studied with particular care for no matter how autocratic some of these admonishments may be, there is a strong reason for their expression and there should be an even stronger reason for interpreting these principles with laxity and ignoring their intent.

As a handbook for those who are attempting to bring their museums into the twenty-first century, it is a splendidly complete guide. For those who are thinking of creating a new museum, which after all is a very easy thing to do, it may be particularly sobering to study and understand the complex undertaking they are contemplating. The acquisition of a building, the development of a collection and the hiring of a staff are but the beginnings of a task which has and can have no end. Once acquired, the collections must be nurtured, the environment stabilized, the social usage expanded with all of the costs, mental, physical and monetary, which this entails. Hence, I view this volume in addition to being a useful guide to sharpen professional practices, as a virtual necessity for those that are contemplating creating new museums.

It is clear to this writer that our most immediate priority is not necessarily to create new museums, but to improve those that exist, to develop closer means of cooperation among them, to heighten their sense of ethical and social responsibility in the preservation, use and interpretation of irreplaceable resources for this and future generations. These goals, implied in the creation of the International Council of Museums in 1946, will be closer to realization on account of this thoughtful and clearly expressed volume.

Paul N. Perrot
October 1993

Preface

> Members of the museum profession have an obligation, subject to due acknowledgment, to share their knowledge and experience with their colleagues and with scholars and students in relevant fields. They should show their appreciation and respect to those from whom they have learned and should present without thought of personal gain such advancements in techniques and experience which may be of benefit to others.[1]

This publication offers a broad base of information designed to present both the theory and practice of the museum profession. It defines the role of the museum worker, describes ethical responsibilities, and reiterates the public service role prescribed by the museum profession. The text offers instruction in the standards and ethics of the museum community. It also reinforces the ideals of responsible stewardship of the cultural and scientific heritage of the world.

Museum workers come to the profession from diverse backgrounds. There is no field of study that is preparatory for a career in museum work. Each person chooses a museum career for a personal, and often ill-defined reason. The common factor is a desire to be a part of special institutions of research and service where new ideas and technology commingle with timeless treasures. It is the complex alchemy that gives the museum profession much of its strength.

The contents of this book are formed around a commitment to professionalism in museum practices. The sections are designed to provide basic information and to prepare the museum workers for a productive future. The methods and techniques described are solidly based on established practices. However, no technology is static. The learning process is continuous. Persons charged with the protection of our common wealth must recognize the positions of authority and trust they hold. They should strive to expand their base of knowledge about museum practices and share that information with the museum community.

"The training of personnel in the specialized activities involved in museum work is of great importance in the development of the profession and all should accept responsibility, where appropriate, in the training of colleagues."

ICOM, *Code of Professional Ethics*, section 8, "Personal Responsibility to Colleagues and the Profession," paragraph 8.2, p. 34.

The text is divided into sections and each section includes Technical Notes, Questions from the Field, and Suggested Reading. The Questions from the Field are questions asked by participants in a course and lecture series conducted in Latin America. They are included in this publication for two reasons: the first is that they document the problems and opportunities shared by most museums. The second is to show that almost every situation occurring in a museum setting is complex and involves more than one act or action.

One of the greatest dangers of publishing a book of "standardized" museum practices and procedures is the perpetuation of past norms without consideration of current needs. The museum community is dynamic. The changing role of museums requires creative and innovative solutions to processes of preserving and interpreting the world's cultural and scientific heritage.

Gary Edson
David Dean
Museum of Texas Tech University
Lubbock, Texas, USA
1993

Note

1. International Council of Museums (1990) "Personal Responsibility to Colleagues and the Profession," *Code of Professional Ethics*, Paris: ICOM.

Acknowledgments

The acknowledgment of the contributions made by many people and organizations to this publication is appropriate. They are as follows.

A special thanks to Elisabeth des Portes, Secretary General of ICOM and Hubert Landais, Chairperson of the ICOM Ethics Committee for allowing us to publish the *Code of Professional Ethics*. Also thanks to the American Association of Museums for allowing the use of the *Museum News* published material: the Code of Ethics for Curators, the Code of Ethics for Registrars, and "Developing a Collection Management Policy," by Marie C. Malaro. The Eiteljorg Museum of American Indian and Cowboy Art was generous enough to authorize the inclusion of their Collection Management Policy. For the job descriptions included in Chapter 2, we owe thanks to those who compiled the information in the 1988 edition of *Museum Studies International* published through the efforts of the Smithsonian Institution and the ICOM Committee on Museum Training (ICTOP). Particular recognition should go to Jane Glaser and Patrick Boylan for their work on that publication.

As the initial work on the material for this book was stimulated by a workshop/course and lecture series in Ecuador, we thank Lucia Astudillo, Presidenta de la ICOM organización regional para america latina y el caribe for organizing the event. Also in Ecuador thanks must go to Juan Carlos Fernandez at the Casa de la Cultura, Jerome Oetgen and Martha Alban at the American Embassy, and all the wonderful museum people of Ecuador and Peru who made the workshop/course so enjoyable and informative. This book is dedicated to them and all the others who will make the museums of tomorrow better than they are today.

The Ecuador trip was funded in part by the United States Information Agency and for their financial assistance we thank them. Without that initial push the workshop/course might never have happened.

The Museum and Museum Science Program of Texas Tech University supported the production of this *Handbook* in many ways and we wish to recognize that assistance. Thanks is also due Dr Donald R. Haragan, Executive Vice President and Provost of Texas Tech University, and Dr Len Ainsworth, Vice Provost, for their support and encouragement with this project.

Finally, thanks is due our wives Miriam Edson and Sue Dean. They allowed us time to work on the material, were patient when we missed appointments, read and commented on the text, and supported us in the process of completing the work. Thank you both!

Section I
Museum role and responsibility

Museums and community

> Museums, in the broadest sense, are institutions which hold their possessions in trust for humankind and for the future welfare of the [human] race. Their value is in direct proportion to the service they render the emotional and intellectual life of the people. The life of a museum worker . . . is essentially one of service.[1]

The word "museum" has had a variety of meanings through the centuries. In classical times it signified a temple dedicated to the Muses; nine young goddesses who watched over the welfare of the epic, music, love poetry, oratory, history, tragedy, comedy, the dance, and astronomy. History notes that the first organized museum was founded at Alexandria, Egypt in about the third century BC by Ptolemy Soter. It was destroyed during civil disturbances 600 years later. The museum had some objects, but it was primarily a university or philosophical community and philosophy in those days referred to all knowledge.[2] It was an institute of advanced study, supported by the state, with many prominent scholars in residence. Euclid headed the mathematics departments and Archimedes was on the faculty.

Following this early museum (mouseion) that focused on education, there was a long period of museological dormancy. Although objects of various kinds were gathered in many parts of the known world, most were either hoard collections accumulated for the monetary value of the objects or collections of curiosities gathered for their uniqueness.[3] In neither case was the primary motive human enlightenment.

The next period of museum development is associated with the Renaissance. The changes in collecting at that time, beginning in the fourteenth century and continuing through the sixteenth century, paralleled the advancements in the fine arts and science. It was a time of great change that saw a revision of world thinking to stress the importance of the role of intuitive knowledge and individual experience in the process of knowing. The focus shifted from a societal-centric to a human-centered universe. In many ways the circumstances were similar to that of today. The change today is from human-centered to global. In any case, the possibilities are so great and the directions so diverse, that although meaningful conclusions may be anticipated, the way of achieving them is confusing.

In the fifteenth century, Florence was the center of intellectual growth that supported the best of the arts and sciences. It was in this city that the word "museum" was first used to describe the collection of the Medici at the time of Lorenzo the Magnificent.[4] The systematic and scientific methodology to the understanding of humankind and nature had evolved by the sixteenth century, and museums as institutions of enlightenment had re-emerged.

In the 200 years between the Medici Gallery and the "public" museum of today there were a number of intermediate steps. The Ashmolean at Oxford in England is considered one of the first public museums of note. It opened in 1683. The British Museum, founded in 1753, admitted only a few selected individuals daily.[5] The Louvre was open to the public on a limited basis, but it was the French Revolution, in 1789, that made it a truly public facility.

The development of public museums was a gradual process. The concept of private collections being made available to the public is generally considered to be a European concept of museum evolution. In the United States, collection growth and public availability tended to go hand-in-hand. This process is exemplified by the museum established by the Charleston Library Society of South Carolina beginning in 1773. This museum promoted the concept of public service and education from the beginning, an attribute generally assigned to the museums of the US.

> "The people's museum should be much more than a house full of specimens in glass cases. It should be a house full of ideas, arranged with the strictest attention to system."
>
> (Attributed to George Brown Goode)[6]

Probably the first museum art exhibit in the United States was held in the Pennsylvania Academy of Fine Arts in 1807. The Institute established two years earlier, was organized to serve as both an art school and exhibition gallery. The featured paintings, at that first exhibit, were Shakespearean scenes by Benjamin West, and other exhibit pieces including a group of plaster casts made from statues in the Louvre. As many of the casts were of nude figures, one day each week was reserved for viewing by ladies, in order to spare them the embarrassment of having to look at the revealing statuary in the company of men.

From Charles Willson Peale's museological and entrepreneurial activities in Philadelphia beginning in 1785 to the establishing of the national museum in 1846, by an act of the US Senate, museum development in the US was a public affair. In the instructions left by James Smithson, the English donor who funded the museum that became the Smithsonian Institution, he described his intention to fund "the increase and diffusion of knowledge among men."

Joseph Henry, first Secretary of the Smithsonian, took the statement as written and began an effort toward research long before the United States had a graduate school in its professional institutions.[7] His plan came into operation eighteen years before a Ph.D. was awarded in the United States. Joseph Henry created a place that fostered research and publication with scholars either in residence or scattered about in a loose working relationship. In the museum, scholars could conduct research and exchange ideas with reference to tangible objects.

In the middle years of the twentieth century there were a number of external factors affecting the museum community. Funding was one factor. The cost of maintaining the collections, hiring qualified staff, and providing for the public began to increase beyond the assistance provided by affluent families or special interest groups. Another factor was television. Rare objects and distant lands were projected into individual homes. The need to visit the museum diminished. To these primary agents of change were added improved printing techniques that produced books with quality reproductions, and a more mobile society.

All these conditions were addressed by a single response – broaden the visitor base. The plan was to attract people to the museums that had not previously been museum-goers. By involving the public in the general well-being of the museum, visitorship and local support increased. There was a discernible movement among museums to address the perceived needs of the communities in which museums were located. For the most part, this effort was, and continues to be, in the form of audience confirmation and reassurance. The museum role is to interpret the familiar, or at least, the already known though not totally understood cultural, historical, and scientific ideas about the constituency. In this way the museum adds to and clarifies the cultural and intellectual prowess of the audience.

Using visitor evaluation as a base, some changes were carefully planned, others were formulated to address assumed needs or opportunities. Exhibitions, for the most part, became more gender, racial, ethnic, and idea inclusive. Museums reacted to their constituency and at the same time came to realize that they (museums) had a viable product to share with their audience – education. This level of museum activities currently exists, to a greater or lesser degree, in most parts of the world.

To prosper, museums must be clear about what they propose to do. Things must be understood before they can be interpreted. The recognition of cultural pluralism has served as the basis for collections, exhibitions, and new museums. The museum community has reacted to the constituency need by providing a forum to document and demonstrate diversity. However, globalization, world-wide economic and cultural interaction requires future thinking rather than response to existing conditions. The museum community has the means to provide leadership for tomorrow as well as documentation of today and yesterday.

Many communities have established museums as centers for learning and information to tell about the past and address current topics. Due, in part, to the many changes in the world order – political, social, cultural, and environmental – museums have an expanded role in human society. This situation has caused museums to rethink and redefine concepts that were thought to be permanent. Some have called the current condition a new paradigm within museology.[8] Others describe this situation as a shift from object-centered to community-centered institutions.[9] In reality, object/community and use/preservation are not contradictory but complementary. They are interdependent ideas – two halves of one whole. The old paradigm viewed from both sides. If there is a new paradigm it is most likely the one already described, the shift from homocentric to tellurian thinking.

> "Involve representatives of various communities and diverse cultural groups in the research and documentation process relative to their cultural experience in order to broaden the range of perspectives and deepen the understanding of museums' holdings."[10]

The concept of "public service" has changed dramatically for museums and museum workers. The changing attitudes and practices of museums reflected the audience being served. In the earliest museums, the collections were private and the audience carefully screened. As the "cabinet of curiosities" idea grew, the public was allowed to enter but only under strict supervision. Exhibitions were prepared for "the good of the visitor," providing information determined by the museum staff to be important to the visiting public. Eventually museum workers came to realize the importance of the visitor and developed exhibitions and programs to address their interests. Many museum activities attempt to explain and justify extant conditions rather than guiding society to find ways of addressing the critical needs of the present.

Museums have a basic role as educational institutions. The saga of the earth through time is told by the objects preserved in the collections of museums. It is a fascinating story told with authentic specimens and artifacts. At the same time, it is important to remember that museums are not ends unto themselves. To accomplish their mission, they must provide pleasure and excitement as well as information and education.

As part of the attitude of public service, museums have proliferated. Museums were formed around special collections to reflect the interests and beliefs of the communities in which they were founded. At the same time the fundamental role of museums began to change. Collections were, and continue to be the heart of museums. However, collections and the collecting process have been reoriented to give substance and purpose to a range of new museums. In this environment of change, traditional attitudes toward research, service, and education have found new means of expression.

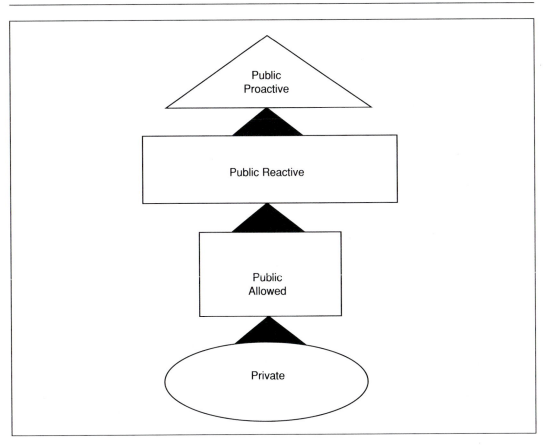

Figure 1.1 Museum types based on audience served

Objects communicate far beyond the walls of the museum in which they are housed. They influence the appreciation and appearance of objects of everyday use, and the level of respect and understanding for the personal and collective natural and cultural heritage of a people or nation.

Information and materials are being gathered to form new collections and museums that will give a redefined perspective to historic people, events, and even the environment. Many of these new museums do not fit the accepted description as places that collect, preserve, and study objects and specimens. Eco-museums, site museums, and non-collection galleries fall into this category. Preservation of historic buildings in the original setting can endow the structure with greater meaning. This is also true of archaeological excavations. The excavation becomes a working museum for research, interpretation, and education.

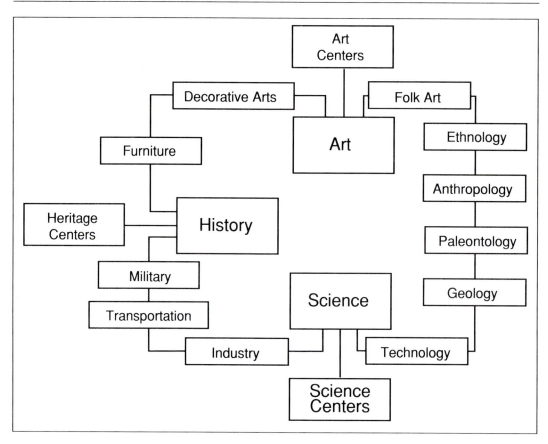

Figure 1.2 Museum proliferation

Of particular importance to the public are museums as community resources. Eco-museums "were designed to preserve economic viability and included facilities to document the areas' histories and for community meetings."[11] These neighborhood museums gained popularity in the 1960s as agents of change that linked education, culture, and community development. The eco-museum concept goes beyond the traditional "museum" idea of collecting objects to establishing conditions for communities to learn about themselves. It builds on the foundation of the community's collective memory and extends to the documentation of physical sites, traditional ceremonies, and social relationships.

> "an ecomuseum recognizes the importance of culture in the development of self-identity and its role in helping a community adjust to rapid change. The ecomuseum thus becomes a tool for the economic, social, and political growth and development of the society from which it springs."[12]

Museums can only be of service if they are used. They will be used only if people know about them, and only if attention is given to the interpretation of the objects in terms that the visitors can understand. Good museums attract, entertain, and arouse curiosity which leads to questioning and thus promotes learning.

The future for museums requires a greater focus on leadership (guidance) and education rather than management and explanation. To be effective, public programs will be proactive and provide direction for the future rather than selective interpretation of past events and activities.

When considering the idea of public service, museums have come to acknowledge the fact that the visiting audience has a variety of cultural or leisure-time opportunities. They may choose a concert, theater, and cinemas, or recreational activities, amusement parks, and sporting events, or they may decide to stay home to read a book, visit with friends, or watch television. While the possibilities seem definable on a local or immediate basis – consider the international or world constituency. The real challenge to museum workers is to have a broad view of global issues and to determine what can be done to make a difference. They must also consider how to make those issues available to the visitor.

As part of the ongoing responsibility of museums, outreach has acquired new meaning. To develop new audiences and provide greater services information must be gained on how people learn and the effective means of communication in a museum setting. "In"-reach is the counterpart of any outreach program. Museum staff require training, leadership, and planning to develop and implement a meaningful outreach program.

> **"Museums have not realized their full potential as educational institutions. Despite a long-standing and serious commitment to their function as institutions of informal learning, there is a troublesome gap between reality and potential that must be addressed by policy makers in education and museums."**[13]

Community perception is often a key element in attracting a particular audience to an exhibition or program. Marketing is the commercial word associated with the idea of attracting a group of people to a product, event, or program. Special attention must be given to nurturing both the impression and reality of public involvement in museum programs, events, and exhibitions.

The perception of an individual museum is the composite of many ideas. Visitors, supporters, the community-at-large, and even the staff present and foster an image of what a museum is and can be. Outreach and perception are opposite ends of the same action. Positive outreach normally generates a positive perception of a museum. Staff that are informed, well-trained, and treated with respect give a positive image of the institution.

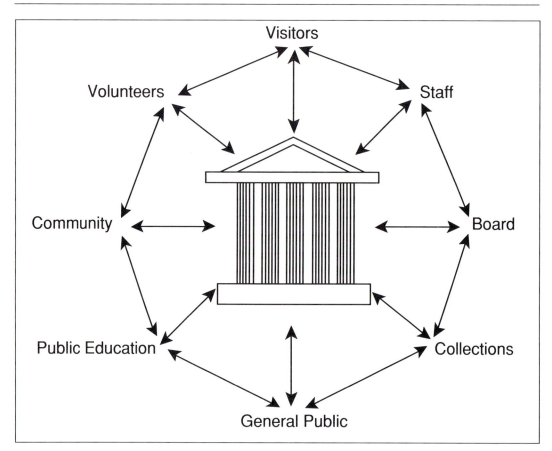

Figure 1.3 Outreach and perception of museums

As part of the outreach process the museum can inform the public of the activities associated with collection care, research, and exhibition preparation. For years, museums have perpetuated the concept of reserve and under–statement when addressing the inner workings of the institution. Few members of the general public have had the opportunity to view the museum from the other side of the exhibition – the working side. Museums must take the initiative in shaping the public perception and perpetuating the image of institutions essential to social and civilized well-being.

> **"Museums represent certainty in uncertain times."**[14]

The close ties that exist between the development of a society and the institutions of culture that represent that society are well documented. That societies evolve at different rates is a factor that impacts both the number and quality of the institutions comprising the cultural section. Progress has been made toward full utilization of museums as institutions of learning and social developments. However, most museums have a long way to go to meet their full potential as:

> **"a non-profitmaking, permanent institution in the service of society and of its development, and open to the public, which acquires, conserves, researches, communicates, and exhibits, for the purposes of study, education and enjoyment, material evidence of man and his environment."[15]**

Notes

1. American Association of Museums (1925) *Code of Ethics for Museum Workers*, Washington, DC: American Association of Museums.
2. Burcaw, G. E. (1975) *Introduction to Museum Work*, 2nd edn 1983, Nashville, Tenn.: American Association for State and Local History, p. 17.
3. Wittlin, A. S. (1970) *Museums: In Search of a Usable Future*, Cambridge, Mass.: MIT Press.
4. Thompson, J. M. A. (ed.) (1984) *Manual of Curatorship*, London: Butterworth Ltd.
5. ibid.: p. 13.
6. Alexander, E. (1983) *Museum Masters*, Nashville, Tenn.: American Association for State and Local History, p. 289.
7. ibid.
8. Sola, T. (1987) "The Concept and Nature of Museology," *Museums*, Paris: UNESCO, Vol. 39, No. 153, pp. 45–59.
9. van Mensch, P. (1988) "Museology and Museums," *ICOM News*, Paris: UNESCO, Vol, 41, No. 3, pp. 5–10.
10. Pittman, B., *et al.* (1991) *Excellence and Equity*, Washington, DC: American Association of Museums, p. 19.
11. Fuller, N. (1992) "The Museum as a Vehicle for Community Empowerment: The Ak-Chin Indian Community Ecomuseum Project," in I. Karp, C. Kreamer and S. Lavine (eds), *Museums and Communities*, Washington, DC: Smithsonian Institution Press, p. 329.
12. ibid.: p. 328.
13. Bloom, J. and Powell, E. (eds) (1984) *Museums for a New Century*, Washington, DC: American Association of Museums, p. 28.
14. Bloom, J. *et al.* (1984) "The Growing Museum Movement," *Museum News*, pp. 18–25.
15. International Council of Museums (1989) "Definitions," *Code of Professional Ethics*, Paris: ICOM, section 1.2. "Museum," p. 23.

Suggested reading

Adams, G. D. (1983) *Museum Public Relations*, Vol. 2, AASLH Management Series, Nashville, Tenn.: American Association for State and Local History.

Burcaw, G. E. (1975) *Introduction to Museum Work*, 2nd edn 1983, Nashville, Tenn.: American Association for State and Local History.

Finlay, I. (1977) *Priceless Heritage: The Future of Museums*, London: Faber & Faber.

Hudson, K. (1977) *Museums for the 1980s*, New York: Holmes & Meier Publishers, Inc.

International Council of Museums (1986) *Public View, The ICOM Handbook of Museum Public Relations*, Paris: ICOM.

Karp, I., Kreamer, C., and Lavine, S. (eds) (1992) *Museums and Communities: The Politics of Public Culture*, Washington, DC: Smithsonian Institution Press.

Karp, I. and Lavine, S. (eds) (1991) *Exhibiting Cultures: The Poetics and Politics of Museum Display*, Washington, DC: Smithsonian Institution Press.

Pearce, S. (ed.) (1991) *Museum Economics and the Community*, London: Athlone Press Ltd.

2

Museum management – part one

"Museums generally derive most of their prominence and importance from their collections, and these holdings constitute the primary difference between museums and other kinds of institutions. The collections, whether works of art, artifacts or specimens from the natural world, are an essential part of the collective cultural fabric, and each museum's obligation to its collections is paramount.

Each object is an integral part of a cultural or scientific composite. That context also includes a body of information about the object which establishes its proper place and importance and without which the value of the object is diminished. The maintenance of this information in an orderly and retrievable form is critical to the collection and is a central obligation to those charged with collection management."[1]

Museum management is a vital element in the development and advancement of museums. Without proper management, museums cannot provide the proper care and use for collections, nor can they maintain and support an effective exhibition and education program. Without proper management, public interest and trust can be lost and the existence of a museum may be jeopardized.

Museums are a reflection of a high level of social development. They require personnel with different and varied educational and managerial backgrounds and it is the balance of these diverse efforts that result in a properly functioning museum. The modern museum by definition must meet and embrace a number of specialized functions. It must be an informative, professional, systematic (in its collection care), enjoyable, and socially acceptable institution. To meet these often seemingly contradictory goals, traditional methods and practices of management are becoming unwieldy and increasingly obsolete.

To meet the challenge a new paradigm of management is evolving that includes the application of principles developed in research, economics, law, education, and physical plant management combined with the latest technology. The exact arrangement of the elements of the model may change but the concern for the management process enjoys equal importance in almost all countries of the world.

> "Employment by a museum, whether privately or governmentally supported, is a public trust involving great responsibility. In all activities museum employees must act with integrity and in accordance with the most stringent ethical principles as well as the highest standards of objectivity."[2]

How do we protect, preserve, and maintain our collections?

How do we make the collections and the information they represent more accessible to the public?

How do we educate the public to the role of the museum?

How can we meet the expectations of our constituencies without jeopardizing the collections?

How can we get more money, staff, space, participants, materials, et cetera?

How can we train and retrain the museum personnel and make them more professional?

How can we integrate new technology into the museum collection management process?

Every museum in every country of the world has many of these problems (or opportunities) regardless of its size, funding source, collections, or visitorship. To better understand the museum management process, it is important to gain greater insight into the way museums operate in different locations.

It is appropriate to view museums first from their source. Who or what authorized their existence and to whom do they report. There are at least four different types of museums based on their authorizing agencies.

1. Governmental – those museums that are authorized and supported by local, regional, or national governmental agencies.

2. Private – museums funded and operated by individuals or private organizations. Church museums are included in this group.

3. University – museums that are attached to colleges or universities and maintained for educational, i.e., study collections.

4. Combination – museums that were initiated by governmental agencies or private organizations and transferred to the other for operational purposes. (This type of museum may be the result of governmental change or the reduction of funding. To continue the museum's operation, a non-governmental organization may be formed to provide funding for the museum.)

It is not uncommon for all of these different types of museums to exist at the same time. No one has a greater or lesser chance of success than any of the others.

Most museums have a management structure that includes at least three components – administration, curation, and operations. All may be the duties of one person or they may include many people.

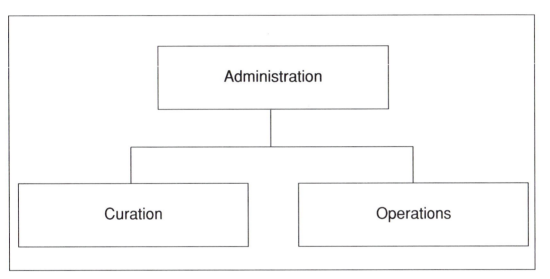

Figure 2.1 Basic organizational plan

The duties assigned to each of these positions may change from institution to institution but a possible arrangement might include the following:

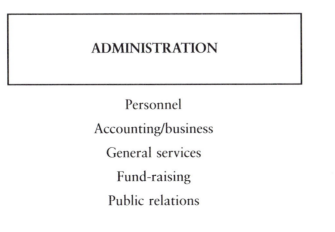

Personnel

Accounting/business

General services

Fund-raising

Public relations

CURATION

Collection registration

Collection care

Conservation

Research

OPERATIONS

Exhibitions

Public education

Technical services

Facility management/security

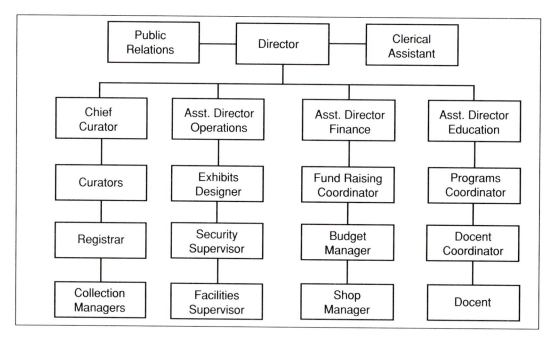

Figure 2.2 Example of compound organizational structure

A more complicated museum management structure may include a cadre of workers; however, the duties are divided along the same lines as the basic structure. The museum management methods and structures may vary among the countries of the world. There is a tendency for the "operational structure" of the organizations and institutions of a nation to reflect the prevailing tendencies of different social structures, concepts of business, and levels of development. Whatever the structure, the personnel should correspond to the needs of the museum and its stated mission.

Museum management should not be viewed as relating only to the institution, but as an administrative responsibility that embraces all the resources and activities of the museum. Proper museum management involves all the staff.

Administrative personnel
Staff of all administrative departments, membership departments, public relations, libraries, publications, et cetera.

Curatorial
Staff of all curatorial departments, registration, cataloging, conservation, research, et cetera.

Education
Staff whose primary responsibility is education, including docents, adult and children's program instructors, workshop leaders, et cetera.

Operations and support
Such personnel as exhibits technicians, preparators, custodians, security personnel, et cetera.

Museum personnel job descriptions

These job descriptions were included (in part) in the Smithsonian Institution/ICOM International Committee on Training of Personnel publication *Museum Studies International 1988*. Special recognition is due Jane Glaser and Patrick Boylan for their work on that publication.

Director

- The director provides conceptual leadership through specialized knowledge of the discipline of the museum and is responsible for policy-making and funding (with the governing board), planning, organizing, staffing, directing, and/or supervising and coordinating activities through the staff. The director is responsible for professional practices such as acquisition, preservation, research, interpretation, and presentation, and may be responsible for financial management. All museum positions report directly or indirectly to the director.

Education

- Advanced degree in an area of the museum's specialization. Coursework and evidence of participation in museum management and administration is desirable.

Experience

- Three years of management experience in a museum or related cultural institution. Additional administrative experience in a related field is desirable.

Knowledge, abilities, and skills

- Specialized knowledge in at least one area of the museum's governing collection or in the management of a particular type of museum.
- Ability to implement the policy established by the museum's governing body and encourage the active participation of the governing body, the museum staff, and the public in realizing the objectives and goals of the museum.
- Demonstrated knowledge of financial development and the ability to interpret budgets and manage ongoing fiscal responsibilities.
- Knowledge of the legal aspects of museum operations and of current and prospective legislation affecting museums.

Curator

- The curator is a specialist in a particular academic discipline relevant to the museum's collections. The curator is directly responsible for the care and academic interpretation of all objects, materials, and specimens belonging or lent to the museum; recommendations for acquisition, deaccession, attribution, and authentication; and research on the collections and the publication of the results of that research. The curator also may have administrative and/or exhibition responsibilities and should be sensitive to sound conservation practices.

Education

- Advanced degree with a concentration in a discipline related to an area of the museum's specialization.

Experience

- Three years of experience in a museum or related educational or research organization.

References

- Evidence of scholarly research and writing.

Knowledge, ability, and skills

- Specialized knowledge (connoisseurship) in one area of the museum's collections.
- Ability to interpret the collections and to communicate knowledge relevant to the collections.
- Knowledge of the techniques of selection, evaluation, preservation, restoration, and exhibition of objects.
- Knowledge of the current market, collecting ethics, and current customs regulations in the area of specialization.

Museum educator

- The museum educator develops, implements, evaluates, and/or supervises the museum's educational programs with the goal of enhancing public access to and understanding and interpretation of the collections and resources. The programs, which may employ a variety of media and techniques, may encompass educational exhibitions, printed materials such as self-guides, demonstrations, classes, tours, films, lectures, special events, workshops, teacher-training programs, school, or other outreach programs as well as docent/guide training. The educator may have administrative responsibilities.

Education

- Advanced degree in education, and knowledge of an area of the museum's specialization, or museum studies with a concentration in museum education.

Experience

- Two years in a museum education department or other educational institution.

Knowledge, ability, and skills

- Ability to devise and carry out education programs, including the preparation and use of publications and exhibitions.
- Knowledge of museum education techniques and resources.
- Knowledge of the learning characteristics of museum audiences.
- Skill in oral and written communication techniques appropriate to various educational levels and objectives.
- Knowledge of the objectives, curricula, and operation of school systems and other educational institutions.
- Knowledge in the area of the museum's collections.
- Skill in using research techniques.
- Knowledge of education evaluation methods.

Museum registrar

- The museum registrar is responsible for creating, organizing, and maintaining orderly forms, legal documents, files, and retrieval systems associated with the following: acquisition, accessioning, cataloging, loans, packing, shipping, inventory, insurance, and storage, pursuant to the care, custody, and control of the objects in perpetuity. A museum registrar organizes, documents, and coordinates all aspects of borrowing and lending objects, which include responsibility for the handling and/or packing of objects, negotiating insurance coverage, processing insurance claims, making shipping arrangements, arranging for security, handling customs procedures, processing incoming and outgoing loans, and processing requests for rights and reproductions. The museum registrar organizes data so that facts and ideas may be usefully extracted.

Education

- Degree in the area of the museum's specialization or in liberal arts.

Experience

- Two years in a museum registration department or in a museum position in which registration was an ongoing responsibility.

Knowledge, ability, and skills

- Knowledge of accepted museum registration techniques.
- Knowledge of conservation and storage practices.
- Knowledge of legal matters related to the collections, copyright laws, and policies governing rights and reproductions.
- Knowledge of records management and data processing systems.
- Knowledge of insurance requirements for the collections, packing techniques, and transportation methods.
- Knowledge of the museum's collections.

Conservator

- The conservator, on a scientific basis, examines museum objects, works to prevent their deterioration, and treats and repairs them when necessary. The conservator sees that objects are fumigated, kept at proper levels of temperature and relative humidity, and protected from air pollutants and exposure to damaging light intensities and wavelengths. The conservator usually has the specialized knowledge to treat a certain class of objects, such as paintings, sculpture, textiles, ceramics, glass, metals, furniture and wood-work, books and art on paper, and should know where to refer materials that cannot be treated in the museum laboratory. In order to keep his or her knowledge current, the conservator may belong to a professional conservation organization which expects adherence to a code of ethics.

Education

- Graduate-level training in a recognized conservation program of two or more years in the theory, principles, and practice of conservation, including a year's training in the principles of general material conservation and a minimum of one year's training or internship in a specialized field; or equivalent training by apprenticeship with one or more qualified practitioners. Undergraduate training should include courses in cultural or art history, scientific studies (chemistry, physics, material science, biology), studio arts, and manual skills.

Experience

- Two years of postgraduate, on-the-job experience (beyond academic training or apprenticeship) under the supervision of a qualified conservator.

References

- Portfolio of current and past work including examination, condition, and treatment reports, and written, photographic, or original documentation.

Knowledge, abilities, and skills

- Manual skill in the treatment of materials.
- Knowledge of the technology and materials of artistic, historic, scientific, and technological objects and of the chemical and physical processes of their deterioration.
- Knowledge of the procedures relating to the examination and preventive and corrective treatment of objects and specimens.
- Ability to write thorough and effective treatment reports.
- Knowledge of environmental requirements and controls for handling, storage, exhibition, and travel of objects and specimens.
- Ability to communicate the required participation of other staff in implementation of approved conservation practices throughout the institution.
- Knowledge of conservation and other relevant literature to assure knowledge of new technology.
- Ability to plan a basic or specialized conservation laboratory and to implement its development.

Exhibit designer

- The exhibit designer translates curatorial and educational staff ideas into permanent, temporary, or circulating exhibitions through renderings, drawings, scale models, lighting, and arrangement of objects and signage. The exhibit designer may supervise the production of exhibitions and have administrative responsibilities.

Education

- Degree or certificate in graphic design, industrial design, commercial art, or communication arts, or in architecture, interior design, theater design, or studio arts with course work in typography and media use.

Experience

- Experience in exhibition design, preferably in or for a museum. Additional experience in exhibit production, related construction work (cabinet-making, wood, metal, or plastic fabrication), model-making, or in media (graphics, advertising, illustration, audio-visual presentations) may be desirable.

References

- Portfolio of current and past work.

Knowledge, abilities, and skills

- Ability to conceptualize exhibition designs appropriate to the aims and style of the institution.
- Ability to make refined aesthetic judgments.
- Ability to specify designs in drawings and written instructions.
- Ability to supervise fabrication and installation of exhibits.
- Knowledge of security and conservation requirements and practices.
- Knowledge of lighting systems.
- Knowledge of tools and techniques for exhibition preparation, shop practices, mechanical drawing, and the use of planning models and mock-ups.
- Knowledge of estimating, budgeting, bidding, and accounting practices.
- Knowledge of the state of the art in exhibition design and related fields.
- Knowledge of communication media and materials.
- Knowledge of the nature and the materials to be displayed.

Collections manager

- The collections manager is responsible for supervising, numbering, cataloging, and storing the specimens within each department or division and may perform the combined functions of registrar and curatorial assistant.

Education

- Degree in the area of the museum's specialization. A graduate degree in museum studies with a concentration in a discipline may be desirable.

Experience

- Three years of experience in a museum registration department or a museum position in which the main functions are the technical duties relating to collections management, such as the handling, storage, preservation, and cataloging of objects and specimens.

Knowledge, abilities, and skills

- Ability to coordinate personnel and plan and administer programs for collections management, including financial planning and budget preparation.

- Knowledge of the organization, arrangement, and nomenclature of specimens and objects in the relevant academic field.
- Knowledge of file and information management techniques used in museum registration and record-keeping.
- Ability to accurately identify specimens and objects within the context of the museum's collections.
- Ability to handle objects appropriately with knowledge of the fundamental principles of conservation, security, and environmental controls.

Regardless of the number of persons involved, the museum workforce must work as a team. If each person works independently, those things that are accomplished will take longer, be less well done, be less museum-specific, and allow more opportunity for individual bias.

Question from the field: one

Question: In most developing museums there are not enough funds to do a completely good job. According to your experience, which is the priority for our museums – exhibitions or storage?

Response: The question of priority is one affecting all museums not just those in the early stages of development. Many of the museums of the world have chosen to add to their collections, develop elaborate exhibition programs, and add larger public galleries. Often these changes have superseded providing proper care of the collections.

Realizing that it may be extremely difficult to give equal attention to both exhibitions and storage, a plan should be devised to meet the important responsibilities to both. The first step is a careful review of the storage needs of the collection. The second is to determine the time and money required to meet the storage needs. Once this information is assembled, a plan for addressing the most critical storage needs can be formulated.

On the exhibition side of the equation, the same type of planning is necessary. How can the exhibition activities of a museum continue while using a smaller portion of the available money and personnel? As examples, exhibits can be extended in length, and gallery furniture reused or reassembled rather than constructing for a particular exhibit. Further savings will result from reducing or eliminating support material, announcements, posters, and gallery guides. It may also be necessary to reduce the number of hours a museum is open to the public. Every aspect of an exhibition program should be analyzed and regulated with the intention of saving human and financial resources.

An important final step in this process is keeping a museum audience informed of the reasons for these changes. There will be fewer questions and complaints if the public understands a museum's program of collection care. Most will view the commitment to meeting the collection storage needs as a responsible act and support the project.

> **Plan carefully.**
> **Keep the public informed.**
> **Achieve the stated objective.**

□   □   □   □   □

Question from the field: two

Question: Our museum has one large storage area. In that space are different materials including paintings, archaeology, ethnology, and various organic pieces. What should we do to maintain levels of relative humidity that are good for everything?

Response: The best level of relative humidity (and temperature) for most objects in a museum's collection is the constant one. Many museum people now realize that to try to maintain a specific (artificial) temperature and relative humidity may not be necessary. For many objects, the "ideal" museum environment of 70° F ± 2° and 45 per cent RH ± 5 per cent is not natural. However, it is a condition determined to be preferable for most objects housed in a museum.

In making environmental judgments, careful thought must be given to the collections, the location, building, exhibition space, and all other elements that will have an impact on the decision-making process. Regulate the environment at a level that can be maintained and one that will address the needs of most of the collection. Inconsistency in temperature and relative humidity is more harmful to collections than a few degrees or percentage points up or down. It is most important to maintain the predetermined environmental conditions.

□   □   □   □   □

Question from the field: three

Question: What is the specific job of the curator? Please give a list.

Response: The curator is a specialist in a particular academic discipline pertinent to one of a museum's collections.

The curator develops a collection plan for a particular area of a museum's holdings.

The curator recommends objects for acquisition and deaccession.

The curator is directly responsible for the care and interpretation of all objects, materials, and specimens relevant to the assigned collection area of a museum.

The curator is the collection expert capable of attribution and authentication.

The curator is responsible for collection-related research and the publication of the results of that research.

The curator also may have administration and exhibition responsibilities and should be sensitive to sound conservation practices.

The curator is responsible for acting in a manner appropriate for a museum professional.

The curator must abide by the policies of the institution of employment and the ethics of the museum community.

Notes

1. American Association of Museums (1978) *Museum Ethics*, Washington, DC: American Association of Museums, p. 11.
2. ibid.: p. 17.

Suggested reading

Alexander, E. (1979) *Museums in Motion, An Introduction to the History and Functions of Museums*, 4th printing 1986, Nashville, Tenn.: American Association for State and Local History.

American Association of Museums (1978) *Museum Ethics*, Washington, DC: American Association of Museums.

Bloom J. and Powell, E. (eds) (1984) *Museums for a New Century, A Report of the Commission on Museums for a New Century*, Washington, DC: American Association of Museums.

George, G. and Sherrell-Leo, C. (1986, 1989) *Starting Right, A Basic Guide to Museum Planning*, Nashville, Tenn.: American Association for State and Local History.

Houle, C. (1990) *Governing Boards, Their Nature and Nurture*, San Francisco, Calif.: Jossey-Bass Publishers.

Lewis, R. (1976) *Manual for Museums*, Washington, DC: National Park Service, US Department of Interior.

Malaro, M. (1985) *A Legal Primer on Managing Museum Collections*, 2nd edn 1987, Washington, DC: Smithsonian Institution Press.

Miller, R. (1980) *Personnel Policies for Museums: A Handbook for Management*, Washington, DC: American Association of Museums.

3

Museum management – part two

> "The ethical duty of museums is to transfer to our
> successors, when possible in enhanced form, the material
> record of human culture and the natural world. They
> must be in control of their collections and know the
> location and the condition of the objects that they hold.
> Procedures must be established for the periodic evaluation
> of the condition of the collections and for their general
> and special maintenance.
>
> The physical care of the collection and its accessibility
> must be in keeping with professionally accepted
> standards."[1]

Museums, as public institutions, exist for the public benefit and to be
successful all aspects of their operations should reflect this obligation and
commitment. Collecting, conservation, and research should be executed with a
public consciousness just as the more visible or public-oriented exhibitions and
educational programming.[2] Any organization operating in the public interest
must manage its affairs properly, but museums as custodians of the cultural and
scientific heritage of a people, region, or nation must function, as nearly as
possible, above reproach. Museums operated or maintained as parts of a
governmental structure are normally required to function according to the
management system of the governing body. There is, however, still a need to
maintain an appropriate system of operations according to accepted
museological practices.

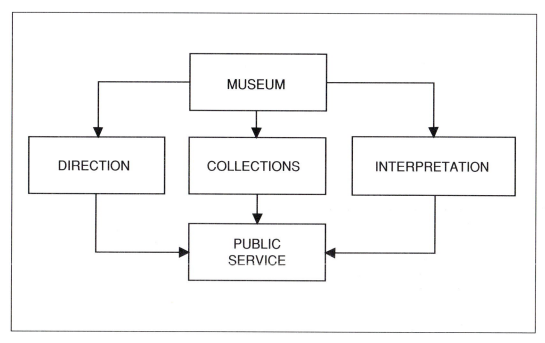

Figure 3.1 Role of museums

To evaluate or re-evaluate your museum consider the following questions:

1. What is your museum's mission and its limits?

2. What sources of support can your museum depend on?

3. What collections are available or need to be found to serve your museum's purpose?

4. What physical facilities will contribute to your museum?

5. Who will have responsibility for the museum?

6. What rules will govern the museum's operations?

7. What division of labor and allocations of authority will there be?

8. How will harmonious working relationships [with staff] be maintained?

9. What will be your collection policy?

10. What conservation needs must you arrange and how?

11. What provision will you make for continuing research?

12. What interpretive methods will you use to reach your public?

13. What time schedule for development will the museum follow?

14. What staff, paid and volunteer, will be needed?

15. What will each part of the [museum] plan cost to execute?

16. Where will the money come from for each part of the plan?

17. How will you maintain good public relations?

18. How will you provide for continual planning?

19. How will you evaluate your museum's activities?

20. How will you keep your museum alive, dynamic, creative, and visionary?[3]

The mission of the museum is its guiding statement of purpose. It describes why the institution exists, what its functions are, and what the scope of activities shall be. A good mission statement answers the questions:

Who is the museum (what is the museum called and who is its base of support?)

What it collects (what objects will be included in the museum's collection?)

How was it formed (is the museum subject to private, corporate, or governmental entities?)

When it collects (what time period(s) or historic epoch will be represented in the museum's collections?)

Where it collects (which collecting locations will be included in the museum's collection constituency – community, regional, national, or international?)

Why it collects (what will the museum do with its collections?)

Rather than begin with the theory of why and how the museum came into existence, it is best to assume the museum exists, there is a building, and there are some objects that constitute a collection. For the purposes of simplification the word "object" may indicate works of art, natural history, science, or history.

Good museum governance begins with a written statement of institutional purpose – a mission statement. It must be supported with other documents, including a manual of policies and procedures, exhibits guidelines, and code of ethics designed for the museum.

Mission statement

The mission statement or statement of purpose of the museum is a document that establishes the limitation of the collection and defines the role of the museum. As an example, the Museo de Oro would have a mission statement that limits the purpose of the museum to collecting, housing, researching, exhibiting, and providing public educational programs relating to gold. A clearly written, well-articulated mission statement will save many hours of discussion and much misunderstanding if as many limitations as possible can be defined.

A mission statement might read like this:

> The Museo de Oro is a not-for-profit institution dedicated to the collecting, housing, researching, exhibiting of object of gold produced in the central regions of the Andean Highlands prior to European influence. The Museum shall use its collections and resources to inform and inspire the general public by exhibiting important works of artistic beauty and excellent craftsmanship produced by persons working in gold. The Museum recognizes its role as a repository of the cultural heritage of the region and is dedicated to serving the people of the area.

It is preferable to keep the mission statement simple and clearly articulated. The meaning of the mission statement should not be open to interpretation.

Once the mission statement has the approval of the museum administration it should be distributed to the staff, supporters, and local, state, regional, and, if appropriate, national authorities so there can be no misunderstanding about the mission of the museum. An exception to this might be when the mission statement is incorporated into the charter or constitution associated with the establishment of your museum. It establishes the intent of your museum and provides a record of the recognition and concern for that responsibility. Broad distribution of the mission statement reinforces the museum's awareness of its public role. Even though a mission statement is not normally a legal document, it is important for all parties to adhere to the mission established for the museum.

Policy and procedures

After the mission statement is written and approved, a series of documents should be developed to define the methods for implementing the mission. Policies list the general rules for applying the mission statement to the daily operations of the museum, and procedures explain how to execute the policies. Policies and procedures should address the following issues:

1. acquisition;
2. accessioning;
3. deaccessioning;
4. collection care and use;

5. loans;

6. facility use;

7. public programming;

8. exhibits;

9. safety;

10. natural disasters and hazards.

Additional policies may be required to meet the specific needs of a particular museum. Together the museum statement and policies and procedures define and explain the levels of accountability the museum has for the collections.

> **The following material is an example of the information that may be included in policies and procedures typical of many public-oriented, publicly-funded museums. The information is offered for reference only, as each museum must design a series of policies and procedures specific to that institution's collections, needs, location, constituency, and mission.**

Acquisitions

Acquisition is the process of acquiring objects for the Museum. Acquisition, except as approved in writing by the director, does not imply accessioning and does not constitute fiduciary, legal, and/or financial responsibility on the part of the museum. Acquired objects may be recommended for accession by the appropriate curator to the director. Objects are normally acquired through donation, fieldwork or research, purchase, or transfer from another institution.

Material may come to the museum from a variety of sources including fieldwork (as in the case of biological specimens or archaeological artifacts), gifts, bequests, or purchases. Each method includes special concerns that must be addressed.

One of the two most common ways used by museums to assemble a collection is fieldwork. The conducting of fieldwork often requires local, state, or national permits. The transportation of field-generated specimens or artifacts may be restricted by international agreement. Local landowners may hold or wish to hold exclusive rights to specimens or artifacts taken on or from their land.

Fieldwork must be well documented, including all required permits, stamps, and verification forms. If the work was done on private property it is advisable to have a signed release from the landowner allowing both the collecting and the removal of the specimens or artifacts. All field records must accompany the specimens or artifacts. They must be considered the property of the museum and given the same care and protection as the objects with which they are associated. Curators or field research personnel may receive photocopies of the field notes to further their research outside the museum as appropriate and determined by the director of the museum. If these notes are published the museum should be acknowledged as the repository for the objects and the rightful owner of the field notes.

Gifts are the second most common way museums amass collections. Objects received by this method may include works of art, historical or ethnological objects, and artifacts. It is not unusual for gift items to have real market value for which a receipt is requested. Gifts of this type may have use restrictions imposed by the donor including being on permanent display or return to heirs after a fixed period of time. It is often very difficult to reject a gift offered by an important community leader or supporter of the museum even though the material or object is not of good quality or appropriate for the museum's needs.

Gifts should only be accepted without restrictions. Museums should not be placed in the position of always having to exhibit certain objects and only under extraordinary circumstances should objects be received into the museum for safekeeping to be returned to the owner at a later date. Certainly natural disaster, social unrest, or war are conditions that might supersede this practice. Gifts of questionable quality or limited use should not be accepted. The attitude of accepting any and all gifts to 'fill space' is ill-advised as the cost of maintaining a poor quality object is the same (or more) than that of a good quality, useful, and/or important object.

Bequests may be assigned to the museum without notice or discussion with the director. The bequest may include inappropriate, inferior quality, or poorly maintained objects that will require a significant commitment of time, space, and/or money by the museum.

If conditions or collections require, bequests can be returned to the estate of the donor. Normally the requirements of the will are nullified by refusal of the museum to accept the objects. This is a situation that should be considered carefully and when appropriate discussed with the heirs. It is very likely that the will includes a codicil that explains or restricts the use or distribution of the bequeathed objects.

Purchases are often the best way to expand certain collections but usually the most difficult as they require immediate funding. Art and occasionally historical objects available on the open market offer an opportunity for a museum to select quality objects of a type, material, and/or origin appropriate to collection needs. However, it is the responsibility of the museum to determine that these objects are offered legally, ethically, and with full knowledge of the general public as the transportation and sale of historical and cultural materials is regulated by international agreement. It is also often the case with purchased objects that pertinent documentation is not available, thus limiting the usefulness of the material.

Responsibility begins with acquisition.

The following procedures are, in every case, to be interpreted to support an attitude of responsible collection management. They are set forth to provide guidance for acquisition by authorized museum personnel. Adherence to these rules will promote responsible collecting and assure the attendant storage, preservation, and conservation accountability inherent in the acceptance of objects. Reference to these restrictions will foster a spirit of understanding and cooperation with prospective donors by serving as a defined justification for acceptance or rejection of donations, gifts, bequests, transfers, or purchases.

1. Acceptance of *any* object places the responsibility on the accepting body for perpetual maintenance and preservation.

2. The museum will acquire no objects for which a valid title cannot be obtained.

3. Restrictive or conditional donations cannot be accepted.

4. The value and provenance of "museum quality" objects are frequently matters of opinion; for the purpose of acquisition, museum curators shall be relied upon for such judgments in their special fields.

5. Acquisitions of the museum are the property and obligation of the museum. The conditions of their care and utilization in the museum are defined elsewhere in this document.

6. Objects donated to the museum will not normally be returned to the donor or heirs. In such cases where the return of an object is deemed appropriate by the director of the museum, a report of that action will be sent to the appropriate governmental agency.

7. The museum will not accept donations of objects of questionable origin (legal or ethical), nor will the museum exhibit or otherwise allow the utilization of such objects.

8. Acquisitions of the museum are subject to the policy of deaccession as set forth in this document, and, except as specifically stated, no objects will be sold, traded, or otherwise removed from the care and protection of the museum.

9. The museum may determine that selected objects are appropriate for designation as educational material. These objects will be given all reasonable care and attention, but, by the nature of their use, are available for selective consumption.

10. The museum will not consider acquisition of personal memorabilia.

11. Donor information is maintained as part of the acquisition file, the accession file, and on the catalog card. It will not be used as part of labeling while the objects are on exhibit without the prior signed consent of the donor.

12. The museum staff is not allowed to give appraisals, either written or verbal. Donors requiring appraisals for income tax purposes must obtain these at their own expense from appraisers of their choice prior to donation.

In view of the non-profit, educational, scientific, cultural, and research status of the museum, a potential donor must be informed of the restrictions under which gifts may be given. The potential donor may either bring the objects to the museum or the appropriate curator may view the material at a designated location. Persons leaving objects with the museum for possible donation should be given a signed receipt indicating that the material was left *only* for consideration and on a temporary basis. The receipt must be signed by the potential donor or their authorized agent and either the registrar or appropriate curator. One copy of the receipt is kept on file in the registrar's office and another copy accompanies the curator's recommendation to the director.

Initial recommendations for object acquisition should be made by the appropriate curator in writing to the director, to address the following:

1. evaluation criteria as stated in the museum policy;

2. significance of objects;

3. relevance of objects to the current collections (research, education, and exhibit);

4. number of like objects in the collection;

5. conservation needs of objects;

6. housing needs of objects;

7. funding for the conservation and care of the objects;

8. legal and social considerations of objects.

Curators may recommend objects for acquisition consideration for their collection area only. Objects to be housed in more than one collection must be evaluated by all involved curators.

A formal letter concerning the acquisition decision will be sent to the potential donor by the director. The director's decision will be communicated in writing to the appropriate museum personnel, including the registrar and curator.

The communication document will become a permanent part of the museum record. If the donation is approved, the registrar will explain, in writing, the procedure for transfer of title and provide the donor with a contract-of-gift form. The contract-of-gift form must be signed by donors at the time the title is transferred and the objects received by the museum. Objects will not be accessioned by the registrar until a signed contract-of-gift is received in the registrar's office. If a contract-of-gift form is not signed within thirty days of notice, the registrar will notify the donor that the museum can no longer be responsible for the donor's property and must return the material. The receipt of the signed contract-of-gift is the official date of transaction, and will be so noted on all donation-related documentation.

Proposed purchases either for or by the museum must also undergo (in advance of actual purchase) the recommendation and review process as for donations and require final approval by the director.

Bequests, preferably, should be approved for acquisition prior to the museum being designated as beneficiary. All objects bequeathed to the museum are subject to the acquisition and accession procedures as defined in the document. In every case, the museum shall observe appropriate confidentiality with regard to accepted testamentary distribution objects, and will attempt to abide by donor request except where those requests are in conflict with museum policy, or the laws of the state.

In the process of acquiring or gathering field specimens, museum personnel will not knowingly or intentionally violate local, state, national, or international laws or statutes. The museum, as an institution, will not knowingly or intentionally receive into its possession any specimen(s) that has been stolen, converted, or taken by fraud. Field collection will not be initiated without the appropriate documentation, including all required permits, and land-use authorization. Permission to collect, preserve, utilize, and subsequently to assume title, without restriction, shall be gained, in writing, from the owner, or legal representative of the owner, on whose land the objects or specimens are collected. These documents are a part of the field notes associated with the collection and as such become a part of the museum's permanent file.

Acquisitions statement

All potential acquisitions must be evaluated in terms of the objectives, purpose, and mission of the museum and must fall within financial and physical limitations of the institution.

All potential acquisitions must be evaluated by the following criteria:

1. Documentation as to origin, previous ownership, use, and pertinent classification information.
2. Ability of the museum to properly maintain and house the objects.

3. Legal standards governing possession and use of objects. (The museum endorses the ethics of acquisitions as set forth by ICOM, and will not knowingly accept any object acquired by either illegal or unethical means.)

4. Willingness of the donor (owner) to transfer complete ownership to the museum without restrictions, limitations, or conditions.

The museum or its employees cannot ethically or legally appraise objects, retain an appraiser for a private citizen, or refer an appraiser to a private citizen, and therefore shall not be involved in appraisal activities.

Purchased objects shall become the property of the museum, will be accessioned, and all bills of sale and appropriate records will be kept by the museum.

Collections and associated documentation, including field records generated by staff research and staff or student fieldwork, are owned by, or held in trust by, the museum, and shall be accessioned.

The director shall have final authority regarding acquisitions and accessions.

The museum maintains, in the office of the registrar, a detailed record-keeping system of all objects accessioned or received by any approved means into its care. Each collection area shall maintain an approved record-keeping system within the collection.

Accessions

Accessioning is the transfer of title of objects, through defined procedures, to the museum or the registration of objects held-in-trust for governmental agencies. Upon accessioning (acceptance of ownership and responsibility), the museum assumes the obligation for the proper management of objects. Accessioning is the function of the office of the registrar.

Complete records of the accessioned holdings of the museum are maintained in the registrar's office. Museum objects are obtained through six primary means: donation, purchase, trade, exchange, transfer, or field-generation. Once an object is recommended for accession and approved by the director, and, where appropriate, a signed contract-of-gift or accessions contract is received, the objects are then accessioned by the registrar into the museum. Accessioning is the transfer of title to the museum. Accession numbers document museum ownership and are an inventory control device for the registrar.

The accession system utilized by the museum is numerical and includes the calendar year of acceptance followed by a number indicating the order of acceptance. The calendar year is written in full, and the number of order of acceptance is separated by a period from the year: for example, 1980.1. Each object or collection is assigned an accession number.

Objects are not incorporated into the museum's collections until they are accessioned by the registrar. It is the responsibility of the appropriate curator to provide all acquisition and identification documentation to the registrar.

The records that accompany accessions are critical. The following are examples of appropriate documentation:

1. A signed contract-of-gift form for those objects donated to the museum; proof of ownership for those objects purchased by the museum; a letter from the trading or exchanging institution transferring title of the objects to the museum; or a signed accessions contract form for those objects held-in-trust by the museum is required.

2. A complete record of all correspondence and transactions involving the acquisitions includes:

   a. name and address of the donor, seller, trading/exchanging institution, or governmental agency for which objects are being held-in-trust;

   b. copy of the permit for held-in-trust objects;

   c. import and export papers on objects from foreign countries;

   d. bill of sale and bill of lading;

   e. all gift restrictions;

   f. copyright considerations;

   g. artist's rights considerations;

   h. provenance information;

   i. history of objects;

   j. dates or ages of objects.

3. For collections acquired by field research by the museum staff, there must be on file in the registrar's office either a copy of the permit giving the staff permission for such research and naming the museum as the official repository, or written documentation that the landowner provided the staff permission for such research and the arrangements for the final disposition of the collected material. The museum recognizes that certain collections generated under governmental permits are regulated by specific laws and are held-in-trust instead of owned by the museum.

4. Black-and-white photographs, color slides, or video record with the assigned accession number visible either in the photographs or inscribed on the face of the photographs are required for some objects. This requirement is to include all type specimens, all works of art, all ethnographic material, significant historical costumes and objects, appropriate archaeological objects, and other objects designated by the director in consultation with the registrar and the appropriate curator.

5. Accession records include an initial condition report, including conservation and fumigation needs. If the object is treated before being incorporated into a collection's holding, the treatment form noting all changes must be filed with the registrar and a copy sent to the appropriate curator. Subsequent treatment of an object that alters its condition should be reported to the registrar.

6. Accession records include the accession number and the collection area to which the objects are assigned and the associated catalog numbers. *Providing the registrar with the catalog numbers is the responsibility of the appropriate curator.*

7. Any other documentation concerning, related to, or accompanying the objects should be included in the accession record.

Once the transfer of title is completed or held-in-trust status established, the objects are entered into the museum's register and assigned an accession number. An accession record worksheet is initiated by the registrar in coordination with the appropriate curator. A brief description of the objects and all background information are recorded on the accession record worksheet. The registrar transfers the accession data to an official accession card that is filed numerically in that office. The frame of the black-and-white photograph or the color slide, or video cassette frame number is attached to the accession card and the negative or duplicate copy is housed elsewhere in an area designated by the director. A source card is filled out by the registrar and filed alphabetically in that office.

Objects accepted for educational uses are accessioned into the museum and assigned to the appropriate collection area. Contract-of-gift or transaction papers of trade or exchange must carry a notation that the objects are accepted for educational purposes that may be of a consumptive nature. The duplicate accession cards for the objects are kept in the files of the assigned collection area even when the physical locations of the objects are reassigned to the museum's education program. When the objects are no longer useful to or needed by the museum's education program, the objects are returned to the collection of origin.

Books to be placed in the museum's library are not accessioned but are recorded by the registrar with the donor's information. A contract-of-gift form is sent to the donor with a complete listing of the books. Records for donated books are kept in the registrar's office in a file separate from the accessions file. Books are cataloged using standard library procedures. Rare books and historic manuscripts appropriate to the collections are accessioned and assigned to the appropriate collection area. They are cataloged into the collection. Accessioned books are not placed in the library.

Deaccessions

A number of reasons create the need for careful removal of objects from the museum collections. The deaccessioning of any object, for whatever reason, is of primary importance to the museum as no object is considered insignificant or unimportant. The only material considered for deaccession will be that to which the museum has clear title.

The museum recognizes the special responsibility associated with the reception and maintenance of objects of cultural, historical, and scientific significance in the public trust. In order for the institution to serve the cultural and educational needs of its various communities, it cannot remain static. Periodic re-evaluations and thoughtful selection are necessary for the growth and proper care of collections. The practice of deaccessioning under well-defined guidelines provides these opportunities. Deaccessioning permanently removes an object from the collections through donation, exchange, sale, repatriation, loss, or deterioration beyond repair and allows the transfer of unrestricted title to the receiving agency.

No object will be donated, exchanged, sold, repatriated, or in any way removed from museum records without careful review, evaluation, and documentation of clear and unrestricted title. Under no circumstances will type specimens and similar objects be deaccessioned; nor will anthropological, historical, or natural science objects be sold. Works of art that are duplicated (in the case of prints, photographs, or other multiple image processes) or original works that are determined not to relate to the mission of the museum may be sold at public auction to either not-for-profit museums, agencies, or institutions or to private individuals.

In consideration of the museum's continuing concern for the preservation of objects, written evidence is required that proper care, maintenance, and environment will be provided for all objects considered for deaccessioning through donation, exchange, transfer, or repatriation. Material transferred for specific use may be reclaimed by the museum if the material is not used for the proposed purpose. Objects under consideration for exchange are subject to the acquisitions and accessions review process. An object must have been accessioned into the museum records for at least seven years before it can be considered for deaccessioning, unless otherwise regulated by state and federal law or transferred to an appropriate institution for educational or research purposes. If a suitable recipient for donation, exchange, transfer, or purchase cannot be found, the museum must keep and maintain the object.

The decision to deaccession is made based on, but not limited to, the following guidelines with the procedures for specific situations as outlined:

1. Objects lacking provenance or location information that are not significant or useful for research, exhibit, or educational purposes in and of themselves may be considered for deaccession.

2. Objects that have been determined not to be authentic may be considered for deaccession.

3. Objects that have limited or no value to the museum because of redundancy in the collection may be considered for deaccession.

4. Objects of sacred or ritual significance requested for return by aboriginal groups or foreign governments may be considered for return to the tribe, community, or country of origin. The requesting group must provide evidence of the validity of their claim and that proper care and maintenance will be provided for all objects considered for return.

5. Objects that do not relate to the stated mission of the museum may be considered for deaccession.

6. Objects that have decayed or decomposed beyond reasonable use and repair or that by their condition constitute a hazard to other objects in the collection may be considered for deaccession. Once deaccessioned, these objects will have all museum numbers removed, and will be destroyed beyond recognition in order to prevent future confusion or rediscovery of the object.

7. Objects that have been lost or stolen from the collections must be reported to the director in writing immediately for notification of similar museums, appropriate organizations, and law enforcement agencies. Objects missing from the museum for a period of three years shall be determined irretrievable and may be deaccessioned.

8. Objects of educational value, but otherwise inappropriate for research or exhibit purposes, may be utilized for that purpose by the concerned collection or the museum education program. If useful to the museum education program, the physical location of the object will be reassigned rather than deaccessioned. If the objects reassigned to the museum education program are no longer useful or needed by that program, the objects must return to the collection of origin. If the objects have deteriorated beyond repair and usefulness, then the objects may be deaccessioned. Duplicate accession cards for the objects are kept in the files of the collection of origin at all times.

Objects without contract-of-gift or other legal document of transfer to the museum may be considered for deaccession. If the original donor is known and no contract-of-gift was signed, an attempt to contact the donor or heirs will be made to determine their willingness to accept the return of the object. Contact will be attempted by certified mail by the registrar; a second contact attempt will be made by the registrar through a notice in newspapers of general circulation in the county of the museum and the county of the last known address of the donor or heirs. Notice will be published at least once a week for two consecutive weeks. If the donor or heirs do not request return of the objects, the museum will require a written statement granting clear and unrestricted title to the institution. If the donor or heirs cannot be located, the object is considered abandoned property. The museum must wait seven years without donor contact before claiming clear and unrestricted title to the object. At that point, the object can be considered for deaccession.

1. Objects without signed contract-of-gift that are returned to the donor or heirs may be returned in whole or in part. While the museum seeks to preserve and maintain the quality of all objects under its care, it is not responsible for the condition in which the objects are returned. If the donor or heirs accept return of the object, they will be required to pay shipping charges.

2. Objects without signed contract-of-gift that cannot be returned to donors or their heirs may be deaccessioned and assigned to interested public or private not-for-profit museums and educational agencies and institutions. The museum will inform regional museums and other not-for-profit agencies and institutions of proposed deaccession actions. Interested agencies will be given appropriate time to contact the museum to request specific objects and outline care and use intentions. Transfer of the objects to the receiving agency is by donation or exchange.

Usable objects that have been deaccessioned may be donated to or exchanged with the following institutions in order of preference:

1. appropriate public museums;

2. appropriate public educational agencies and institutions; and

3. private museums and educational agencies and institutions.

If the donation or exchange option fails, only works of art may be sold at a widely publicized public auction conducted by a reputable purveyor. The purveyor will be responsible for determining a fair market value based on his judgment and that of an in-house evaluation and two outside appraisals. The donor or heirs or the executing artist, if contemporary works of art are involved, will be notified of the intention by the museum to sell. As part of the notification process, the donor or heirs will be given assurance that:

1. The money acquired from the sale of art objects will be used solely to obtain works of art for the collections or to conserve art works already in the collection.

2. Funding for newly acquired and accessioned objects will be attributed to the original donor.

The initial recommendation for deaccession shall be submitted by the appropriate curator in writing, with photographic documentation attached, to the director. The request shall include an evaluation of the object and the reason for recommending deaccessioning. The final decision on deaccessioning of any object is made by the director after consultation with appropriate personnel. If a contract-of-gift was signed the donor or heirs will be contacted if possible.

The deaccessioning process is as follows:

1. Deaccessioning must be documented in writing and the original documents kept on file in the registrar's office. A duplicate set will be on file in the appropriate collection. The deaccession record must include, but is not limited to:

   a. name(s) and title(s) of persons involved in initiating and sanctioning the process and date of deaccession;
   b. initial recommendation by the curator;
   c. reason for deaccessioning;
   d. description of object being deaccessioned;
   e. catalog and accession numbers;
   f. evidence of clear and unrestricted title of the museum to the object;
   g. photo documentation of deaccessioned object.

2. If appropriate, the following must also be included:

   a. formal request for repatriation by aboriginal group or foreign government;
   b. name and location of the receiving museum, agency, institution, or purchaser, or aboriginal group or foreign country;
   c. written evidence from receiving agency or aboriginal group or foreign government of their ability to properly care for and use the object;
   d. document that transfers clear and unrestricted title to the receiving agency.

3. The accession card must be marked "deaccessioned" in red ink by the registrar with the date of transaction and the disposition of the object. While the object is no longer physically part of the collections of the museum, the accession number and card must remain a permanent part of registration records. An accession number will not be reassigned. It is the responsibility of the registrar to conduct the process of deaccessioning and to keep and maintain all deaccession records.

4. All duplicate accession cards of a collection area must be returned to the registrar's office. The catalog must be marked "deaccessioned" in red ink with the date and disposition of the object. This action is taken only by the curator. The catalog number remains a permanent part of the collection's records and is not reassigned.

Loans

Borrowing and lending objects are inherent practices in a museum and require specific procedures to assure object management. Loans do not involve transfer of title but are the temporary reassignment of objects from the museum (outgoing) to another institution or to the museum (incoming). All loans are for a defined period of time and for the stated purposes of exhibition, research, and/or education.

Loans are by authority of the director and are effected through the office of the registrar. Loans are initiated by a curator and transmitted in writing to the registrar. A written loan agreement must accompany every loan with specifications on the rights and responsibilities of each party. The loan contract must stipulate the conditions of the loan to ensure adequate storage, environmental protection, and safety precautions during transit, handling, and use. Loan contracts are kept on file in the registrar's office with a copy in the collection area. It is the responsibility of the curator to notify the registrar of the return and completion of a loan. The registrar establishes the procedures for packing and transportation of all loans.

Any loan arrangement (outgoing or incoming) that will require a financial or physical commitment by the museum or will obligate the museum to other than normal care, maintenance, or protection of objects, must be approved by the director.

Under no circumstances will objects and related accessioned documentation be loaned from or received into the museum collections without prior written approval from the appropriate curator, and notification to the registrar and the director.

Initiation of loan requests is made through the curator of the collection from which the materials are to be derived or in which the materials are to be housed, and coordinated through the registrar of the museum. The director will be kept informed of all loan negotiations.

Loans will be made for exhibition, research, and educational purposes only and for a stated period of time.

Loans will be made to institutions only, except as requested by a curator for an individual engaged in recognized research and/or educational activities, and as approved by the director.

A written loan agreement will accompany every loan and will define the rights and responsibilities of each party involved in the transaction. All contracts of loan will be through the registrar's office.

Loan objects may not be lent to a third party without advance written permission from the curator of the museum from which the objects are derived.

All commercial exploitation of loan objects is prohibited. Photographing or reproducing objects may not be done without advance written permission from the appropriate curator.

Damage or loss of loan objects must be reported to the appropriate curator. The registrar will immediately be notified of any damage or loss.

The museum reserves the right to cancel or deny renewal of any loan.

The museum will be credited in all publications and exhibitions associated with loan objects from the collections.

Requests or offers from individuals to place personal property in the museum usually will not be honored.

Objects left in the care of the museum without a signed contract for a period of seven years will be considered abandoned property and subject to acquisition and accession review. Prior to review the museum will provide normal curatorial care for these objects but cannot be held responsible for their condition.

Records of incoming and outgoing loans will be maintained by the registrar's office. Monitoring of object condition will be the responsibility of the appropriate curator.

Type materials and comparable objects will not be loaned.

Outgoing loans

Museum collections are maintained for the benefit of the public and objects are loaned to reach a wider audience and facilitate research. While on loan, objects must be afforded the same level of care and protection as provided by the museum. Because of these considerations, loans are made only to other similar institutions, non-profit agencies, and educational organizations. Loans for research purposes are made to the institution with which the individual is affiliated and that institution assumes full responsibility for the proper administration of the loan and the care and security of the objects. Requests for exceptions must be submitted in writing by the curator to the director for consideration who will respond in writing to the curator with notification to the registrar. The written request must contain full justification for the exception, length of loan, and evidence of the ability of the individual to provide appropriate care and security for the objects.

Objects considered for loans must be the property of the museum and accessioned into the museum's record, or must be assigned to the museum as the agent of another authorizing entity. All objects considered for loan must be acquired by legal and ethical means, and in stable condition to withstand the rigors of being on loan. Neither non-cataloged museum collections nor type specimens and comparable objects will be loaned. Each collection area may further restrict the kinds of objects or materials eligible for loans based on nature, rarity, monetary value, research priority, and/or management considerations of the objects.

The museum has an obligation to take precautions to assure that objects requested for loan receive proper care and security. It is incumbent on the requesting institution to present verification of their environmental, storage, exhibition, and security conditions and procedures for handling and transit of objects. Exhibition or research conditions must be stated clearly on the loan agreement and evidence of adherence may be requested. The length of time and other conditions of loan (such as periodic checks to monitor the safety of the objects, use of objects for stated purpose, condition of the objects, and to assure that insurance valuations are current) must be stated on the loan agreement and adhered to by the borrowing institution.

Packing and transportation methods that must be approved by the registrar will be stated clearly on the loan agreement. The objects must be packed and transported in the safest possible way in accordance with the nature and condition of the objects.

Loans generally are for a six-month period with an option to extend for an additional six months without having to return the objects for inventory and evaluation. Requests for longer periods must be in writing from the borrowing institution and fully justified. These renewal loans may be subject to restrictions including written evaluation (condition report) or the return of the objects for inventory, in-house evaluation, and assurance of current insurance valuation prior to the extended loan period. No objects shall be on exhibition loan for longer than one year or research loan for two years.

A condition report on objects going on loan, prior to packing for transport to the borrowing institution and after return to the museum, which is the responsibility of the registrar, is required. A condition report may be required from the borrowing institution upon receipt of the loaned material and prior to packing for return to the museum. Damage or loss of objects while in transit or during the loan period must be reported in writing to the curator with immediate notification to the registrar. Damage or loss of objects while in transit or during the loan period must be verbally reported immediately to the registrar with a subsequent written explanation directed to the curator. The registrar is responsible for providing appropriate information to the borrowing institution relating to a loan. Insurance claims for damaged or lost objects are the responsibility of the registrar. Objects on loan cannot be altered, cleaned, or repaired unless permission to do so is authorized in writing by the curator in the loan agreement.

Objects on loan must be returned promptly when the loan period expires. As appropriate, a reminder letter is sent to the borrowing institution. The museum reserves the right to cancel or deny renewal of any loan.

Loans that will radically alter or destroy objects may be permitted only with the written approval of the director. Requests must be made in writing by the curator to the director, and must contain full justification for the destruction and a description of the method to be used. The director will respond in writing with notification to the registrar. Although the object may not be returned to the museum, the information gained from the analysis will be provided to the museum in its place. It is the curator's responsibility to monitor materials on destructive loan, to assure their correct use, and to record the returned data in the collection records under the object's catalog number with notification to the registrar. The object is not deaccessioned. The museum does not in any way relinquish ownership of the object, and retains the right to recall the object, or its modified forms, if not used for the stated purpose within the loan period or if other circumstances warrant it. For objects held-in-trust for governmental agencies, a letter from the appropriate agency must be on file in the registrar's office approving the request prior to initiating the in-house documentation.

Field-generated, scientific collections, and associated ancillary material may require specialized knowledge (for example, sediments), and this may necessitate transport to specialists for data extraction and analysis. It is the curator's responsibility to monitor these materials and to record the returned data with the appropriate collection. If these materials are not accessioned, a formal loan agreement is not required. However, if objects (for example, seeds, insect parts, bones, snails) are returned with the data, they are accessioned with their appropriate collection and cataloged. Any field material accessioned prior to being sent for analysis must be accompanied by a loan agreement.

Because of security precautions and management considerations, third party loans are discouraged and seldom authorized. Written requests are to be made in advance to the curator by the original borrowing institution with full justification for the third-party loan. Subject to written approval by the director, the curator will respond in writing to the original borrowing institution with notification to the registrar. A third-party loan is subject to all loan conditions outlined in this document. A new loan agreement must be prepared by the registrar covering the third party, informing that institution of its rights and obligations. Return of the objects for inventory and evaluation prior to being lent to the third party may be required. Under no circumstances will a third-party loan be made to an individual.

Except for use in condition reports, all photography, reproduction, or replication of borrowed objects must be with prior written approval by the curator with notification to the registrar and director. Lighting, photographic conditions, environmental, and/or applied chemical alterations, and other conditions of reproduction and replication must be specified by the curator in writing. Photographs, reproductions, and replicas can be used only for research, exhibition, and educational purposes. Commercial use of loan objects is prohibited.

The museum must be credited in all publications and exhibitions associated with the loan objects including photographs and reproductions, and must receive two copies of any publication. The objects should be identified by their catalog or accession numbers. The proper name of the museum to be used in all acknowledgments is, "Museo de _____ ."

Incoming loans

Objects are received into the museum on loan from both institutions and individuals. In the event the lending institution or individual does not have a loan form available, the museum will adapt its form to provide documentation associated with the incoming loan. The museum will exercise the same care with objects on loan as it does in the security, handling, and storage of its own objects.

Requests for loan objects to the museum are initiated by the curator in writing to the lender with notification to the registrar. Normally, curators accept objects being placed on loan to the museum and sign the loan agreement form as the representative of the museum.

Under no circumstances will loan objects be received into the museum that have been acquired by other than legal and ethical means. Loan objects cannot be received from anyone other than the legal owner or their authorized agent.

Except for unusual circumstances, objects will not be received on loan from museum staff members. Exceptions for loans from museum-affiliated personnel must be requested by the curator in writing to the director who will respond in writing to the curator with notification to the registrar. The request must contain full justifications, loan purpose, and loan period.

It is the responsibility of the lender to set object valuations. The type of valuation should be stated on the loan agreement. The lender will monitor loan valuations and will notify the museum immediately if any changes occur during the loan period. If a valuation is not forthcoming or not mutually acceptable between the lender and museum, the director will reconsider pursuit of the loan. The registrar will notify the lender that failure to provide valuation(s) will result in non-acceptance of the loan. The museum will not provide evaluations or appraisals for loan objects.

Loans of personal property from individuals for warehousing in the museum *will not* be honored.

The registrar may require the lending party to certify that the loan objects can withstand ordinary strains of packing, transportation, and handling. The registrar may request that the lending party send a written condition report prior to the transportation of the objects. It is the responsibility of the curator to monitor the condition of the loan objects. Upon receipt of the loan, the objects must be inventoried, inspected, photographed (where appropriate), and written notations made of the findings. A copy of these findings must be maintained by the registrar.

Any inconsistency in the loan inventory, such as number or types of objects, damage or suspected damage, or any change in the condition of the loan objects, must be reported immediately to the registrar. The registrar must notify the lending party and, when appropriate, notify the insurance company and prepare a full condition report. *It is the responsibility of the registrar to handle claim negotiations.*

The curator is responsible for the prompt return of the loan objects. The objects must be inventoried, inspected, photographed (where appropriate), and written notations made of the findings. A copy of these findings must be maintained by the registrar. Any inconsistency in the inventory, damage, or suspected damage must be reported immediately to the registrar. The registrar must notify the lending party and, where appropriate, notify the insurance company and prepare a full condition report.

The museum reserves the right to cancel a loan or remove the loan objects from display at any time. All outgoing loans are for a set period of time that cannot exceed two years. Regular evaluation of each loan situation should occur to determine if loan renewal or updated insurance valuation is needed.

Normally, permanent incoming loans are not permitted. However, the museum recognizes that, by statute, some agencies are not permitted to deaccession objects but may offer such objects on permanent loan. Although title is not transferred, all other rights of possession follow. In this situation, although termed a permanent loan by the governmental agency, the objects are subject to the museum's acquisition policy, must undergo consideration by an appropriately designated museum committee, and, if accepted, the objects are accessioned into the museum collection.

When returning loaned material, the objects must be packed and transported in the same or a more suitable manner as the one in which they were received. Questions concerning packing and shipping arrangements of loan objects will be addressed by the registrar. The registrar will send the lending party a copy of the shipping list and a museum receipt form. If the lending party retrieves the loan objects in person, the museum receipt form must be signed prior to removal of objects from the museum.

The registrar may notify a lender of the museum's intent to conclude an incoming loan for which a written agreement exists that was made for a period that is unspecified or in excess of seven years. The statement of termination of loan must include the following information:

Records indicate you have property on loan to the museum. The museum wishes to conclude the loan. You must contact the museum, establish your ownership of the material, and make arrangements for return of the property. If you fail do so within sixty-five days from the date of this notice, you will be deemed to have donated the property to the museum.

Property on loan to the museum for seven years or more, and for which no written loan agreement exists, and to which no person has made claim according to the records of the museum, is considered abandoned and subject to conditions of ownership by the museum. (The exact period of time for determining abandoned property differs. Local laws should be consulted and the advice of an attorney should be sought prior to irreversible action.) The lender is given notice if the museum sends a letter to the lender at the lender's last known address. Should the museum not have a current address for the lender the museum will publish a notice at least once a week for two consecutive weeks in a newspaper of general circulation in the locality of the lender's last known address. The notice of the unclaimed loan will contain the lender's name, last known address, description of the loan objects, the date of loan, and the name, address, and telephone number of the registrar.

As part of a loan agreement, the lending party has the responsibility to maintain contact with the museum. If there is a change in ownership of the objects while on loan, as exemplified by the following conditions:

1. transfer of title,

2. death of the individual lending party, or

3. dissolution of the lending institution,

the lending party or its authorized agent must give prompt notice to the museum. In such cases, the museum will either negotiate a new loan agreement or return the objects.

Exhibits and public programs

Exhibits and public programs using space, funding, personnel, and facilities of the museum will be developed by designated individuals or committees appointed by the director.

All exhibits and public program requests will be evaluated on the following criteria:

1. Relevance to mission and community obligation of the museum.

2. Ability of the museum to properly develop, install, and maintain the objects or execute the program in a public environment.

3. Sociological and ethical implications of objects exhibited or public programs.

4. General value of exhibition or program to the museum and the public.

5. Type material and comparable objects will not be exhibited.

The director shall have the final authority for selection and implementation of all exhibitions and public programs in the museum.

As a general statement, in matters relating to the selection of objects to be exhibited in the museum, every effort will be made to maintain the confidence of the constituents. Exhibit decisions will be weighed not just in the view of what the museum perceives to be best for the people, but also with consideration of what the people perceive to be in their best interests. The desire of the museum to maintain the "good will" of special interest groups must be balanced with its obligation to carry out its responsibilities to the general public, and the greater community of national and international museums. Every reasonable effort will be exerted to avoid the appearance and fact that favoritism and commercialism rather than merit and scholarship dictate exhibit selection.

Facility use

This statement is intended to establish a written basis for use of facilities, grounds, equipment, supplies, and services of the museum. The policy is designed to support museum policies, and to clarify facility and grounds use standards and practices. In all cases, the primary decision-making factor regarding facility use shall be *support of the mission of the museum*. Under no circumstances shall extraordinary use of the facilities interfere with general accessibility during public hours. The director of the museum is the designated agent in determining appropriate practices regarding museum personnel, facilities, and equipment.

Museum grounds and facilities may only be used for public educational, research, and enjoyment purposes. No *personal* uses of facilities, equipment, or grounds are permitted. The concept of *no use for personal reasons* shall extend to those groups or organizations requesting use of the facilities simply as a convenient location to conduct activities having nothing to do with the purpose, intent, or mission of the museum. This restriction shall apply to all requests regardless of sponsorship.

Use or modification of the grounds adjacent to museum facilities must be approved by the director of the museum.

Reservations for space and services may be made by civic, support groups, and other non-profit organizations, as they qualify under museum policies. Museum facilities, equipment, grounds, and personnel may not be used for commercial interests.

Specific rooms and areas of the museum are designated for special events, meetings, catered meals, lectures, and symposia. The museum will maintain a list of available spaces, make reservations for their use, keep records, assess charges, and coordinate facility preparation activities.

All activities at the museum require the presence of security personnel. No substitutions may be made for security staff, nor may staff members volunteer their services to serve in a security role.

Modification or rearrangement of museum facilities, equipment, or materials for special events or group activities must be approved, in advance, by the director of the museum.

Groups that reserve museum space will be responsible for the care of that space during the event and for clean-up afterwards. Reparations for damage to the facility through negligence or abuse will be assessed to the responsible group.

Specific areas of the museum grounds have been designated for outdoor activities. Priority use of these spaces will be given to school children on prearranged tours. Use is on a first-come basis and no charges will be assessed. Clean-up is the responsibility of the school group using the facility.

Live, human-controlled animals, other than laboratory animals or seeing-eye, hearing, and security dogs, are not authorized to be housed in museum buildings or on the grounds. Laboratory animals may not be kept in the building beyond the immediate needs of research.

It must be restated that the above material is for information only. Each museum should design and execute a mission statement and the appropriate policies and procedures to implement that policy.

Each institution must respond to the governance, collections, and constituency to which that museum is responsible. Each museum is unique and must define its own operation practices within the limitations of proper collection care, maintenance, and interpretation.

Question from the field: four

Question: What are the advantages and disadvantages for a museum that has funding from a private foundation?

Response: Often the advantages and disadvantages of funding from a private foundation are the opposite sides of the same situation. A private foundation often has greater flexibility in setting priorities. Funds are easier to spend due to the lack of bureaucratic layering often found in public agencies. Private foundation funds may be under the control of one individual who may or may not support the activities of the museum. When a conflict occurs it is often difficult to resolve. Public agencies are somewhat impersonal, causing delays and frustrations. However, they are less likely to overreact when an extraordinary situation arises.

Tendencies in museums funded by private foundations verses public agencies might be considered in the following terms:

Private foundation	*Public agency*
• Personal	• Impersonal
• Flexible	• Bureaucratic
• Unstable	• Stable
• Responsive	• Pragmatic

Private foundation funds for museums are usually derived from interest generated from investments – as the market varies so does the level of funding. In extreme times the private foundation may decide to deaccession valuable works of art to regain fiscal stability. In contrast, public agencies are less dramatic in their fluctuations allowing for greater continuity.

□   □   □   □   □

Question from the field: five

Question: How do you deaccession objects without selling or exchanging them?

Response: First it is important to consider why the decision has been made to deaccession an object. The first assumption is that the material no longer has collection-related value and keeping it in the museum will waste space, time, and money. A second possibility is that the object has deteriorated beyond possible use. The third reason may be the acquisition of a better example, making the first piece either obsolete or redundant. Each of these situations is likely to prompt a different action.

Deciding the preferable method of removing objects from the collections requires careful consideration and good judgment. The value of a particular object may change and once the object is removed, it is lost forever.

An object that has lost its value to one museum may still have great significance to another. Transfer to another museum based on that institution's need is an ideal way to remove redundant objects. Instituting an agreement with a museum that will allow exchange without concern for immediate value-for-value transfer can be a very worthwhile arrangement.

In some instances, an object is worth retaining as museum property, but with limited usefulness. It should be in reasonably good condition and can be maintained with minimum care. The objects may be loaned to another institution for an extended period subject to periodic evaluations.

Objects and specimens having no scientific, historic, aesthetic, or educational values or those that have deteriorated beyond use may be destroyed.

> By definition one of the key functions of almost every kind of museum is to acquire objects and keep them for posterity. Consequently, there must always be a strong presumption against the disposal of specimens to which a museum has assumed formal title. Any form of disposal, whether by donation, exchange, sale, or destruction requires the exercise of a high order of curatorial judgment and should be approved by the governing body only after full expert and legal advice has been taken.
>
> ICOM, *Code of Professional Ethics*, section 4. "Disposal of Collections," paragraph 4.1, p. 29.

□   □   □   □   □

Question from the field: six

Question: Who decides what will be exhibited?

Response: The person with the final authority for deciding which objects will be exhibited is the director of a museum. The source of the information on which the decision is made depends on the individual institution and the policies of that museum. In many museums it is the curator who makes that recommendation. In others it may be the conservator, the collection manager, or the registrar, depending on the assigned duties of the persons involved.

> Stephen Weil notes, "Preservation serves the future at the expense of the present. Exhibitions serve the present at the expense of the future."[4]

By using a team approach to developing exhibits, the decision on which objects to use can be made at an early stage of the planning process.

Notes

1. American Association of Museums (1978) *Museum Ethics*, Washington, DC: American Association of Museums, p. 11.
2. Lewis, G. (1984) "Introduction to Museum Administration and Management," *Proceedings of the Annual Meeting of ICOM International Committee for the Training of Museum Personnel*, Leiden: Reinwardt Academie, p. 1.
3. George, G. and Sherrell-Leo, C. (1986, 1989) *Starting Right, A Basic Guide to Museum Planning*, Nashville, Tenn.: American Association of State and Local History.
4. Weil, S. (1983) "Introduction," *Beauty and the Beasts*, Washington, DC: Smithsonian Institution Press, pp. xiii–xiv.

Suggested reading

Appelbaum, B. (1991) *Guide to Environmental Protection of Collections*, Madison, Conn.: Sound View Press.

Bandes, S. (project director) (1984) *Caring for Collections*, Washington, DC: American Association of Museums.

Beibel, D. (1978) *Registration Methods for the Small Museum*, Nashville, Tenn.: American Association for State and Local History.

Lewis, G. (1984) "Introduction to Museum Administration and Management," *Proceedings of the Annual Meeting of ICOM International Committee for the Training of Museum Personnel*, Leiden: Reinwardt Academie.

Lord, B., Lord, G., and Nicks, J. (1989) *The Cost of Collecting, Collection Management in UK Museums*, London: Her Majesty's Stationery Office.

Malaro, M. (1985) *A Legal Primer on Managing Museum Collections*, 2nd edn 1987, Washington, DC: Smithsonian Institution Press.

Research and Education Association (1982) *Handbook of Museum Technology*, New York: Research and Education Association.

Thompson, J. M. A. (ed.) (1984) *Manual of Curatorship, A Guide to Museum Practice*, London: Butterworth & Co.

4

Museum security

Museum security is the philosophy and activity of providing an environment in which people and objects may be as free from threat of harm or damage as possible. Using this as a broad definition, there are several elements involved in such security. These include:

- staff
- barriers
- signage
- collection management practices
- housekeeping activities
- environmental monitoring
- alarms and surveillance
- security plan.

These components are interrelated with each other and with all other factors of museum management. Security is not only the job of security personnel, it concerns everyone who works at the museum. Security involves not just the publicly accessible parts of the institution, but all other parts as well.

Staff

The security personnel are the public faces of the museum. Inattentive or surly security staff members evoke like attitudes in visitors. Security personnel who are friendly, business-like, and helpful encourage the best response in the visitor. This adds to the appeal of the museum experience for the patrons, while increasing the probability that they will act appropriately during their stay.

In some museums, security personnel are trained to be public- or customer-relations specialists. The formidable, suppressive glare has been replaced by a demeanor that projects helpfulness as well as authority. Although security personnel are necessarily rule enforcers, they need not be unpleasant in executing their duties. Most people respond positively to a quiet word of correction, because they are usually unaware of the potential harm they pose to the objects or to others.

Alertness and observation are the principal tools of museum security personnel. If an institution's visitation varies from heavy traffic to virtually no visitors, the tendency is to become complacent and disinterested in the slow times, and to be resentful of the interruptions occasioned by busy ones. It is wise to give security personnel a variety of tasks to accomplish. These should be tailored to the sort of activity levels usual in the museum. Tasks for low activity periods may include detailed gallery checks and facility inspections. Such assignments help stimulate interest in the overall management of collections, provide valuable information about actual conditions in galleries, and give the security personnel a sense of their importance to the institution.

All staff members must share in museum security matters. Every person on the museum's staff should be alert and conscious of changes in the collections, environment, and behavior. Security personnel are primarily public-oriented in their scope of activities. That leaves the largest part of the institution – storage, workrooms, offices, etc. – as the concern of other staff members. Without an attitude of sharing the responsibility between all staff members, adequate security is virtually impossible. This means that every staff person, regardless of job or department, should appreciate their security role and support that of fellow staff members.

Barriers

An effective and time-proven method of safeguarding both people and objects is using barriers. A barrier is anything that comes between a person and an object. It is easy to imagine physical barriers as barricades: fences, railings, plates of glass or plastic, or even space. It is more difficult to picture a barrier that is implied, that is psychological rather than physical. Yet, such barriers can be more effective than physical obstacles.

Designing physical barriers for exhibitions that provide protection and avoid undesirable behavior, but that still allow maximum visibility will avoid negative audience response. Concerns to be aware of include providing an unobstructed view of objects and avoiding the impression that visitors are not welcome. Planning and building barriers into exhibits is an excellent way to both limit accessibility and enhance enjoyment of an exhibition without implying an assumption of wrongdoing on the part of the visitor.

People have a tendency to lean on anything that is convenient. If a surface is available at about the right height and size, people will lean on it, put their feet on it, or sit on it. This behavior is a response to actual, imagined, or anticipated fatigue. Constructing barriers that afford convenient places to sit or rest is often unintentional. Adequate seating in a gallery lessens the predisposition to use barriers (or exhibitions) as props for tired feet and backs. In many museums, barriers are designed to serve as both barricades and as places to lean while examining the exhibitions. Often it is better to work *with* human inclinations, rather than try to overcome them.

Humans display certain behavioral tendencies that can be used to create psychological, or implied obstacles. For example, as a rule people do not like to enter areas that are dimly lit or dark. They are uncomfortable with the unknown. Using this behavior, a designer can create spaces into which the public will not readily enter, or by applying the reverse, create spaces that visitors are more likely to enter readily. Areas of dark color are less inviting than brightly colored ones. Also floor color can provide subtle hints about the proper direction and appropriate behavior. Carpeted floors are more inviting than hard surfaced ones. Patterns in floor covering can act as directional guides and as limits to traffic flow. Varying levels of flooring can serve to separate people from objects. Stores and shopping centers have used all these devices quite effectively for controlling people and increasing the exposure of their wares.

Barrier designs are deceptive. What appears obvious to the designer is not always so to the visitor. It is usually wise to try out various barrier strategies and devices before investing a great deal of time or money in their purchase or construction. Observing visitor behavior around trial barriers, either real or implied, can provide valuable information about their effectiveness and suggest changes for improving them.

Signage

Signs provide information and direction, thus avoiding the uncomfortable experience of feeling lost. Signs may include large words placed at easy to see heights, labels or text panels requiring a closer approach, or even graphics and symbols that give clues about proper behavior or direction.

People are pummeled by signs on all sides. Words are the most familiar form of signage. Street signs, business signs, logos, door signs, billboards, etc., are part of daily life nearly everywhere in the world. We expect signs to instruct, inform, and direct us in most aspects of public life. It is not surprising that when people visit museums, they expect to find signs that inform them where to go, what to see, and how to act.

A major function of signage is to provide wayfinding information for visitors. Pointing the way to restrooms, first aid services, and administrative offices is important to those not familiar with the facility. Helpful signage shows a genuine interest by the museum toward the visitor, and adds to the comfort of the museum experience.

Another use of signs is as behavioral indicators. Displaying rules about acceptable and appropriate behavior is a way that signage can be a benefit and prevent the need for confrontation. In instances where incorrect activities occur, signs reinforce staff responses, removing the personal slant from necessary corrective actions.

Signs should be of sufficient size for visibility and legibility. This correlates with both the size of the whole sign and the height of the lettering. For high visibility signage, usually placed at an elevated level for wayfinding purposes, 2 to 6 inch (5.08 to 15.2 cm) letters are correct. For signs warning of the dangers of touching objects, or giving instructions about safety, 18 to 36 point types are advisable.

Color is also important. Exit signs are normally back-lit in eye-catching red. Wayfinding signs for restrooms are not often brightly colored, depending more on their size and placement to attract attention. Informational signs often use a color-code strategy to assist in easy recognition. Danger signs are normally large and brightly colored. Signs, such as "Please, do not touch the paintings," are often subdued in color but placed in highly visible locations. The specific design of signage should be carefully considered and some uniformity incorporated to avoid confusing messages.

As with barriers, it is important to research the effectiveness of the signage and be ready to make changes as indicated.

Collection management practices

Security in collection management encompasses the safety of collection objects in their environment, correct handling practices, and proper documentation of object movement and treatment.

In the area of environmental control, several factors must be considered. They are:

- temperature and relative humidity
- dust and pollution
- biological organisms
- reactivity of materials
- energy levels.

As discussed in the chapters on collection management, various control measures may be used to maintain a constant and stable environment. Environmental security can be ensured by using careful and proven collection management standards and practices.

A major aspect of collection security is control of access. Keep collections as isolated from handling as possible. Locking doors and issuing keys only as needed, and storing items in ways where they can be seen without handling are standard practices. There are several very practical reasons for limiting access to collections. Every time a door, vitrine, or storage case is opened, the internal climate changes. Dirt, bacteria, mold spores, and pollution pour into the space. Insects easily travel on trouser legs or shoes and are introduced to the collections by daily traffic. Open doors invite theft, vandalism, and untrained handling of objects. When people enter collection storage areas, lights are turned on causing raised energy levels, and fluctuations in temperature and humidity. In effect, any human activity around collections creates the potential for damage to objects.

The ideal situation for preservation of most collection items would appear to be keeping them in a darkened room with tightly controlled temperature and humidity levels. Some collection care-givers would say this is the correct solution. Due to the need for monitoring and use, this is not possible. Yet a measure of stability is needed. It is needed to slow deterioration of objects and to prevent introduction of damaging factors. In fact, collections need to be continuously monitored to intervene when deterioration begins, before it becomes serious. The normal compromise is to limit access to collections, whether in storage or on exhibition, allowing only the people needed to monitor collection conditions. The usual method is to lock doors and cases, and to control the issue of keys. When objects must be handled for conservation or preparation purposes, they should be removed from the storage area and taken to a workroom separate from the storage room.

Handling objects is a necessity if they are to be collected, monitored, maintained, conserved, and exhibited. Objects are most vulnerable to damage when people are holding them. At least two considerations are appropriate in this respect. One is that the human hand secretes body fluids such as sweat and oils constantly, no matter how dry one's skin feels. Such fluids are caustic and over time will begin to erode most substances, causing subtle damage at first, but later growing into severe conservation problems. The answer to this concern is to wear gloves of non-reactive materials, such as cotton or latex.

Another handling problem is properly supporting objects as they are carried. Collection objects should always be handled as though they might easily break. When picking up a lightweight object, two hands are required, one supporting from below, the other stabilizing at the weakest point. Never lift an object with one hand except in rare instances. Heavier objects should be carried with two hands supporting the objects from below at the points of greatest structural strength. With chairs, for example, one hand on either side of the seat is normally correct. Chairs should never be carried by their armrests or backs. Framed paintings should be carried by their sides, rather than picked up by the top of the frame. All such handling procedures may appear simple and based on common sense. However, before handling any collection object, it should be examined for the best and safest way to handle it.

One other consideration concerns the amount and frequency of handling. The less an object is moved the better. In storage it is helpful to contain objects in ways that permit them to be inspected and identified without touching them. Pots or baskets can rest in ethafoam collars that both support and stabilize the object, as well as providing a place for accession or catalog numbers for easy reading without picking up the items. Drawers, boxes, and cases should include lists of the items stored in them for quick verification of object locations and conditions. When possible, tags should be attached to objects to permit identification without the need to search for markings on the items themselves. Archival folders should be marked for identification so that frequent removal of the paper or photograph is not required. For items on exhibit, diagrams of the installation with identifying numbers denoting the objects in use eliminate the need to move the objects.

In addition to the physical handling of the collection objects, maintaining proper documentation is needed to ensure current, verifiable knowledge of the locations and conditions of all objects in the museum. Any time an object is inspected or moved from one location to another, the changes should be included on its permanent record. This will aid not only in keeping track of the object, but will often give clues to conservators should problems later arise.

Housekeeping activities

Housekeeping practices apply across the entire museum organization. Most of the time, housekeeping activities are considered the realm of the custodial or janitorial staff. Training housekeeping personnel is important. They should be instructed about the proper methods and materials to use around collections. It is equally important that every staff member be aware that good housekeeping begins with him- or herself. Picking up and disposing of trash, keeping food and drink containers and smoking debris out of the building (especially collection areas and exhibitions), and reporting cleaning needs are actions every museum person can take.

Removal of dust from the collection storage areas and exhibitions is important. Dust contains many and varied chemical products, as well as being an abrasive. Dust left to build up on cabinet and case tops, in corners, and in cracks provides a ready source of contaminants for collection objects when they are removed for inspection or use. Dust also provides sustenance and shelter to living organisms. Crumbs of food, dried beverage residue, and organic compounds from the collection objects contain nutrients. It is important to have regularly scheduled housekeeping activities. Collection areas should be routinely vacuumed or damp-mopped to remove floor dust. Tops of cases and cabinets should be cleaned with damp clothes, and lining or wrapping materials changed to remove contaminants. It is important to use cleaning aids that will remove the dust rather than redistribute it back into the atmosphere. It is equally important to avoid cleaning fluids and methods that pose dangers to the collections. Water-based products are usually best, but careful consideration and study should be applied before introducing products into collection areas.

Environmental monitoring

As already noted, regulating the environment surrounding collections is vital to object security. The wider concern is controlling the climate within the whole facility. In some instances, this may be a very difficult problem, especially if a mechanical air-conditioning and ventilation system is not present. Whether or not a mechanical system exists, control can be attempted. Before control measures can be instituted, however, monitoring is required to determine the actual conditions in the facility. For temperature and humidity, a useful tool is a hygrothermograph. This machine monitors environmental conditions over a period of days, recording conditions on a strip of graduated paper. From the record, one can determine fluctuations in temperature and humidity over several 24-hour increments and develop comparable data of the daily conditions. This will give the information necessary to address controlling fluctuations deemed potentially damaging to collections.

Another monitoring tool is the thermohygrometer. This device, often quite small, can be placed inside micro-environments for easy readings of their climatic conditions. The thermohygrometer does not make a paper record, but gives the current temperature and humidity levels. The advantage of these instruments is that they are small enough to be included inside exhibitions and storage containers. As a person does a daily inspection, he or she can get an accurate picture of the conditions to which the collections are being exposed.

The other piece of atmospheric test equipment needed is a psychrometer. These devices come in several models and styles, but they all operate in the same manner. By using a dry thermometer side-by-side with a thermometer covered with a damp cloth, a highly accurate and immediate reading of the environment can be made. By using the psychrometer as the absolute measurement, the other monitoring devices can be accurately calibrated for maximum effectiveness. Also, the psychrometer provides a valuable "spot-check" service when conditions are in question.

Monitoring includes other activities and materials as well. Sticky traps and light traps can reveal insect invasions before they become a collection problem. Light meters can inform about light levels on and around objects. Always, the chief monitoring activity is the collection inventory. This should be never-ending. Collections should be completely inspected and inventoried at least once yearly, and more often if possible.

All of the monitoring devices and methods suggested require that people study and respond to the results, otherwise nothing is accomplished. To provide responsible collection care, hygrothermograph charts must be read and responded to, light levels checked and adjusted, and sticky traps examined and appropriate actions taken.

Alarms and surveillance

Alarm systems are often considered the best method of providing security for people, collections, and facilities. The use of alarms is, of course, an old and continually evolving technology that steadily becomes more sophisticated. The only way alarms can be beneficial to museums, however, is if they alert a human being to a problem in time to prevent excessive damage. Unfortunately, most alarms call attention to events already taking place instead of sounding before they occur.

60

Surveillance equipment such as closed-circuit television systems (CCTV) also enjoy an overrated status as security systems. Again, CCTV is only helpful if a person is watching. Unfortunately, human attention spans are limited, making most video surveillance systems only partially effective at best. The danger is that sole dependence on CCTV leads to complacency. There is a false sense of safety engendered by the mere possession of alarm and surveillance equipment. In fact, nothing replaces the presence of an alert security staff member as a means of providing real security.

While alarm systems and surveillance networks are valuable tools, they do not, of themselves, provide security, except as potential deterrents. Visitors who notice a CCTV camera or a sign indicating the presence of an alarm apparatus may be more inclined to act appropriately, based on the likelihood that someone is watching them. A vandal or criminal will not be deterred by such factors unless, when the system is tested, there is an immediate and organized response. Only then will the equipment have a real deterrent value.

Security plan

Each institution should have a written plan for dealing with security. This should include not only what to do in response to problems, but also how to prevent problems from occurring. A code of conduct for security personnel should clearly state what is expected from those staff members. The procedures for opening and securing the facilities should be included. A copy of the reporting forms and instructions for their use needs to be in the plan. The pertinent institutional policies and procedures ought to be part of the plan, as well as diagrams of the facility for quick reference. Planned responses to the various situations that might occur should be devised and included.

An element of security planning sometimes overlooked involves foreseeing disasters. Most museums do not have enough personnel or equipment to deal with major disasters, whether caused by human or natural agencies. It is important that the museum have a well thought out plan of action for every foreseeable contingency: a disaster plan. The plan must be ready and available should the unthinkable happen. It should include what to do and whom to notify in case of fire, flood, threatening weather, bomb threats, earthquakes, or personal assaults, and any other of the many possible events that might occur in and around the museum.

Evacuation routes should be planned in advance, places of shelter should be clearly marked, and telephone numbers for emergency agencies should be easy to find. In addition to the provisions for personnel safety, the plan needs to include procedures for protecting, and if necessary, securing and salvaging collections. Collection documentation should be duplicated and stored off-site in the event the museum is destroyed. The location of those records should be noted in the plan.

No one enjoys contemplating the possible problems that might arise, but it is a necessary exercise if any viable response to a disastrous situation will be possible.

☐ ☐ ☐ ☐ ☐

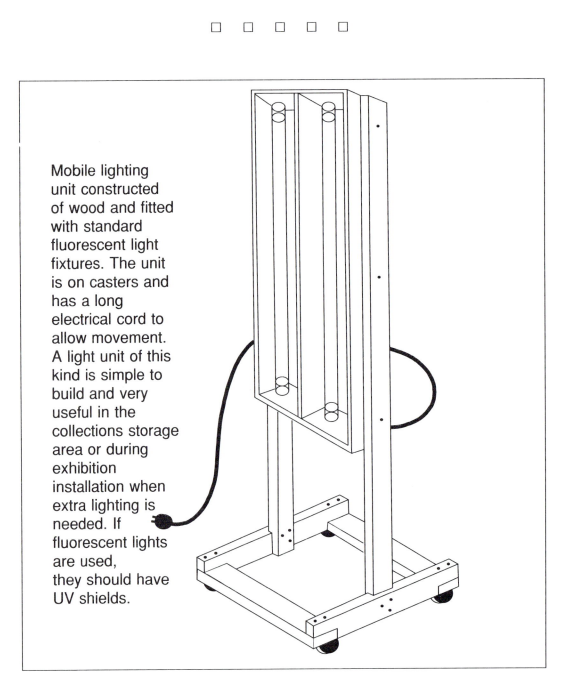

Mobile lighting unit constructed of wood and fitted with standard fluorescent light fixtures. The unit is on casters and has a long electrical cord to allow movement. A light unit of this kind is simple to build and very useful in the collections storage area or during exhibition installation when extra lighting is needed. If fluorescent lights are used, they should have UV shields.

Figure 4.1 Mobile lighting unit

Question from the field: seven

Question: What type of artificial light is advisable for use in archaeology storage?

Response: Probably the best commonly available lighting for most storage areas in a museum is fluorescent with ultraviolet filters. The light is relatively inexpensive, the bulbs (lamps) are easily obtainable in most places, and the light is even in distribution. Due to the high level of ultraviolet rays produced by fluorescent light, either tubes or film UV filters are extremely important.

To meet special lighting needs construct a mobile lighting unit with either fluorescent or incandescent lights. The unit can move about the storage or work area to provide the needed lighting. In this way the light level is kept low except in the area of immediate activity.

Suggested reading

Howie, F. (ed.) (1987) *Safety in Museums and Galleries*, London: Butterworth & Co.

International Committee on Museum Security (1986) *A Manual of Basic Museum Security*, London: ICOM.

Olkowski, W., Doar, S., and Olkowski, H. (1991) *Common-Sense Pest Control*, Newton, Conn.: The Taunton Press.

Schröder, H. (1981) *Museum Security Survey*, Paris: International Council of Museums.

Thompson, G. (1978) *The Museum Environment*, London: Butterworth & Co.

Thompson, J. M. A. (ed.) (1984) Manual of Curatorship, A Guide to Museum Practice, London: Butterworth & Co.

Tillotson, R. (D. Menkes ed.) (1977) *La Securité dans les musées* (Museum Security), Paris: International Council of Museums.

Zycherman, L. (ed.) (1988) *A Guide to Museum Pest Control*, Washington, DC: Association of Systematics Collections.

Section II
Museum collection management and care

5

Collections management

The International Council of Museums (ICOM) defines a museum as:

> "a non-profit making, permanent institution in the service of society and of its development, and open to the public, which acquires, conserves, researches, communicates, and exhibits, for purposes of study, education and enjoyment, material evidence of people and their environment."[1]

The most difficult part of maintaining a museum is the proper care and use of the collections that are called "material evidence of people and their environment." The care of collections is the primary responsibility of all museums. Collections come in many forms and may represent the most sacred and profound of a society's cultural heritage or embody the common elements of everyday life. Fine art objects, natural history specimens, aboriginal artifacts, or common use articles require the same special care once placed in the custody of the museum.

A metamorphosis takes place when objects, no matter what their intrinsic value, are transferred from personal possessions to museum objects. All acquire a uniqueness that exceeds previous existence. The level of care for all museum objects must be adequate to ensure their existence in the future.

As no museum can be all things to all people, basic decisions must be made concerning what can and cannot be done, particularly in the area of collection management, if a measure of public confidence is to be achieved. For a museum, a major step in this direction is the formation of a collections management policy.

A collections management policy is a detailed, written statement that sets forth the purpose of the museum and its goals, and explains how these goals are interpreted in its collections activity. The policy serves not only as a guide for the staff, but, more important, as a public statement of the museum's professional standards for objects left in its care.

A collections management policy includes specific information to cover the following:

- defines the purpose of the museum;
- explains the collection scope (what, where, when, and why);
- describes the uses of the collections;
- outlines acquisition strategies;
- recounts the loan policies for both incoming and outgoing loans;
- establishes the record-keeping requirements;
- delineates the method of disposing of items from the collection.

The collection policy is a basic planning document that contributes to the understanding and interpretation of the museum's mission. The policy is closely aligned with the mission statement of the museum. It should be used as a guide for curatorial activities and define, in concert with other planning documents, the goals of the museum. The collection policy may evolve from the historical collection pattern of the museum. It may also reflect a more current attitude of selectivity and focus for acquisitions.

> **"Each museum authority should adopt and publish a written statement of its collecting policy. This policy should be reviewed from time to time, and at least once every five years. Objects acquired should be relevant to the purpose and activities of the museum, and be accompanied by evidence of a valid legal title."[2]**

In writing the policy, there are several factors to be considered:

- The policy should be written in a way to serve as a useful guide for staff members and interested members of the public.
- The policy should be viewed as an opportunity to clearly state the goals of the museum and the methods to achieve those goals.
- The policy should consider effective procedures for evaluating collection care, maintenance, and needs.
- The policy should review and define the administrative structure of the museum and delineate the duties of the chief administrative officer.
- The policy should examine the needs of individual collection areas in the context of the goals of the museum as a whole.
- The policy should be flexible enough to accommodate unusual opportunities.
- The policy should reflect the records maintenance procedures for all activities that affect collection objects.

- The policy should explain the museum's responsibilities for items left in its care.
- The policy should appraise constituency needs and clearly state collection accessibility.

☐   ☐   ☐   ☐   ☐

The following part of this section is reprinted with permission from *Museum News*, the American Association of Museums. The article "Collections Management Policies," by Marie C. Malaro appeared in the November/December 1979 issue of *Museum News*. All rights reserved.

Drafting the policy

(1) **Statement of Purpose:** State the purposes of the museum, the present scope and uses of its collections, and the more immediate goals of the museum as these relate to the collections. The statement may refer to pertinent statutes or the museum's charter, for instance, and, where appropriate, the role of boards or committees involved in the collection procedures should be explained. It may also be helpful to refer to or attach bylaws or procedures adopted by such boards or committees.

If the museum maintains more than one type of collection (e.g., permanent collection, study collection, school collection), this should be explained along with the rationale for each such type of collection. Differences, if any, in the handling of these collections should be noted appropriately in the collections policy.

(2) **Acquisition of Items:** As a rule, objects may be added to the collections by means of gifts, bequests, purchases, exchanges or any other transactions by which title to the objects passes to the museum. In establishing criteria for determining whether an object should be added to a collection, at least the following points should be considered:

(a) Is the object consistent with the collection goals of the museum?

(b) Is the object so unusual that it presents an exceptional opportunity for the museum and thus should be given preferential consideration?

(c) If the object is offered for sale, might it or a comparable object be obtained by gift or bequest?

(d) Can the proper care be given to the object?

(e) Will the object be utilized in the foreseeable future?

(f) Is the provenance of the object satisfactory and how is this decision made?

(g) Is the object encumbered with conditions imposed by the donor regarding use or future disposition?

69

(h) Is the use of the object restricted or encumbered by intellectual property rights (copyright, patent, trademark, or trade secret) or by its nature (obscene, defamatory, potentially an invasion of privacy, physically hazardous)? How are decisions regarding such matters resolved and by whom?

(i) Will the acceptance of the object in all probability result in major future expense for the museum?

(j) What records must be made in the accession process, when are they to be made and by whom, and where are they kept?

In determining the procedure and the appropriate level of authority for acceptance of items for the collections, distinctions may have to be made on the basis of such factors as size or number of the objects, value, cost of maintenance and restrictions on use. Where appropriate, the museum's policy should set forth instructions on such matters.

As a general rule, an object should not be accepted unless it is destined for a particular collection. Exceptions to this rule should be rare and should be granted only after careful consideration, which includes satisfactory arrangements for disposition of unwanted objects.

Advice should be given regarding the appraisal of objects by the staff in response to outside requests. As a rule, museums avoid doing formal appraisals, especially at the request of donors or prospective donors. (This rule protects both the donor and the museum. Because the museum is the recipient of the gift, the objectivity of its appraisal is open to questions.) Deviations from this rule should require the approval of an appropriate museum official.

(3) **Deaccessioning:** As a general rule, unless there are specific restrictions to the contrary, collection items may be deaccessioned. However, in this area particularly, a museum should be very aware of its role as trustee of the collections for the benefit of the public. For example, when significant items are being considered for deaccessioning, it may be prudent to assure that museum procedures provide for appropriate outside comments before decisions are made.

In stating criteria for determining whether an object should be removed from a collection, some basic considerations are:

(a) Is the object no longer relevant and useful to the purposes and activities of the museum?

(b) Is there danger of not being able to preserve the object properly?

(c) Has the object deteriorated beyond usefulness?

(d) Is it doubtful that the object can be used in the foreseeable future?

(e) Is there a need to improve or strengthen another area of the collections in order to further the goals of the museum?

The collections policy should state clearly the procedures to be followed in deaccessioning, what records must be made of the process, when the records are to be made and by whom, and where the records are to be maintained. The type or value of the object under consideration may dictate additional precautions, such as:

(a) a higher value of approval than ordinarily required;

(b) the need for outside appraisals.

The question of acceptable methods of disposal may also be addressed:

(a) May disposal be by exchange, donation or sale?

(b) Will preference be given to any particular method of disposal?

(c) Will scholarly or cultural organizations be preferred recipients rather than private individuals or commercial entities?

(d) Will local or national interests be weighed in deciding on the recipient?

(e) If disposal is to be by sale, should preference be given to public auction or private sale?

(f) If an object has seriously deteriorated, may it be designated for educational "hands-on" use within the museum or donated to another educational organization for such purpose? May it be destroyed?

Additional questions associated with disposal procedures that may be considered are:

(a) If donors of items to be deaccessioned are alive, are they, as a courtesy, to be notified of the intent to deaccession?

(b) How are funds realized from deaccession sales to be used?

(4) **Loans:** In summarizing loan procedures (both incoming and outgoing), at least the following matters should be addressed:

(a) To whom will loans be made and for what purposes?

(b) Who has the authority to approve incoming and outgoing loans?

(c) If unusual restrictions are placed on a proposed incoming or outgoing loan, who must approve the loan?

(d) How are decisions arrived at concerning the provenance of items that may be the subject of an incoming loan?

(e) Will items be loaned or taken in on loan if it is doubtful whether they can withstand travel, climate changes, the circumstances of exhibition? How are such questions resolved?

(f) In order to insure proper accounting for both incoming and outgoing loans, should all loan transactions be for specified periods of time (with option for renewal)?

(g) What procedures must be followed by the staff in processing an incoming or outgoing loan? When must certain records be made and by whom?

(h) Who has the responsibility to monitor a loan?

(5) **Items Placed in the Custody of the Museum:** Ideally, every item placed in the care of the museum should be recorded in some predetermined manner within a reasonable time. This means that there should also be a registration method for items, other than loans, that are left temporarily in the custody of the museum for such purposes as attribution, identification or study. The registration method should be designed to control the acceptance of such deposits in accordance with the museum's policy and to encourage periodic review of the deposits in order to insure expeditious handling.

(6) **Care of the Collections:**

(a) At all times, staff members should be aware of their responsibilities to preserve and protect collection objects. This rather obvious point might warrant repetition in the collections management policy.

(b) Are the collections, whether on exhibition or in storage, adequately protected against fire, theft, vandalism and natural disaster? Are there established procedures for handling such emergencies? Who in the museum has oversight responsibilities in these areas?

(c) Conservation of collection items is a continuing responsibility. Should there be a delegation of responsibilities to appropriate staff members to monitor conservation needs?

(d) Appropriate attention should be given to the packing and shipping of collection items moving in or out of the collecting unit. Who bears the responsibility for monitoring this?

(e) Ideally, no collection item should ever leave its assigned collecting unit unless a written record is made and recorded of such movement.

(7) **Records:** The following comments may be helpful in judging the adequacy of a museum's records system.

(a) Each museum should have established systems for preservation of data on collections. Collection records may be divided into two general categories. The first includes records which are commonly associated with registration functions. These primarily document the legal status of an object within the museum and that object's movement and care while under the control of the museum. The second category includes records associated with curatorial functions. These provide a broad body of information about an object which establishes the object's proper place and importance within its cultural or scientific sphere.

(b) Good registration records normally include a descriptive catalog record as well as evidence of legal ownership or possession of all objects. These record systems should relate to objects by a unique museum number (e.g., accession number, loan number) and should provide for easy retrieval of object information as well as current object locations. Records of accessioned objects should further reflect the prior history of ownership of each object and all activity of such object (loan, exhibit, restoration, deaccession). Records of objects on loan to the museum should reflect all activity of such objects while under the control of the museum.

(c) Collection records should be made in a timely manner, housed in secure locations and physically preserved by proper handling and storage methods.

(d) If possible, a duplicate copy of registration records (e.g., microfiche) should be made and stored outside the museum as a security precaution.

(8) **Insurance:** Some questions concerning insurance that may be addressed are:

(a) If funds are limited, what is the proper role of insurance versus, for instance, protection, conservation, packing and transportation requirements?

(b) Is insurance to be carried on the museum's collections when these collections are in the custody of the museum? If so, are collections insured at full value or at a fraction of value?

(c) Must outgoing loans be insured? If so, by whom? Who pays?

(d) Must incoming loans be insured? If so, by whom? Who pays?

(e) Are objects left in the custody of the museum insured?

(f) What records must be kept regarding insurance and by whom?

(g) Who has authority to approve deviations from general insurance policies?

(9) **Inventories:** In order to police collections activities, the museum may wish to establish inventory procedures. These procedures may address such topics as:

(a) uniform method of maintaining inventory records,

(b) periodic comprehensive inventories,

(c) spot-check inventories,

(d) procedures to be followed if collection items appear to be missing.

(10) **Access to the Collections:** This section may address such topics as:

(a) Who has access to the collections? (Actual physical access as well as copies of collection or collection-related material.)

(b) When can access be denied and by whom?

(c) Are fees to be charged for record reproduction work? Before answering these questions, any "freedom of information" and/or "privacy" laws in effect in your locality should be reviewed. (A government controlled museum may have more complex problems in the area of access.)

☐   ☐   ☐   ☐   ☐

The production of a viable collection management policy is a difficult and time-consuming task. It can require many hours of careful study, clear thinking and cooperative effort.

Example of a policy

The following is an example of a Collections Management Policy courtesy of the Eiteljorg Museum of American Indian and Western Art in Indianapolis, Indiana. The policy has been altered to be generic in nature rather than specific to the collections of the Eiteljorg. The policy is reproduced with the permission of the museum.

COLLECTIONS MANAGEMENT POLICY

for the

_____Museum

1. STATEMENT OF PURPOSE

The_____ Museum is dedicated to the preservation and interpretation of the_____ of the_____. The purpose of the museum is to increase the knowledge and understanding of the_____ . To achieve this purpose the museum will actively pursue the establishment, the expansion, and the maintenance of its collections in _____ _____ . Accordingly, the museum's collections are to provide a basis for its exhibition and educational programs, for research and study, for special lectures and symposia, and for cultural and educational enrichment of the community.

2. PURPOSE OF COLLECTIONS POLICY

A) Establish the museum's methods of acquiring works of art and artifacts for the collections.

B) Establish the museum's methods of deaccessioning works of art and artifacts from the collections.

C) Establish procedures by which works of art and artifacts may be lent to other museums or borrowed from other museums, institutions, and private sources.

D) Establish procedures for a comprehensive record keeping system of all objects placed in the museum's custody. Insuring the optimum care and management of the museum's collections is always the primary concern of the staff [and board of directors].

E) Establish ethical and legal procedures for an effective collections management system.

F) Provide a basis upon which all questions concerning the museum's collections and collecting activity are answered.

3. CRITERIA FOR COLLECTIONS

A) The museum shall maintain three specific types of collections:

   a) The Permanent Collection

   b) The Research Collection

   c) The Education Program Collection

for the purpose of providing and expanding the foundation for the museum's exhibition program, and establishing a valuable educational and cultural resource for the community.

4. DEFINITION OF TYPES OF COLLECTIONS

A) *Permanent Collection*: designates all objects for which the museum has exclusive ownership, which are assigned a museum accession number, and which are maintained on the current files of the registrar's office. The museum shall pursue, through purchase, exchange, gift or bequest, objects in this category that significantly contribute to the museum's collection and that possess the visual integrity and physical condition necessary to be incorporated into the museum's exhibition program.

B) *Research Collection*: designates all objects for which the museum has exclusive ownership, which are assigned a museum accession number, and which are maintained on the current files of the registrar's office. The museum shall pursue, through exchange, gift or bequest, or purchase objects that significantly contribute to the teaching and the related study of _____

_____. These objects may be used to supplement temporary exhibitions and/or utilized for research purposes by the museum's staff, visiting academic scholars, and museum professionals in the course of study for publications or teaching programs.

1) Objects from the Permanent Collection may be placed in the Research Collection category given the following procedure:

   a) A thorough evaluation of the object's importance to the Permanent Collection is made by the collections staff in cooperation with the director.

   b) It has been determined that the object no longer possesses its original high degree of visual integrity or physical condition or it has been replaced by a similar object of greater significance.

   c) A recommendation of transfer has been accepted by the director and the board of directors.

C) The museum shall maintain a separate Education Program Collection. Objects in this collection may be obtained through gift or bequest or purchased only through funds allocated for educational purposes. Objects in this collection will not be assigned a museum accession number nor will they be maintained on the files of the registrar's office. The director of education shall have complete discretionary powers to accept, reject, utilize, or dispose of objects in this category. All records of such objects shall be maintained by the Director of Education.

5. SCOPE OF COLLECTIONS

   A) The museum shall actively collect _____
       that relates to the history, the development, and the cultural significance of the _____ .

   B) The museum shall actively collect works of art and artifacts that relate to the artistic, cultural and historical understanding of the _____
       _____ . Prehistoric objects and archeological material shall be considered on an individual basis.

6. ACQUISITION OF OBJECTS
   A) Only those works of art and artifacts which meet the following conditions and governing rules of acquisitions will be accessioned into the museum's collections:

1) The object(s) must have intrinsic value.

2) The object(s) must be consistent with and be relevant to the stated purpose, scope, and activities of the museum.

3) The object(s) must be of "museum" quality. Primary consideration will be given to the museum's ability to provide proper care and storage for any work of art or artifact. No object(s) should be considered for acquisition if its physical condition exceeds the museum's financial ability to provide for its care and preservation.

4) The museum must be able to provide proper storage for any acquisition under consideration.

5) The object(s) must have a verifiable record of authenticity and provenance. The provenance of acquired objects shall be a matter of public record.

6) The object(s) must have a free and clear title.

7) The museum acknowledges its responsibility to ascertain that objects offered, whether by purchase, exchange, gift, or bequest, are not stolen, wrongfully converted, or are in the United States illegally. The acquisition of cultural property of foreign countries is to be guided by the policies of the UNESCO Convention of November 14, 1970.

8) The museum will decline to accept archeological material if there is reasonable belief that the circumstances of its recovery involved the recent unscientific excavation or intentional destruction of sites either within or without the United States.

9) The museum shall, at all times, be aware of and sensitive to the concerns of indigenous persons when considering the acquisition of artifacts. Under no circumstance shall the museum pursue the acquisition and/or display of aboriginal skeletal remains, burial objects, or other highly sacred artifacts.

10) If the museum should discover that it has inadvertently acquired an object that is proven to have been obtained in violation of rules 7, 8, or 9 above, the museum shall seek to return the object(s) to its legal owner or shall seek to determine, through outside recognized and competent authorities, the proper means of disposition.

11) If possible, an examination period of 45 days should be required for any acquisition under consideration for purchase. If possible,

and practical, a second appraisal of the object's monetary and aesthetic worth should be secured from a recognized and unbiased authority by the museum at its expense.

12) The donor is responsible for appraisals of value. Under no circumstance shall the museum provide an appraisal of a donation. It may offer only suggestions concerning outside appraisal services.

13) All acquisitions are to be outright and unconditional.

14) No objects shall be accepted into either the Permanent Collection or the Research Collection if the immediate intent is to sell or exchange it for another object(s). Potential donors may donate object(s) to the museum with the intent and understanding that such object(s) will be sold to provide contributions to the acquisitions fund.

15) All donations to the museum's collections are irrevocable upon the formal and physical transfer to the museum.

16) All legal instruments of conveyance and warranty of title, signed by donor/seller/agent setting forth an adequate description of the objects involved and the precise conditions of transfer shall accompany all acquisitions.

17) Acquisitions by gift or bequest to the Permanent Collection must remain in the possession of the museum for a minimum of five years or as long as they retain their physical integrity and authenticity, and as long as they remain useful for the purposes of the museum.

18) Vendors offering works of art or objects for sale to the museum must be established and reputable merchants. The museum shall avoid acquiring objects from known or recognized independent "artifact traders" and "pot hunters."

7. PROCEDURE OF ACQUISITION

A) The director and collections staff are ultimately responsible in the search and identification of sources for acquisitions. Such tasks shall be conducted under the supervision of the Board of Directors. Both the director and the curator of collections have discretionary power to refuse objects which do not meet the stated criteria and procedures for acquisitions.

B) All objects under consideration for acquisition, either through gift or purchase, will be subject to the thorough examination, research, and recommendations of the collections staff and director before a formal decision is made. No object shall be accepted for consideration with out the full knowledge of the director.

C) The director shall provide the Board of Directors, prior to each regular meeting, with a written summary of appropriate information concerning works of art or artifacts offered as gifts, bequests, extended loans, or for purchase along with the recommendations of the registrar and curator of collections.

D) All acquisitions must receive approval by the Board of Directors before being formally accepted into the collections, except that the director may formally accept, on behalf of the museum, gifts or bequests under $10,000 and may purchase, within guidelines established by the Board of Directors. In such cases, the director will provide the Board of Directors a written report detailing the acquisition activity.

E) The Board of Directors' recommendations concerning the acceptance or rejection of object(s) under consideration will be set forth in the minutes of their meetings.

F) The curator of collections, in cooperation with the registrar, will prepare or assist in the preparation of all legal instruments of conveyance, transfer of title, and letters of acknowledgment, acceptance or rejection, and submit those records appropriate to the donor/vendor.

G) The museum shall extend to any donor the right of anonymity.

H) Once an acquisition is formalized, the museum must obtain immediate physical possession. No objects shall remain in the possession of the donor or vendor beyond the minimum time (not to exceed two weeks) needed to relocate items to the museum's collection storage facility.

I) It shall be the primary responsibility of the museum staff to ensure the authenticity of an object prior to its formal acceptance or rejection, to ensure that a valid "Deed of Gift" is created to document transfer of ownership of objects donated to the museum, or to ensure that a valid "Bill of Sale" is secured for objects purchased by the museum.

J) All acquisitions will be assigned an accession number, properly documented, and all appropriate records permanently maintained by the registrar's office.

K) The curator of collections, in cooperation with the registrar, will submit at the end of each fiscal year an annual report detailing that year's collections activity including acquisitions, deaccessioning, documentation, conservation needs, and future plans for the museum's collections.

L) The museum must be made aware of any copyright restriction (either through vendor notification or staff research) and must be conspicuously noted in the registrar's files. The public relations department must be made fully aware of any object which bears a copyright restriction.

8. PROCEDURE FOR DEACCESSIONING

A) The museum reserves the right to deaccession any object under the following criteria:

1) Objects shall be considered for deaccessioning for the purpose of improving the museum's collections and exhibition programs.

2) Objects may be deaccessioned only if they are not relevant and useful to the purposes and activities of the museum, or have failed to retain their physical integrity and authenticity and cannot be properly stored, used, and preserved.

a) The director, the registrar, and the curator of collections must recommend that the object be disposed of and give direction for its disposal. The object, accompanied by the recommendations shall be presented to the Board of Directors or a duly authorized committee.

b) The deaccessioning of any object shall require approval by the Board of Directors.

c) If the Board votes that the object shall be retained, an explanation stating specifically their reasons and recommendations shall be set forth in the minutes of the Board's meeting and shall be submitted to the director to guide the staff in future use of the object.

d) All records of any deaccessioned object shall continue to be permanently maintained by the registrar's office.

3) Disposal of deaccessioned objects shall be made by one of the following means which are listed in order of preference:

a) Exchange with another non-profit institution.

b) Donate to another non-profit institution.

c) Sale to another non-profit in-state institution.

d) Sale to another non-profit out-of-state institution.

e) Sale or exchange to a reputable for-profit institution.

f) Make available at public auction outside the museum's immediate locale.

*Any item acquired as a direct result of deaccessioning of another object shall be noted as "provided by" the donor of the original item.

4) Under no circumstance may a member of the Board of Directors, member of an advisory committee, museum employee, or their representative or immediate family be sold, given, or otherwise obtain possession of deaccessioned objects.

5) No private sales may be conducted under any circumstances.

6) All monetary gain realized from the sale of any collections object shall be added to the Acquisitions Fund.

9. CONFLICT OF INTEREST

A) No Board of Director, advisory board member, museum employee, or their immediate family member shall take advantage of information available to him or her concerning the acquisition or deaccessioning of collections object(s) for his or her own personal collecting activities.

B) No Board of Director, advisory board member, museum employee, or their representative or immediate family member may compete for personal gain in the purchase of any object which is being considered or is likely to be considered for the museum's collections.

C) No Board of Director, advisory board member, museum employee, or their representative or immediate family member may, directly or indirectly, purchase or otherwise acquire objects from the collections through the act of deaccessioning or any other means.

D) Should conflict develop between the needs of an individual and the museum, those of the museum are always considered priority and shall always prevail.

E) All employees who actively collect in the same area as the museum must submit to the director a summary of objects which they currently possess. Such a document is to be maintained by the director and secure from disclosure to any other individual.

10. INCOMING AND OUTGOING LOANS

A) It shall be the policy of the museum to borrow objects from other museums, galleries, and private sources for the purposes of exhibition, research, or public education. In addition, the museum shall lend objects from its collections to responsible institutions for the purposes of exhibition, research, or public education.

1) Specific terms of agreement between lender and borrower for incoming and outgoing loans shall be negotiated on an individual basis.

2) All incoming and outgoing loans must be approved by the director in consultation with the registrar and curator of collections.

3) Loans will be made only if and when a formal written loan agreement has been executed.

4) Copyright restrictions are to be observed at all times.

B) Incoming Loans

1) Incoming loans shall be for specific purposes and time periods.

2) Objects on loan will receive the same care as those which are owned by the museum.

3) If damage occurs to a loan object (or group of objects) it is the responsibility of the collections staff to contact the lender at the earliest possible date. No conservation work may be undertaken without prior consent of the owner.

4) No modification of a loan object shall be made by the museum unless it is of a cosmetic nature (i.e. matting/or framing) and it is carried out with the complete and written consent of the owner.

5) The museum shall not borrow any object which is physically unstable and in need of conservation.

6) Long-term or "permanent" loans are to be executed only after careful consideration and a full discussion by the director, the collections staff, and the Board of Directors of the perceived "advantages" and "disadvantages." Recognizing that many long-term loans are attempts to secure free storage, care, and preservation for personal collections, the museum will only accept loans offered if there is reason to believe that the object(s) will be

regularly exhibited. Such loans are to be accepted for a one year period renewable only if the need of the institution warrants such renewal.

7) The museum will comply with all restrictions and conditions placed on borrowed objects. The museum will comply with any credit citation requested by the lender.

C) Outgoing Loans

1) Objects from the museum's collections may be loaned to other museums and institutions for a finite period of time.

2) All requests must clearly state in writing the intended use (which includes both exhibit and publication purposes and period of use).

3) The borrower must complete and return a Facility Report noting fire and police protection; lighting, temperature, and humidity control; trained personnel; etc., before preliminary consideration of a loan will be made. The museum may place certain restrictions on a loan object regarding how it is to be exhibited.

4) Loans will be considered on the basis of the best interests of the museum and the public it serves.

5) No loan request will be approved if it exposes any object to undue risk because of exhibit conditions, means of transportation, or any other factor which falls below the prescribed standards for care and maintenance set by the American Association of Museums.

6) A thorough examination and an assessment of the physical condition of the object(s) must be made before formal approval is given. Any pre-existing weaknesses, imperfections, deterioration, inconsistencies, fractures, tears, repairs, or other alterations must be thoroughly documented in a written report and photographed.

7) The borrower will bear full cost for handling, crating, insurance, and transportation of objects, and must comply with those methods adopted by the museum.

8) Requests to borrow "works of special importance" to the museum's collections must be approved by the Board of Directors.

9) The borrower may not clean, restore, or make any modification to an object in any way either for exhibit or research purposes.

10) The borrower is to bear full responsibility for any object that is lost or damaged during transit or while in the physical custody of that institution.

11) If damage occurs, the borrower must immediately notify and comply with the wishes of the museum. The registrar's office must be notified at the earliest possible date of the damage and the actions to be taken to correct the problem.

12) The museum may require that certain loans be accompanied by a staff member(s), both outgoing and incoming, and that packing and unpacking, mounting and dismounting be supervised by such a staff member(s) at the borrower's expense.

13) When the loaned object(s) is returned to the museum, it shall be the responsibility of the curator of collections to examine it for any changes in physical condition. The director shall be immediately notified of any such changes to allow for appropriate action by the museum and the borrower.

14) The borrower will be furnished with two condition reports. One is to be completed, signed, and returned upon the initial un-crating of the object(s). The second report is to be completed and signed upon re-crating and returned with the object(s) to the museum.

11. INSURANCE

A) The Board of Directors, upon recommendation from the director, shall determine the insurance program. The policy shall be reviewed on an annual basis through the cooperative efforts of the director, the registrar, director of finance, and the curator of collections.

B) A record of the purchase value, appraisal value, or in some cases, an estimated value of each object or group of objects in the Permanent Collection and the Research Collection shall be maintained by the registrar's office and placed under limited access.

12. ACCESS TO COLLECTIONS AND RECORDS

A) The director shall have discretionary power to designate any additional staff member(s), in addition to the registrar, curator of collections, and collections assistant, who may have access, either on a restrictive or nonrestrictive basis, to the collections storage facility. The collections staff shall make every effort to comply with requests (for such access or information), from within and without, that are in keeping with the stated objectives of the museum's goals, programs, and activities.

B) Other individuals, including staff members, and visitors, may only enter storage areas when accompanied by the director, curator of collections, or the registrar.

C) Access to objects in the Research Collection shall be granted by the registrar's office on an appointment basis to qualified researchers. Such requests must be made two weeks in advance and access must be supervised by a member of the collections staff. Objects may not leave the collections facility. The museum reserves the right to request recommendations of a researcher from an established institution.

D) Collections records shall remain restricted in use to all other individuals, both within and without the museum, with the exception of the director, registrar, and curator of collections. Only the basic accessioning information shall be made available for viewing. Donor files, object appraisals or values, location records, and insurance records shall remain confidential.

E) The museum reserves the right to obtain copies of scholarly publications which result from the utilization of information and/or materials from its collection.

13. REPRODUCTION AND PHOTOGRAPHING OF COLLECTIONS ITEMS

A) The collections staff shall maintain a comprehensive schedule of fees to be charged for reproducing or photographing items in the collections. Extreme care must be taken to ensure the protection of copyrights, patents, or any other property rights.

B) A full credit line, as authorized by the registrar's office, is required when any object from the collection is published or reproduced.

C) Authorization of use of photographs or reproductions is granted on a basis of ONE TIME USE ONLY.

D) Exhibits may be photographed by visitors for non-commercial purposes only. Flash equipment and tripods are PROHIBITED in the galleries. Photographers must not obstruct other museum visitors and be at least three feet away from exhibits.

14. CARE OF COLLECTIONS

A) The museum shall maintain in its annual budget funding for the on-going care and conservation of objects in the collections. It shall be the responsibility of the collections staff, through regular periodic inspections, to assess the physical needs of objects in the collection and make the appropriate recommendations to the director and Acquisitions Committee.

B) It is the responsibility of the museum to ensure that the collections are adequately protected against fire, theft, vandalism, natural and/or environmental disasters. Proper exhibition and storage facilities along with adequate environmental control systems must be a HIGH PRIORITY at all times. Consideration must be given to provide a well trained security staff and maintaining a high level of awareness and understanding of professional collections standards and procedures. A review of these measures shall be made throughout the year.

C) An important part of the collections care procedure shall be the establishment and implementation of a comprehensive records system which includes at least the following: documents recording the legal status of title of an object(s); all correspondence, minutes and documents pertinent to an accessioned object; accessioning and cataloguing records; deaccessioning records; photographic documentation; exhibit, condition, and conservation history; insurance records; current location and loan records; and an annual inventory record. The curator of collections and the registrar are responsible for the establishment and maintenance of the records system on a daily basis. The director and Board of Directors shall be responsible for its enforcement.

D) A duplicate copy of all vital collections records shall be made and stored outside the museum in a secure and appropriate institution.

☐　　☐　　☐　　☐　　☐

Question from the field: eight

Question: When you acquire an object where does it go first for accessioning?

Response: All objects entering a museum should go first to the receiving room. This room should be separate from the collection storage area. In that location, the curator, registrar, and conservator should review the object to determine its condition and the level of care required before introducing it to the collection. (In museums with limited personnel, the object should be carefully checked by the person responsible for collection supervision.) Many pests enter the collection area by way of newly acquired objects that have not been properly and thoroughly examined.

As the object is being reviewed, the registrar assigns an accession number, makes the proper entry into the accession book, and completes the necessary accession forms.

Once the review is completed and the accession number applied, the most critical treatment should begin. Direct action like cleaning, fumigating, or disassembling should take place before transferring the object to the collection storage area.

Question from the field: nine

Question: Is it necessary to have a fixed terminology to manage the registration of collections?

Response: Semantics is a major problem for registering many non-scientific collection objects. For samples and specimens in scientific collections, standard terminology exists and is in common use. Common names are often used to describe artifacts in history, clothing, art, and ethnology collections. Later, those names may lose their significance making the descriptions useless. Generic names are often used that describe a type of object rather than a specific object. The word may have specific meaning to the person using it, but mean nothing to others.

A vocabulary should be formulated that is appropriate to a museum's collection needs. As the nomenclature for each type of object is set up, it must be recorded, alphabetically, in either a reference book or card file. The files for collections processed without benefit of common nomenclature should list all variations of the accepted vocabulary. The preferred words are marked on the file and the date of its first use noted in the margin. In this way, new or more acceptable terminology can supersede that used before.

To clarify the process, the object identification card should include an object classification as well as an object name. As an example: an object may be identified as "kitchen ware" as a general classification and "frying pan" or "skillet" as the specific nomenclature. As long as the vocabulary is used regularly and commonly applied, it is acceptable. The best situation is to have a nomenclature that is universally, or at least nationally, recognized.

An important factor about nomenclature to remember is that objects described by the same name should be identifiable in the collection. This is achieved by using an object card filed by general category name and specific name. Computerized collections can be sorted by name.

☐   ☐   ☐   ☐   ☐

Question from the field: ten

Question: How do you inventory a museum collection?

Response: The inventory process must start with good and complete record-keeping. The work of inventorying a collection is greatly reduced when the files are complete. For small collections a systematic comparison of catalog card with object is the easiest method. This is done by starting with the first catalog entry and finding the object using the location listed. The date of the inventory is noted on the back of the catalog card. The process continues until every catalog card is checked against the appropriate object. The system is slow but thorough.

Storage Unit Number	Object Numbers
Unit FA–1	1976–3
	1968–527
	1959–328–5
	1959–328–6
	1989–555–36
	1992–4
Unit FA–2	1937–90–50
	1952–425–7a
	1952–425–7b
	1990–6–23
	1927–333–36

Figure 5.1 Example of computerized location system based on storage unit contents.
Note: FA–1 notes the first fine art storage unit. The object numbers are those of the objects housed in that particular case.

Collections are also inventoried using the storage unit locating card. Compare the object number to the number noted on the storage unit card, and write the date next to the catalog number. This process can be very efficient if a location file is a part of the cataloging process. The location file will list all the objects in any particular storage unit. This method is also used for computerized collections by doing a data search based on the location field.

A location-based computerized index of collections can be very effective. Objects can be quickly located with a minimum of object disturbance. A location system should be as simple and easy to use as possible.

☐　　☐　　☐　　☐　　☐

Question from the field: eleven

Question: Is the use of a computer necessary to maintain a good collection record and do a proper inventory?

Response: No! A computer is a tool that can help the record-keeping process. The primary benefit of using a computer for collection management is the speed of information recovery. However, the time required to enter the information in the computer is hardly different from that needed to type a pre-printed index card.

Careful record maintenance is the key to being able to conduct an inventory with few complications.

☐　　☐　　☐　　☐　　☐

Question from the field: twelve

Question: If you register each collection according to its specialty, that is art, history, textiles, archaeology, et cetera, what is the method you use when a collection is a mixture of all materials? Do you keep the collection together or do you distribute it according to its discipline association?

Response: Accessioning a collection into a museum is by numeric sequence based on the year and time of arrival. When a particular collection has several kinds of objects they are numbered as part of the same collection. Depending on the nature of the objects, they may be separated for storage and cataloged separately. Objects with research or historical affiliation may be housed in the same collection area. As an example: an historic painting may have more informational value than aesthetic merit. For that reason a decision could be made to house the painting with a related collection in the history storage area rather than in the art storage room. Decisions of this kind are made by the curators involved and the registrar of collections. Regardless of the conclusion, a careful listing of all objects and their locations are included as part of the catalog record. No object should be moved, deaccessioned, loaned, or exhibited without the proper curatorial and registrarial involvement.

☐　　　☐　　　☐　　　☐　　　☐

Question from the field: thirteen

Question: What kind of forms should you use to catalog objects in addition to an accession form?

Response: It is not the number of forms but the amount of necessary information that is important. The primary factor of cataloging is to amass adequate documentation to allow rapid and accurate recovery of both the object and the related information. This process can be done with two or more forms. Cross-referencing objects is an accepted method of collection control. Forms (cards) are developed based on year of acquisition, object material (wood, bone, stone, metal, ceramic, et cetera), site (origin), donor, age, style, period, or other designation depending on the object.

Each form (card) should include the location of the object and the appropriate identification material. Another entry of importance is a shelf or cabinet location card. This form (card) is attached to the shelf or cabinet. It documents the exact location of each object in a particular storage unit.

56–10–2	69–352–25		69–352–26
75–11–6a	73–426	70–69–4	69–352–27
75–11–6b	73–426–5	85–34	
75–25–2	90–397	85–35a	85–35b

Figure 5.2 An example of a simple shelf location card

☐   ☐   ☐   ☐   ☐

Question from the field: fourteen

Question: Is it correct to cover wood shelves with plastic or flannel?

Response: Wood shelving has several interesting characteristics. It is flammable. It will rot. It is perfectly suited for insects. It contains acetic acid, formic acid, and small amounts of propionic acid, isobutyric acid, and formaldehyde. The level of release of these organics depends on the type of wood and the temperature and relative humidity. None of these concerns is satisfactorily addressed by covering the shelves with plastic or flannel.

Wooden shelving used for anything other than wood– or silica–based objects such as ceramics, glass, or some stones, should be sealed or covered with mylar or glass. Many plastics will not prevent off-gassing and will trap moisture and promote rot and mold. Flannel adds to the chance of infestation by certain types of insects, and traps and holds moisture. It cushions objects but provides little else in the way of protection.

There are no surface coating materials that will completely seal wood against "off-gassing." Oil-based paints, polyurethanes, or alkyd paints are not satisfactory. Vinyl-acrylic paints are somewhat effective, but the best protection is provided by two-part epoxies. The latter are expensive, difficult to apply, require careful ventilation during application, and an extended time (up to six months) to cure before contact with collection objects.

If a padding material is needed, shelves or drawers may be lined with acid-free paper, cardboard, blotters, or unbleached muslin. The muslin is the least desirable as it has many of the same disadvantages as flannel. New materials made of polystyrene are somewhat more expensive but provide good padding and protection. However, care must be taken in selecting "polyfoam" products for collection use to assure the chemical integrity of the product.

Question from the field: fifteen

Question: Where do you put the accession number on a piece painted on all sides?

Response: An accession number should not be applied directly to an object if the artifact will be damaged or if the numbering process cannot be reversed. As an example: coins, stamps, or photographic negatives may be damaged beyond use by the addition of an accession number. It is preferable to place the objects in a proper receptacle to which the number is affixed. Objects can be kept in plastic sleeves, acid-free folders or boxes, plastic vials, or specially formed support systems. In all cases, care must be taken to mark clearly the container and note the location in the storage unit with a small photograph of the objects.

The registrar normally places the accession number on incoming objects. When there is a question about where to locate the number the curator must be consulted.

Notes

1. International Council of Museums (1990) *Statutes*, Paris, ICOM: article 2, paragraph 1, p. 3.
2. International Council of Museums (1990) "Acquisitions to Museum Collections," *Code of Professional Ethics*, Paris: ICOM, section 3, paragraph 3.1. p. 27.

Suggested reading

Appelbaum, B. (1991) *Guide to Environmental Protection of Collections*, Madison, Conn: Sound View Press.

Bandes, S. (project director) (1984) *Caring for Collections*, Washington, DC: American Association of Museums.

Genoways, H., Jones C., and Rossolimo, O. (eds) (1987) *Mammal Collection Management*, Lubbock, Tex.: Texas Tech University Press.

International Council of Museums (1990) *Statutes*, Paris: ICOM.

Kühn, H. (1986) *Conservation and Restoration of Works of Art and Antiquities*, Vol. 1, London: Butterworth & Co.

Lewis, R. (1976) *Manual for Museums*, Washington, DC: National Park Service, US Department of Interior.

Light, R., Roberts D., and Stewart, J. (eds) (1986) *Museum Documentation Systems*, London: Butterworth & Co.

Malaro, M. (1985) *A Legal Primer on Managing Museum Collections*, 2nd edn 1987, Washington, DC: Smithsonian Institution Press.

Thompson, J. M. A. (ed.) (1984) *Manual of Curatorship, A Guide to Museum Practice*, London: Butterworth & Co.

6

Museum conservation

> "One of the essential ethical obligations of each member of the museum profession is to ensure the proper care and conservation of both existing and newly-acquired collections and individual items for which the member of the profession and the employing institutions are responsible, and to ensure that as far as is reasonable the collections are passed on to future generations in as good and safe a condition as practicable having regard to current knowledge and resources."[1]

"There's a silent thief stealing away with millions of dollars of art work each year. The thief's name? Poor conservation." The *Museums for a New Century*[2] writers continue to express this concern by saying, "The same villain is at work in museums of history and natural history."

> Conservation is an attempt to prolong the life of objects of historical and artistic value. The primary job of saving them can be done by their curators or owners through providing proper safeguards for the objects against environmental extremes: such as strong light, humidity and temperature fluctuations; insects, animals, and micro-organisms; vandalism or burglary and curatorial ignorance or carelessness – the ravages of man.[3]

Collections are central to museums. If collection objects are destroyed or allowed to be destroyed not only does the museum lose a valuable asset, but humankind loses an element of its cultural or scientific heritage that may be irreplaceable. Protection of objects depends on a long-term commitment to preservation of objects by the museum. Conservation treatment usually requires the services of a conservator who is trained to address the problems associated with a particular class of object. However, museum personnel are responsible for ensuring that museum objects receive the proper care.

> Caring for collections is part of the definition of a real museum.

Museums for a New Century addresses collection care by saying, "Care connotes everything from providing controlled environmental conditions to ensuring adequate security, maintaining necessary catalog records and repairing damage."[4] To ensure the objects receive the treatment necessary for their preservation and use, and that each treatment is appropriate, the object's condition, history, significance, and role in the collection must be considered. It is also imperative that all preservation treatments are competently performed and properly documented.[5]

Past attempts to repair, restore, and/or stabilize objects have often been detrimental to the long-term preservation of the museum object. Often no treatment would have been better and less damaging. Many treatment techniques and materials have proved to be inadequate for the task to which they were applied. Consequently, important features of the objects have been lost forever.

> Preservation,
> Conservation,
> and Restoration.

There are three words that are used in discussions when talking about conservation. These are preservation, conservation, and restoration.

What are the differences?

> Preservation is defined as: "The act of preserving, or keeping in safety or security from harm, injury, decay, or destruction."
>
> Conservation is defined as: "The act of preserving, guarding, or protecting; preservation from loss, decay, injury, or violation."[6] The word origin is from the Latin, meaning: to keep or to keep together.
>
> Restoration is defined as: "restoring or being restored; reinstatement; a putting or bringing back into a former, normal, or unimpaired state or condition."[7]

In the museum community, conservation is the technology of preserving collections. The primary objective of all museum conservation should be to preserve the object in as stable condition as possible. It should never be the first choice of museum personnel to alter or reconstruct an object. Preventive conservation is the first step in the ongoing process of object care supplemented by conservation treatment and lastly by restoration when warranted and desirable. Restoration should never be viewed as an allowable substitute for proper care and maintenance of museum collections.

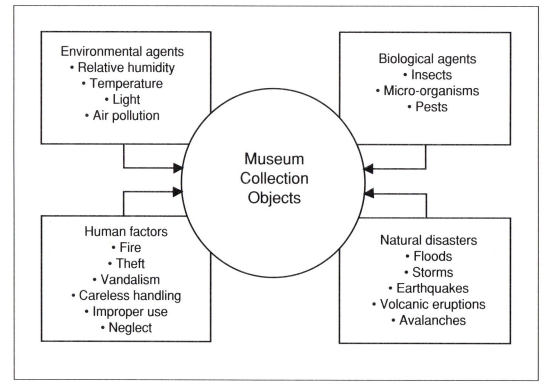

Figure 6.1 Agents of deterioration[8]

Edward Alexander[9] makes the following statement:

> Closely connected with collection was the function of conservation. Collectors have always taken care of their hoards, often times with miserly devotion. The techniques of conservation were at first little understood, and nearly all the panel paintings of antiquity have disappeared. The Greeks made crude attempts to preserve votive shields by coating them with pitch to prevent rust, and they placed vats of oil at the feet of Phidias' *Athena Parthenos* to reduce excessive dryness. By the sixteenth century, paintings were being cleaned and re-varnished, but not until nearly 1750 was the re-backing process perfected that could transfer the layer of paint from its original location to a new surface.

> Closely connected with collections *is* the function of conservation.

In the book, *Caring for Collections: Strategies for Conservation, Maintenance and Documentation*,[10] is the statement:

> The conservation of collections takes place on four different levels. The first level treats collections as a whole to maintain them in an unchanging state by providing controlled environments and adequate housing for the objects, either in individual display cases or entire storage facilities. The second level is object preservation, which has as its primary goal the preservation and retardation of further deterioration or damage to the object. The third level is actual conservation restoration; action taken to return a deteriorated or damaged artifact as nearly as is feasible to its original form, design, color and function. This process may alter the outward appearance of the object. The fourth level is in-depth scientific research and technical examination of the object.

Level one

The first level of collection object conservation requires evaluation and modification of the conditions surrounding the object rather than alteration of the object itself. This phase of collection care is museum-wide and maintaining collections in an unchanging state is central to the process. To achieve and sustain this level of care, the museum environment, temperature and humidity, must be regulated, and collection objects should be adequately housed in either exhibition cases or storage cabinets. Handling of objects, even by museum staff, should be carefully regulated. Lighting conditions, too bright or too hot, or with excessive ultraviolet must be monitored both in the collection storage area and galleries. Smoking and eating in collection areas can add to deterioration of objects.

> Museums should not, except in very exceptional circumstance, acquire material that the museum is unlikely to be able to catalogue, conserve, store or exhibit, as appropriate, in a proper manner.

The underlying logic of level one collection care is based on the fact that deterioration is often a gradual process that occurs over a number of years and in ways that are hardly perceptible to untrained observers. The goal of level one conservation is to prevent harm to an object before it occurs or in the case of an object that came to the museum with damage to prevent further deterioration.

A program of collection care at level one should include the following elements:

- Establish proper and complete records for all collection objects (accession records, inventory, condition reports, research documentation, and use records).
- Inspect (inventory) collection objects on a regular schedule.
- Train collection care and exhibits personnel to recognize the symptoms of object deterioration.
- Employ proper procedure in handling, storing, exhibiting, and transporting objects.
- Monitor and regulate the museum's environment.
- Provide appropriate security and fire protection for collections.

It must be emphasized that level one conservation is the responsibility of everyone in the museum. From custodian and security staff to exhibits personnel and curators, care must be taken to protect items from improper treatment. Most damage is done to objects due to thoughtless acts that seem inconsequential at the time but that have long-lasting detrimental effects.

There are three primary ways of addressing level one collection care:

- One is proper facility operation that includes consistency in temperature and relative humidity levels. It is more important to minimize fluctuation than it is to attempt to meet unattainable levels for temperature and relative humidity.
- The second is training. In-house training for all persons coming in contact with museum collections will provide the foundation for better care for objects.
- The third is proper housing for collections. Storage units can be clean and well organized regardless of the material of which they are constructed or the associated costs. There can be no excuse for poor housekeeping.

> **Good housekeeping is a primary step for proper collection care.**

Level two

The second level of conservation is preventive. The goal at this level is to prevent or retard deterioration or damage to the collections. At this level the object itself may receive some form of *minor* treatment. As examples, objects may be isolated in a dust free micro-environment, objects may be cleaned, objects may be treated for pests or atmospheric induced deterioration (i.e., removing a faded or light-damaged painting or UV burned or discolored paper object from exhibit and placing them in a darkened storage area), and objects may be remounted with acid-free mat or unglazed to remove them from a potentially damaging situation.

G. Ellis Burcaw[11] offers a brief definition of preservation – "Preservation consists of techniques to prevent undesirable changes from occurring."

Training is a mandatory part of this level of collection care. It may be at a minimal level as required to re-mat and re-glaze works of art or consist of instructions of basic object cleaning techniques. More substantive treatment including fumigation and rehousing should be carefully considered prior to initiation. In all cases it is best to consult a qualified person for advice as the most well-intended act may result in damage to irreplaceable objects.

> It is imperative that any preventive treatment that impacts directly on collection items be carefully considered prior to initiation. No process should be considered without consulting a qualified individual for advice and instructions.

Housing or rehousing the collections can be a major part of the preventive conservation of collections. Although placing an object on exhibit has certain inherent conservation problems, storing an artifact in optimum conditions is not only desirable but possible. Good storage is a key to long-term preservation of collections. Good storage is preventive conservation and it must be viewed as a necessary part of the museum's responsible care of collections. Proper storage planning will reduce the risk of object deterioration and ensure the accessibility of objects for exhibition, research, and inventory.

Collection storage must be considered as a museum-wide undertaking that considers all aspects of collection care. There are at least four issues to be considered when appraising collection storage needs.

1. Collections
   a. What type collections the museum houses?
   b. What collection expansion is anticipated, planned, desired?
   c. What and how much research will the collections require?
2. Facilities
   a. What type space is available in the museum for storage?
   b. How usable is the available space for storage?
   c. How accessible is the available space?
   d. How safe is the available space?

     e. What physical support is included in the available space: electrical, mechanical, et cetera?

3. Equipment

     a. What funding can be dedicated to collection storage equipment purchase?

     b. What kind and type of storage cabinets are available locally or without additional funds?

     c. What are the special storage needs of the museum's collections?

4. Containers

     a. What folders, sleeves, or boxes will be needed to store collection objects?

     b. What specimen trays may be required to prevent objects from moving or damaging other objects?

     c. Will special mounts or supports be necessary to prevent objects from falling or slumping?

     d. Will special hangers be needed to suspend objects?

     e. Are racks an economic and safe way to store museum objects?

To provide safe and secure storage for museum collections the assigned space must be dedicated to storage and serve no other purpose. The storage area must be separated from all other museum activities including exhibition, research, administration, and work.

> **40–40–20 an equation that relates to conservation.**

The well-known proportion, 40–40–20, means that of the total amount of space in the museum, 40 percent should be for collections, 40 percent for exhibits, and the remaining 20 percent for everything else (offices, rest rooms, hallways, janitors' closets, lobbies, auditoriums, lunchrooms, workrooms, receiving rooms, et cetera). This proportion is to be used as a "rule of thumb" for planning and organizing the museum. The concept here is that adequate space for storage and collection care is one of the best conservation measures available to the average museum.[12]

50 lux (5 foot-candles) for especially light-sensitive materials (for example, dyed and treated organic materials, textiles, watercolors, tapestries, prints and drawings, manuscripts, leather, wallpapers, natural history specimens, including botanical specimens, fur, and feathers).

200 lux (20 foot-candles) for undyed and untreated organic materials, oil and tempera paintings, and finished wooden surfaces.

Generally, other materials (for example, metals, stone, ceramic, and glass) are less light-sensitive and may be exposed to higher levels up to a maximum of 300 lux. However, when these materials are exhibited with light-sensitive materials, light levels must be controlled at the levels acceptable for the most sensitive materials.

Ultraviolet (UV) radiation: controlling the level of ultraviolet radiation by installing filtering materials between the light source and the museum objects is mandatory if the ultraviolet radiation exceeds 75 microwatts/lumen.

Except for the short duration required for access or housekeeping, light-sensitive objects in storage should be kept in total darkness. Lighting in the storage area should be turned off when not in use.[13]

Level three

This level includes actual restoration to return a damaged object to its original form. A trained restorer can provide the most appropriate treatment to damaged collection objects. However, the first step to gaining the assistance of a professional restoration technician is recognition of the deterioration or damage sustained by an object.

Deterioration in some form is inevitable. All things deteriorate. The degree of deterioration and the harm done in the process is a major concern for museum personnel. The first step in determining the condition of an object and the level of deterioration is observation and record maintenance. Good record-keeping provides the information necessary to review change in object condition.

Object + Care + Use = Worth of Museum[14]

In the *Belmont Report* there is the statement:

> In part this situation [deterioration of objects] exists because physical facilities for conserving museum objects are inadequate. Some means of controlling temperature and humidity is essential if paintings and aging historical objects are to be preserved. It is less of a problem in a science museum, but there, too, extremes in temperature and humidity or high concentration of sulfur dioxide in the air can, for example, cause irreparable damage to an insect collection.[15]

> "The scientific examination and treatment of museum objects and the study of the optimum environments for their preservation constitutes the field of study known as conservation."[16]

The success of an active conservation program depends on data management – the gathering, recording, and evaluating of pertinent information relating to collection care. The first step in that process is understanding the types of materials that comprise museum collections. Many museum workers believe works of art are the most subject to damage and therefore the most in need of conservation, or that historical material is more likely to require conservation attention due to the age and nature of the material. Others view ethnographic objects or natural history specimens, pottery, rocks, fossils, glass containers, or steel armor as the most vulnerable.

Which materials are the most likely subjects for deterioration and therefore the most likely to be in need of conservation? In fact, all objects are vulnerable to some form of deterioration, infestation, or decay.

In *The Care of Historical Collections*,[17] subtitled *A Conservation Handbook for the Nonspecialist*, H. J. Swinney of the Strong Museum states in the Foreword, "It follows that every museum has an imperative duty to take intelligent and effective care of the things in its possession, both while they are in storage and while they are on exhibition. Museums call this sort of care 'conservation'."

Level four

This level is to further scientific knowledge and professional practice in the field of conservation internationally. The goals are to strengthen conservation resources and to develop new programs that will be of long-term benefit to conserving cultural property – both movable and immovable – including fine art collections, historic buildings, archaeological artifacts and sites, and ethnographic material.

"[Conservation] includes three explicit functions: examination, preservation, and restoration. Examination is the preliminary procedure taken to determine the original structure and materials comprising an artifact and the extent of its deterioration, alteration, and loss. Preservation is action taken to retard or prevent deterioration or damage in cultural properties by control of their environment and/or treatment of their structures in order to maintain them as nearly as possible in an unchanging state. Restoration is action taken to return a deteriorated or damaged artifact as nearly as is feasible to its original form, design, color, and function with minimal further sacrifice of aesthetic and historic integrity."[18]

Object Materials	Deterioration	Primary Air Pollutants	Environmental Factors Accelerating Damage
Metals	Corrosion/ Tarnishing	Sulfur Oxides and Other Acid Gases	Water, Oxygen, Salts
Stone	Surface Erosion, Discoloration	Sulfur Oxides and Other Acid Gases	Water, Temperature, Salts, Vibration, Micro-organisms, Carbon Dioxide
Paint	Surface Erosion, Discoloration	Sulfur Oxides, Hydrogen Sulfide, Ozone, Particulate Matter	Water, Sunlight, Micro-organisms
Textiles	Weakened Fiber Strength, Soiling	Sulfur Oxides, Nitrogen Oxides, Particulate Matter	Water, Sunlight, Mechanical Ware
Paper	Embrittlement	Sulfur Oxides	Moisture, Mechanical Ware
Leather	Weakening, Powdered Surface	Sulfur Oxides	Mechanical Ware
Ceramics	Changed Surface Appearance	Acid Gases	Moisture

Figure 6.2 Deterioration to museum objects caused by air pollution[19]

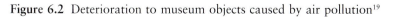

101

> Endemic is the phenomenon of treating the symptom, rather than diagnosing the problem. For example, scientific understanding of the deterioration process – fundamental for conservation – and the chemical behavior of certain materials used by the profession is as primitive as was medicine in the time of Molière. We are still operating on a trial-and-error basis, trying to apply pharmacopoeia without knowing the diagnosis of the situation.[20]

In the article "Conservation's Cloudy Future,"[21] the author states:

> Continued neglect for collection maintenance is a generic museum ailment. The fact remains, collection maintenance as a whole is an onus too great for any director, board of trustees or upper-echelon administrator to shoulder willingly. It has often been the nightmare of sensitive curators. It will always be the world-without-end.

History has played an important role in the environmental conditions that are significant to the conservation dilemma. One epoch in history has been identified which contributed the most to the deterioration of museum collections. It is a floating point in time that differed from nation to nation. That epoch is the Industrial Revolution. Edward Alexander states in *Museums in Motion* that "the Industrial Revolution brought high-intensity lighting, central heating, air pollution, and other unfavorable conditions that could speed the deterioration of collections. Yet the Revolution also brought scientific study and knowledge of the composition, conservation and restoration of objects."[22]

ICCROM

ICCROM, the International Centre for the Study of the Preservation and the Restoration of Cultural Property, is an intergovernmental organization created by UNESCO in 1959. It has seventy-five member states and sixty-four associate members (non-profit conservation institutions) throughout the world. Its headquarters are in Rome. ICCROM's statutory functions are: "to collect and disseminate documentation on scientific problems of conservation; to promote research in this field; to provide advice on technical questions; and to assist in training technicians and raising the standard of restoration work."[23]

While it may be assumed that conservation addresses only those forces that attack, contaminate, or destroy in-museum collections, the XVth General Assembly of ICOM meeting in Buenos Aires, October 26 through November 4, 1986, approved the following resolutions:

Resolution No. 2 The Future of Our Cultural Heritage: Emergency Call.

- *Noting* that all of humankind's cultural material heritage is in great danger, threatened by negligence, inadequate maintenance, natural decay and acute

lack of any preservation treatment and preventive care;
- *Recognizing* that only a coherent preservation policy on all levels can provide the necessary remedies;

The 15th General Assembly of ICOM, meeting in Buenos Aires, Argentina on 4 November 1986,

1. Calls on local, national and international authorities to give the highest priority to the preservation of the cultural material heritage;

2. *Recommends* appropriate education and advanced training to all personnel concerned with these endeavors;

3. *Recommends* that education authorities develop curricula at all levels of education with a view to fostering appreciation of the cultural heritage;

4. *Encourages* all related professions in fields such as architecture, anthropology, archaeology, art history, etc., to formally recognize that no training in these disciplines be considered complete without at least an introduction to the basic principles of conservation, not in the sense of conservation practice, but with the aim of generating an awareness and understanding of conservation and its importance to other disciplines;

5. *Recommends* as the highest priority the creation and promotion of conservation centres, workshops, information networks, and international conservation organizations as well as a network of assistance for disasters;

6. *Recommends* that conservators and other related specialists be involved at every stage of planning and construction of exhibit facilities, storage space, and during archaeological excavations.

From the same document Resolution No. 3:

Whereas there is a grave and immediate threat of the loss of a great proportion of our people's natural heritage through the rapid destruction and degradation of our natural environment, particularly in those regions of the world that have not yet been significantly altered, and

Whereas the quality of all peoples is reduced and endangered by the continuing indiscriminate and unplanned elimination of great numbers of plant and animal species, and

Whereas little is known even today of the great majority of plant and animal species with which we share this globe, and

Whereas the responsibility of discovering, describing, and preserving examples of this biological diversity rests today almost exclusively with the world's natural history museums and their scientific personnel, and

Whereas the university training of young scientists has changed focus so that the number of those who are able to understand and record this diversity of has rapidly declined in the past decade;

Therefore this, the 15th General Assembly of ICOM,

Urges natural history museums and zoological and botanical gardens and natural reserves throughout the world to work together and with both public and private entities to train young scientists in the essential research of documenting the earth's biological diversity and to develop mechanisms for preserving sufficient habitats for this diversity to continue to exist and flourish for future generations.

(From *ICOM News*, Bulletin of the International Council of Museums, Vol. 39, No. 4, 1986, published by ICOM, Paris)

□　　　□　　　□　　　□　　　□

Technical note: one

Types of materials that comprise a museum collection from the Museum Handbook, *National Park Services, 1990*

An understanding of the properties of the materials which comprise an object enables one to take certain actions which will slow or halt the deterioration of that object. Museum objects are divided into three material type categories: organic, inorganic, and composite.

a. *Organic Objects*
    Origin:　　　　　*Plant (e.g., cellulose) or Animal (e.g., protein)*
    Material Types:　*Wood; paper; textiles; leather and skins; horn, bone and ivory; grasses and bark, lacquers and waxes, plastics, some pigments, shell, natural history specimens.*
    Characteristics:　• *Contain the element carbon*
    　　　　　　　　　• *Combustible at normal temperature*
    　　　　　　　　　• *Made of complicated molecular structures that are susceptible to deterioration from extremes and changes in relative humidity and temperature.*
    　　　　　　　　　• *Absorb and emit water vapor from and to the surrounding air in an ongoing attempt to reach an equilibrium (hygroscopic)*
    　　　　　　　　　• *Sensitive to light*
    　　　　　　　　　• *Source of food for mold, insects, and rodents.*

b. *Inorganic Objects*
    Origin:　　　　　*Mineral*
    Material Types:　*Metals, ceramics, glass, lithics, stone, some pigments, geological specimens.*

Characteristics:
- *Have undergone extreme pressure or heat*
- *Not combustible at normal temperature*
- *Ceramic and stone are porous and will absorb water, salts, pollution, acids*
- *Glass and metal can be chemically modified and are susceptible to corrosion*
- *Except for certain types of glass, not sensitive to light*
- *Susceptible to mechanical damage (e.g., breakage and abrasion).*

c. *Composite Objects*

Composite objects (mixed media objects) are common in museum collections. These objects are made of two or more materials. For example, a painting is comprised of a wood frame and stretcher, a canvas support, a variety of pigments of organic and inorganic origin, and a coating. A book may be comprised of several materials (e.g., paper, leather, glues). Composite objects are subject to all causes of deterioration. Besides individual effects, each material of the object reacts to environmental extremes and changes at different rates. These different materials can react in opposition to each other, setting up physical stresses and causing chemical interactions that may cause deterioration.

□   □   □   □   □

Technical note: two

Preventive conservation role and responsibility

The responsibilities of preventive conservation are institution wide. Once the decision is made to take a more active approach to the care and maintenance of collections key museum personnel must know their roles and work as team members to make the operation effective. Preventive conservation is an ongoing process.

MUSEUM ADMINISTRATOR

Supervise museum staff and facilities to assure:

- *Stable environment.*
- *Secure environment.*
- *Proper housekeeping.*
- *Properly trained personnel.*

CURATOR

- *Monitor condition of objects (inventory).*
- *Monitor environment.*
- *Practice proper techniques for handling and storing.*

- *Monitor condition of objects on exhibit.*
- *Prepare and maintain proper documentation.*
- *Train personnel in proper collection care techniques.*
- *Develop and implement housekeeping plan.*
- *Prepare emergency plan for collection.*

CONSERVATOR

- *Assess condition of collection (Conservation Survey).*
- *Determine level of deterioration or damage.*
- *Train collection staff to identify cause of damage.*
- *Provide technical advice on environment, storage, and collection care.*

☐   ☐   ☐   ☐   ☐

Questions from the field: sixteen

Question: What can be done to keep insects out of the collections?

Response: Insects are a problem in most museums. The damage done by insects can be immediate and devastating to collections. By the time the infestation is recognized it is often at an emergency level requiring dramatic treatment. Insects will attack all collection objects made of organic material. The type of insect and the level of infestation will depend on the location of the museum and the control measures. In many parts of the world the common cockroach is the major pest. In other areas, moths, termites, powder-post beetles, dermestid beetles, and silverfish add to the problem.

The first step to controlling insects is awareness of their presence in the collection area. The control of insects requires at least seven levels of action.

1. Develop a pest management plan.

2. Restrict food consumption in the collection storage area just as in the exhibition galleries.

3. Clean the storage area regularly.

4. Require all staff to look for and report insect activity in the museum.

5. Inspect and treat, if necessary, all objects entering the museum prior to introducing them to the storage area.

6. Visually inspect collections on a regular basis.

7. Have periodic inspections by trained exterminators.

An important preventive step is good housekeeping. Careful cleaning is the best defense against insects. Food remnants and wrappers, soft drink containers, sugar for coffee, and other forms of "human food" are attractive and nourishing to cockroaches and silverfish. Human hair, lint, and neglected packing materials will nurture the larvae of carpet beetles, dermestids, or clothes moths.

Every museum will eventually experience some level of insect problem. To deal with the situation, an effective pest management plan is necessary. Proper planning reduces the delays that result from indecision and lack of essential information. Museum conservators and curators, along with other staff, working with entomologists and insect control agents should determine the most appropriate methods for post-infestation extermination of the insects. The pest management plan should focus on pre-emptive measures to avoid infestation. No matter how effectively a museum deals with an infestation, once the damage is done the value of the collections for research and exhibition is lessened. Good pest management must begin before infestation.

CAUTION: **When chemistry is used to control pests, considerable care should be taken to avoid substances harmful to collection materials and humans. Many common insecticides that are considered harmless under normal conditions may be toxic to humans in concentrated doses. Some pest control chemicals may react negatively with silks, metals, plastics, painted surfaces, and colorants. Read the instructions, and if in doubt test the insecticide for reaction with sample materials.**

☐   ☐   ☐   ☐   ☐

Question from the field: seventeen

Question: What is the best way to store ceramic fragments?

Response: The way to store ceramic fragments is to lay them on a cushioned surface, adequately separated, in a metal storage unit. Each piece is assigned a number and clearly marked. However, realizing that some institutions have thousands of ceramic fragments, the ideal may be difficult to attain.

A "second best" method could include wrapping each piece individually in acid-free or buffered paper. The piece or collection number is noted on the paper. The wrapped pieces can be packed tightly without abrasion. Fragments should not be piled one on the other but may be separated by a layer of acid-free corrugated board placed on supports. Ceramic kiln shelf supports (stilts) are good, inert, and relatively inexpensive separators. Another storage method requires the fabrication of a storage box with lift-out shelves.

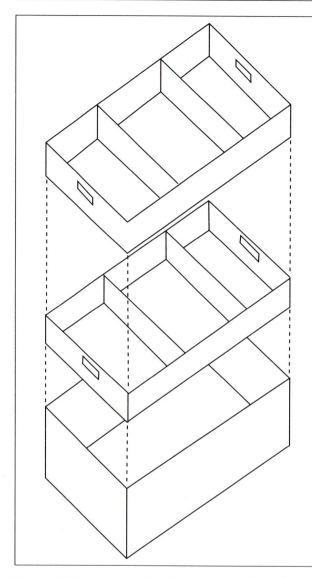

A storage unit can be constructed to store ceramic and bone fragments. Two or more shallow trays can be constructed to fit into a box for easy and safe storage. The trays should not be more than 5 cm. deep and of a size that can be lifted when filled. The trays stack in the box and rest on the dividers avoiding contact with the contents. The construction must be sturdy enough to withstand the weight of the fragments.
Use acid-free or buffered construction material and avoid the use of glue.
Handles will make lifting the trays easier.

Figure 6.3 Storage container for pottery or bone fragments when collections are large and space is limited

Question from the field: eighteen

Question: In a museum that has many different parts, what process do you use for climatic adjustment when transferring the objects from storage to the exhibiting area?

Response: Extreme climatic changes between one area and another require careful handling of objects. The normal process is to allow time for objects to adjust from one condition to another. As with traveling exhibits, conditioning can be done by leaving the objects in closed containers for 24 hours. Crates or closed transport carts on wheels are ways to accommodate the gradual reconditioning of objects.

The material to be moved is placed in a closed container in one climatic condition, moved to the other, and left enclosed for at least 24 hours. During the holding period the conditions inside the container gradually change to that of the surrounding atmosphere.

Another option is to establish a holding room in which the atmospheric conditions are the same as the area from which the material has been removed. By gradual adjustment the conditions can be altered to match that of the receiving area. Again the change must be slow. The major damage is done by rapid fluctuations of temperature and humidity.

Question from the field: nineteen

Question: Should objects be stored in closed containers? What kind of box should be used?

Response: The answer to this question depends on the object. Some objects can be stored in boxes made of acid-free material. Other objects, due to their material composition, "off-gas" (that is, produce a gas by the reaction of unstable compounds). These gases are often detrimental to the object. The closed container holds the gas in contact with the surface of the object potentially causing damage. The amount of damage depends on the surface treatment, the composition of the object, and the amount of off-gassing.

Objects such as clothing, textiles, and some ethnographic materials are well suited for storage in "boxes." This is especially true of objects that are flexible and when the flexing may cause damage. Costumes, ornate dresses, and textiles that combine fiber and non-fiber materials are better protected by storing them in boxes. Often it is necessary and preferable to build a box for the particular object rather than folding or rolling the material.

Building a storage box is a simple process but it is advisable to start with the right material. Use the highest quality "cardboard" available at the price the museum can afford. Acid-free, lignin-free, 100 percent rag, pH balanced are qualities to be considered when selecting material to construct storage boxes. Avoid corrugated cardboard of the kind used for commercial boxes or cardboard stock with obvious wood particles. If no high-quality construction material is available, it is preferable not to "box" the object.

Cut the box shape from a flat sheet of construction material and score fold-lines with a blunt instrument. Fold the end tabs around the sides and stitch them in place with cotton thread or string. Avoid using glue, tape, or other joining substances as they may damage the enclosed material. Label the box for easy identification. *Note:* give careful consideration to each object before placing it in a closed container.

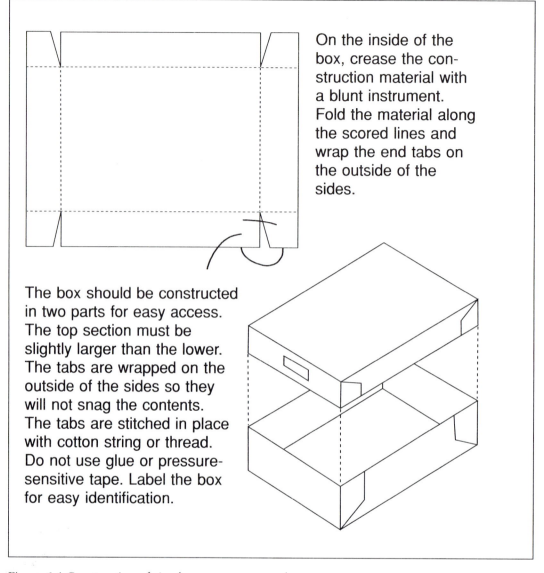

On the inside of the box, crease the construction material with a blunt instrument. Fold the material along the scored lines and wrap the end tabs on the outside of the sides.

The box should be constructed in two parts for easy access. The top section must be slightly larger than the lower. The tabs are wrapped on the outside of the sides so they will not snag the contents. The tabs are stitched in place with cotton string or thread. Do not use glue or pressure-sensitive tape. Label the box for easy identification.

Figure 6.4 Construction of simple two-part storage box

☐   ☐   ☐   ☐   ☐

Question from the field: twenty

Question: What levels of humidity and temperature do you recommend for modern art including painting, textiles, metals, and paper?

Response: Probably the foremost challenge in dealing with "modern" art is with the wide variety of materials. It is almost impossible to achieve and maintain the "ideal" environmental conditions for all works of art. The problem is compounded by "mixed-media" works of art. However, the better the control, the greater the longevity of the art work. An optimum environment will lessen deterioration and increase the usability of the objects for future generations.

For works of art, the acceptable levels for temperature and relative humidity are 65 to 75 degrees Fahrenheit (18 to 24 degrees centigrade) and 40 to 55 percent relative humidity (RH).

No works of art should be stored on the floor. Most works of art are susceptible to moisture, dust, or insects. By building storage units on feet rather than solid platforms the area below can be inspected and cleaned quickly and efficiently. Storage units should be at least 6 inches (15.24 cm) off the floor.

Store paintings vertically in bins that will hold no more than three pieces. In this way the weight of the paintings is distributed against the outside walls reducing the potential damage. Attention must be given to protecting both the front and back of works of art – paintings, prints, drawings, or photographs. Properly built and located storage units will help that process.

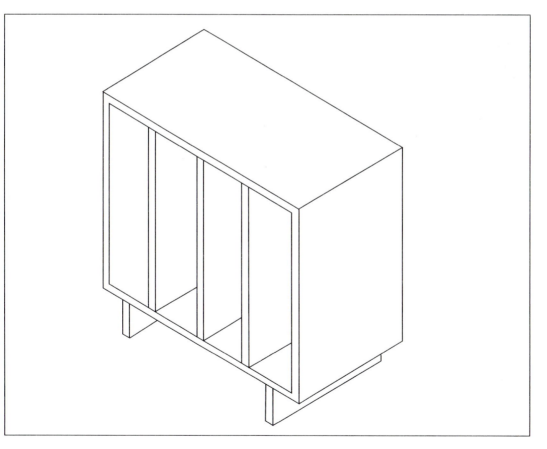

Figure 6.5 Simple storage unit for paintings

If budgetary constraints prevent the use of metal storage units, wood can be used. The construction is simple and multiple storage units can be stacked to accommodate an expanding collection. When wood is used all surfaces must be sealed with two or more coats of polyurethane with either aliphatic hydrocarbons or xylenes as solvents.[24] The coating must be applied under carefully regulated conditions and dried in the open air. An extended time (normally six weeks) is required for the polyurethane to "cure."

Question from the field: twenty-one

Question: Is it OK to wrap paintings in plastic to protect them from dust?

Response: No, even though this was a fairly common practice not long ago. The "off-gassing" of solvents used in the painting or heat may soften the plastic. The softened plastic can adhere to the surface of the painting causing extreme damage.

For short-term protection during transit, paintings can be cushioned with plastic wrap as long as there is no contact with the painted surface and the wrapping is not sealed. It is preferable to move a painting protected in this way vertically rather than horizontally. In this position the plastic will not sag and touch the painting surface.

□   □   □   □   □

Notes

1. International Council of Museums (1990) 'Conservation and Restoration of Collections,' *Code of Professional Ethics*, Paris: ICOM, p. 32.
2. Bloom, J. and Powell, E. (eds) (1984) *Museums for a New Century*, Washington, DC: AAM Publications, p. 42.
3. ibid.
4. ibid.: p. 40.
5. National Park Service (1990) *Museum Handbook*, Washington, DC: National Park Service, p. 8:1.
6. Webster, Noah and McKenhnie, Jean (eds) (1977) *New Twentieth Century Dictionary*, Collins World Publishing Co., Inc., p. 388.
7. ibid.: p. 1544.
8. National Park Service, *Museum Handbook*.
9. Alexander, E. (1979) *Museums in Motion*, Nashville, Tenn.: American Association for State and Local History, p. 9.
10. Bandes, S. (project director) (1984) *Caring for Collections: Strategies for Conservation, Maintenance and Documentation*, Washington, DC: American Association of Museums.
11. Burcaw, G. E. (1975) *Introduction to Museum Work*, Nashville, Tenn.: American Association for State and Local History, p. 97.
12. Burcaw, G. E. 'Care for Collections,' in ibid.: p. 93.
13 National Park Service, *Museum Handbook*, p. 4:39.
14. Burcaw, G. E. (1983) *Introduction to Museum Work*, 2nd edn, Nashville, Tenn.: American Association for State and Local History.
15. Bobbins, M. (ed.) (1968) *America's Museum: The Belmont Report*, Washington, DC: American Association of Museums.

16. Bloom and Powell (eds), *Museums for a New Century*, p. 40.
17. Guldbeck, P. (1976) *The Care of Historical Collections*, 2nd edn, Nashville, Tenn: American Association for State and Local History, p. vii.
18. Bandes, S. *Caring for Collections*.
19. Lewis, R. (1976) *Manual for Museums*, Washington, DC: National Park Service, US Department of Interior, p. 4:51.
20. Monreal, L. (1989) 'Filling the Gap,' *Museum News*, January/February, p. 50.
21. Keck, C. (1980) 'Conservation's Cloudy Future,' *Museum News*, May/June, p. 36.
22. Alexander, *Museums in Motion*, pp. 9–10.
23. ICCROM (1987) *Training in Conservation of Cultural Property*, Rome: ICCROM.
24. Bachmann, K. (ed.) (1992) *Conservation Concerns – A Guide for Collections and Curators*, Washington, DC: Smithsonian Institution Press.

Suggested reading

Appelbaum, B. (1991) *Guide to Environmental Protection of Collections*, Madison, Conn.: Sound View Press.

Bachmann, K. (ed.) (1992) *Conservation Concerns – A Guide for Collections and Curators*, Washington, DC: Smithsonian Institution Press.

Brill, T. (1980) *Light – Its Interaction with Art and Antiquities*, New York and London: Plenum Press.

Guldbeck, P. (1972) *The Care of Historical Collections, A Conservation Handbook for the Nonspecialist*, 2nd edn 1976, Nashville, Tenn.: American Association for State and Local History.

Horie, C. V. (1987) *Material for Conservation*, London: Butterworth & Co.

Kühn, H. (1986) *Conservation and Restoration of Works of Art and Antiquities*, Vol. 1, London: Butterworth & Co.

Mills, J. and White, R. (1987) *The Organic Chemistry of Museum Objects*, London: Butterworth & Co.

Olkowski, W., Doar, S., and Olkowski, H. (1991) *Common-Sense Pest Control*, Newton, Conn.: The Taunton Press.

Shelley, M. (1987) *The Care and Handling of Art Objects*, New York: Metropolitan Museum of Art.

Thompson, G. (1978) *The Museum Environment*, London: Butterworth & Co.

7

Exhibit conservation

Any finite space, whether it is a box, a room, or a building, contains an environment, the totality of the surrounding conditions and circumstances. There are two basic elements in an environment: matter, both organic and inorganic; and energy. Since no matter–energy system is completely inert, all the parts and activities form a chain of action–reaction. The conservation mission of a museum requires that such interactions be kept to a minimum. This means controlling the factors that promote interaction. Those factors are:

> temperature
> relative humidity
> dust and pollutant gases
> biological organisms
> reactivity of materials
> light

These are the same factors of primary concern to all collection management activities.

It is always preferable to identify potential problems and to take preventive steps. However, in many instances, the problems are not recognized until after they occur. To decide upon the best means of control, whether proactive or reactive, problems need to be identified and their scopes defined.

Identifying potential problems

The first step in identifying collection maintenance problems is to be familiar with the sorts of things that cause them. Refer to the list of environmental factors above. These are the factors to watch. In any system of materials and energy, the best that can be accomplished is to slow down the natural deterioration of objects. By prioritizing collection management activities based upon the potential for harm from the various factors, the process of decay can be slowed down dramatically. Such things as temperature, humidity, and light levels have dramatic effects on many objects.

The effects of dust and pollutant gases, biological organisms, and the reactions of one material with another, are not always easy to detect to the untrained eye. It is important to be aware of the danger signs to be able to detect problems early.

The size of a problem or its potential varies with the size of the environment it exists within. A museum building may contain several rooms. These are smaller environments with their own set of factors. Inside the rooms will often be cases, vitrines, or containers for collection objects. Each container is a smaller environment with a unique set of factors. The larger environments, room-size and building-size, may be referred to as macro-environments (macro = large + environment). The smaller ones, cases and vitrines, may be called micro-environments (micro = small + environment).

The whole concept of micro-environments existing within macro-environments is called a "box-in-a-box" configuration.

Controlling the various environments within a museum is the basic problem to be addressed. The main idea is to try and keep the conditions in the various boxes as near constant as possible; consistency is the key. If the conditions change quickly and dramatically, the objects are subjected to a great deal of stress, which invariably results in deterioration. A consistent environment slows down damage.

Each case, or box, in a gallery has its own climate. The tighter the box is sealed, the more self-contained the environment is. Since the case is present in the larger box, the gallery, the macro-environment plays a role in the smaller environment of the case. The ideal is to control an entire building's environment so that all parts are under the best conditions. However, in many instances, it may be best to control the micro-environments rather than trying to control the whole building, especially if the latter is not feasible. The control of macro- and micro-environments poses separate and distinct considerations. What is best for a case is not adequate for a building, and vice versa.

Controlling macro-environments

To determine control measures, it is necessary to have certain information available. The regional climate is especially important. Whether the climate is humid or dry, cold or hot, polluted or the air is clean are all important points. Knowing what is best for the collection objects is the other information needed, for example, the optimum temperature requirements (ideal = 21°C ± 2°), relative humidity (ideal = 50% RH ± 5%), the proper light levels, and the effects of pollution in the air on the collections.

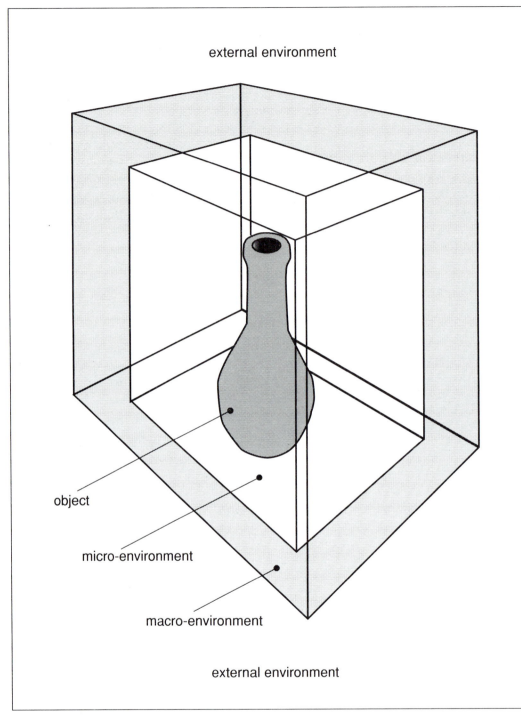

external environment

object

micro-environment

macro-environment

external environment

Figure 7.1 "Box-in-a-box" configuration of exhibition elements

Normally, the characteristics of a region are well known, and the curator, collection keeper, or other staff can provide information about the objects. Matching the collection requirements with the best possible environment is what is needed. If a building has air-conditioning equipment in it, controlling temperature variations is easier to accomplish. If not, then creative solutions must be used to try and keep the collections protected from dramatic changes in temperature. The same is true for humidity, cleanliness of the air, and the amount of light in a museum. Good housekeeping, enclosing of delicate objects in cases, limiting the amount of natural sunlight, and other such practical precautions can help prevent damage when ideal conditions are not possible.

An important activity in collection care is monitoring the environment. Methods include the use of thermometers and humidity sensing equipment such as hygrometers. A careful study of the changes in temperature in a building over a full day at various times of year will help in determining the measures for controlling heating and cooling.

Management of environmental factors

Temperature and humidity

If a museum has a Heating, Ventilation, and Air-Conditioning system (HVAC), the staff needs to have an in-depth knowledge of the type and capabilities of the system. If an HVAC system is not present, other measures to control temperature and humidity will be needed. These might include using fans to move air about, blocking windows that allow sunlight to enter the galleries, and insulating the attic to reduce heat fluctuations. What methods are available and useful is a determination that must be made for each facility by its staff. The more consistent the conditions, the more the collections will remain stable.

There are a number of reasons for humidity and temperature control. From the collection care standpoint, the main reason is moisture stability in materials. Moisture moves from an area that is more humid to an area that is dryer. It is this movement of moisture that causes woods, leathers, ivory, and the like to swell and shrink. If the swelling and shrinking are rapid, as over a 24-hour period, then the material will usually crack. Another reason for control is that bacteria and fungi grow best in moist conditions. Mildew, a type of fungus that thrives in high humidity, is extremely detrimental to most collection items.

Without an HVAC system, controlling humidity is difficult but not impossible. Delicate objects can be sealed into reasonably air-tight containers to control the rate of change. It is important, however, that the space around the objects be fairly small. Putting a small object in a large container will not protect it from humidity changes. Regulating the temperature will have a direct effect on the relative humidity in the air.

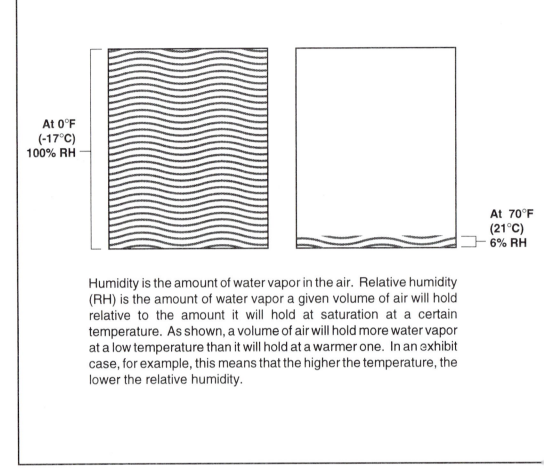

At 0°F
(-17°C)
100% RH

At 70°F
(21°C)
6% RH

Humidity is the amount of water vapor in the air. Relative humidity (RH) is the amount of water vapor a given volume of air will hold relative to the amount it will hold at saturation at a certain temperature. As shown, a volume of air will hold more water vapor at a low temperature than it will hold at a warmer one. In an exhibit case, for example, this means that the higher the temperature, the lower the relative humidity.

Figure 7.2 What is relative humidity?

Dust and pollutants

Particulate matter (dust) and pollutants (airborne chemicals) can generally be removed from the air by passing the incoming air through filters before it enters the building. Whether HVAC is present or not, good housekeeping will assist in preventing particulates and pollutants from building up on collections. Sweeping and damp mopping the floors will help reduce dust. Using damp cloths to clean furniture and cases, will also help. Cleaning collection objects should be done in a manner consistent with proper collection care.

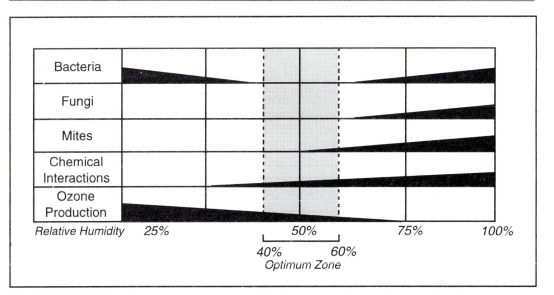

Figure 7.3 RH ranges for potential collection threats[1]

Light

Light is another critical environmental factor. Natural sunlight is the most harmful form of energy for museum collections. It contains all frequencies of electromagnetic energy including heat and ultraviolet light. If sunlight is not necessary, it is best to keep it out of the galleries altogether. If it is required, collection objects such as textiles, paintings, drawings, woods, and such materials should not be placed in direct sunlight. Metals and some ceramics are not greatly impacted by sunlight, but it is best not to expose anything to direct sunshine.

If sunlight is eliminated as illumination, then artificial light sources must be used. There are two principle types of artificial lighting: fluorescent and incandescent.

Fluorescent lighting is good general illumination. It does not cast strong shadows, and is relatively economical to operate. However, most fluorescent light bulbs emit ultraviolet light that is harmful to many museum objects. Using filters made of a plastic called UF-3 on the bulbs will solve that problem, but fluorescent lighting is usually bland and lacks drama.

Incandescent lighting, produced by tungsten-filament bulbs, is a more interesting lighting source. Its main deficiency is the amount of heat it produces. To overcome that problem, ventilation and distance can be employed. Incandescent bulbs come in a variety of different types such as spots, reflector floods, and floods, and in many different strengths. This allows much more dramatic and interesting lighting for exhibitions.

From the conservation point of view, visible light is not the most harmful sort of energy. All energy is expressed as a spectrum of electromagnetic radiation. The portion of the spectrum humans see is called the visible light spectrum (VLS). Frequencies just below VLS are called infrared radiation (IR) or heat. Heat excites or energizes molecules within materials and makes them more reactive, volatile, and vulnerable. Frequencies immediately above the VLS are referred to as ultraviolet (UV) light. This is a harmful type of light because it causes molecular damage in substances. In living organisms UV light causes sunburn, mutations, and cancers. In non-living substances, it can seriously degrade the internal make-up of objects.

Obviously, it is desirable to prevent heat and UV from interacting with collections. However, light is necessary for the human eye to perceive objects, so a certain amount of damage can be expected. Some materials are very sensitive to UV light such as silks, pigments, hairs, feathers, leathers, ivories, some dyes, watercolor paints, paper goods, and textiles. In those materials, as with all non-living materials, deterioration is cumulative and irreversible.

Added to obstructing or filtering harmful light, limiting exposure time can also have a positive effect on reducing damage. Keeping light levels as low as possible, lowering levels when the gallery is not occupied, and using buttons and switches that visitors can activate are methods currently available. Also, limiting the period of display for highly sensitive materials is important. A common principle is limiting exposure of an object for exhibit purposes to six months, then allowing it to "rest" in storage for three years between showings. This exposure principle should be applied whenever feasible. If it is not followed, remember that damage is cumulative and irreversible. That is a strong justification for limiting exposure of collections.

Recommended light levels: [2]
Objects insensitive to light – no limits except heat.
Objects moderately sensitive to light – 150 lux or 15 f-c.
Objects very sensitive to light – 50 lux or 5 f-c.

To adjust light levels, one must be able to discern what levels exist. A good, affordable tool for this is a light meter. Light meters are a common photographer's instrument and are generally available. There are types that measure all frequencies of visible light. The best meter for museum purposes measures in lux or foot-candles.

Use the minimum amount of light necessary. Brightness and dimness are a matter of perception, not fixed levels of lighting. If a gallery is lit at about 3 foot-candles, then a case in which an object is illuminated at 5–10 foot-candles will seem bright. Lighting should be designed with regard to conservation guidelines.

Control of organisms

In any museum, there are unwanted, uninvited guests that can often cause serious damage to collections in storage and on exhibit. Controlling such pests consists of three main activities:

1. monitoring,

2. prevention, and

3. elimination.

The most readily available method of monitoring is through observation. Inventories and spot checks of exhibitions should be routine. If any change in an object is observed, a thorough examination should be performed. Another useful tool is trapping. Sticky traps and light traps should be a routine part of facility and collection management. Such devices will often reveal the presence of insect pests that might otherwise go unnoticed.

Collection inventories will reveal infestations of insects, mammals (rats and mice), and microflora (fungi and molds). If problems show up in collection storage, then exhibitions must be observed carefully.

The primary method of controlling pests is through prevention. This involves several considerations. Reducing the opportunity and the resources for pests to invade and thrive is a fundamental task. Food wastes, soft drink containers, gum, candy wrappers are all sources of sustenance for many creatures. Food should be prohibited from collection storage and exhibition areas. If this is not possible, then cleanliness is imperative.

The environmental conditions for pest survival are important. High humidity and warmth are ideal conditions for many organisms, especially insects. Regular cleaning of collection and exhibits areas is an essential means of controlling the environment, as is controlling access to collections. Uncontrolled access to collections provides opportunities for introducing pests. Any materials entering either storage or exhibition areas should be carefully examined and, if organisms are found, should be treated before introduction to the collections.

Extermination is a useful means of controlling access and treating infestations. Perimeter extermination, using a commercial form of insecticide, should be routinely conducted. Placing mouse- or rat-traps around the facility is advisable, though such devices must be regularly checked. Use of baits such as rat poison and mouse bait are useful but must be carefully regulated. Baiting of sticky traps is useful for controlling insects.

When an infestation is found, spot extermination or fumigation may be required for control. The chemicals used to fumigate are toxic to people as well as to animals. The person applying the fumigant should be well versed in the safe handling of such materials, and in some places must be licensed to use them. After treatment, collection materials should be stored in enclosures to prevent re-infestation until the problem is well under control.

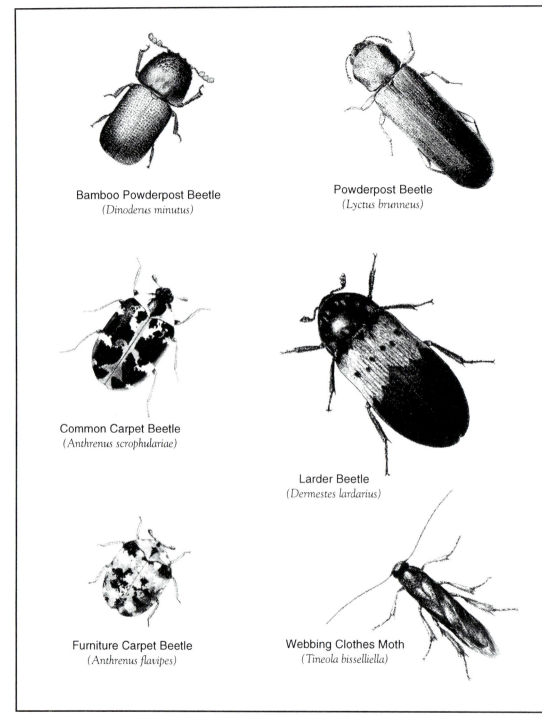

Bamboo Powderpost Beetle
(*Dinoderus minutus*)

Powderpost Beetle
(*Lyctus brunneus*)

Common Carpet Beetle
(*Anthrenus scrophulariae*)

Larder Beetle
(*Dermestes lardarius*)

Furniture Carpet Beetle
(*Anthrenus flavipes*)

Webbing Clothes Moth
(*Tineola bisselliella*)

Figure 7.4 Museum insect pests

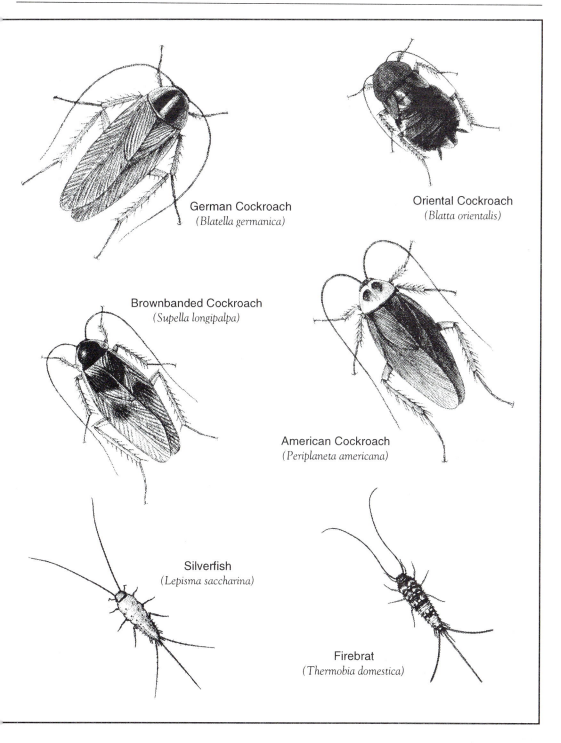

German Cockroach
(*Blatella germanica*)

Oriental Cockroach
(*Blatta orientalis*)

Brownbanded Cockroach
(*Supella longipalpa*)

American Cockroach
(*Periplaneta americana*)

Silverfish
(*Lepisma saccharina*)

Firebrat
(*Thermobia domestica*)

123

Another consideration is the effect that extermination and fumigation chemicals have on collections. Substances such as ethylene dichloride and carbon tetrachloride are harmful to many of the materials found in museum collections. Care should be exercised in choosing insecticides. It is often best to ask a conservator about the correct chemicals to use when treating an infestation. Testing samples of similar materials with the proposed insecticide is a good idea, if time allows. In all instances where control of pests involves chemicals, the expediency of extermination must be weighed against the damage that the pests are causing.

A safety measure that is always appropriate when the use of a pesticide is planned is to post a notice and evacuate personnel while the application is made. This can be as simple as putting up a sign prior to the application stating that an insecticide will be used. This allows people who feel that they might be affected by the chemicals to avoid the area until the pesticide has evaporated.

It is good procedure to keep records of all activities involving infestation control. Records should include the type of collection materials affected, the extent of the infestation, the kinds of organisms involved, and the actions taken to control them. Such documents are best kept in the file for the objects treated (see sample infestation form, p. 280).

Reactivity of materials

Materials used in constructing exhibits pose their own set of potential hazards to collections. Depending upon the building type and materials used, the facility itself may pose a potential problem. Paints, adhesives, and other such products contain solvents and corrosives. The atmosphere may hold gaseous pollutants from industry nearby. The processes employed in manufacturing materials used to construct cases, vitrines, and the like may present possible dangers as well.

In the use of paints, adhesives, and the like, potential problems can be reduced by allowing time for harmful chemicals to evaporate before placing them in contact with collections. In instances where wood, papers, or other acidic materials are used, sealing or placing inert substances between the materials and collection objects can prevent problems. Adequate ventilation is an important means of control as well. The possibilities and solutions are endless, and each structure is unique. Being aware of potential problems is the best way to prepare for and prevent their development.

Controlling micro-environments

An exhibit creates small environments within larger ones – the box-in-a-box configuration – whenever a case or vitrine is part of the gallery. The smaller space, the micro-environment, reacts to the larger one, the room or macro-environment. A micro-environment is a complex of variables and materials to which collection objects are normally directly exposed.

A case or vitrine is usually sealed except for energy entering and leaving. In a cased exhibit, where the lighting devices are inside, heat is a major factor. For a vitrine, where lighting is external, enough heat energy is trapped to significantly affect the interior temperature. In both instances, the higher temperatures cause drying conditions. Although in a sealed environment the amount of moisture remains the same, the higher temperature has the effect of drying the air so that the relative humidity is actually lowered. Add to this the fact that lights will be switched on and off, causing rapid fluctuations in both temperature and relative humidity, and the result is a very dynamic and potentially destructive micro-environment for collections to be placed in.

Methods of controlling a micro-environment usually involve two approaches: 1) separating energy sources from the container as far as possible; and 2) creating a buffer between the macro- and micro-environments to slow the rate of change. Depending upon the sensitivity of an object, one or both of these methods may be necessary.

Since a constant energy level resulting from continuous lighting is neither preferable nor cost-efficient, it is desirable to have a method of controlling temperature and humidity that will automatically react to varying conditions. The use of such a method is called "buffering." One of the chief methods of buffering is using the object and its encasing materials as a sort of energy and moisture reserve. As heating induced by lighting occurs, the substances in the micro-environment absorb energy and release moisture. During times of low energy, as at night when lights are off, the materials will release energy and absorb humidity. This will occur in virtually all instances except where cases or vitrines are constructed of metal. However, an important factor in this "natural" buffering is the amount of air space around the object. In a case where the object is small and the case is large (a volume ratio of 500:1), the object will react as though no buffer was present; the object will suffer. If the case is tighter fitting, that is, the volume is a few times larger than the object (for example, 5:1), then the buffering effects are substantial, protecting the object from rapid changes.[3]

There are several substances that are referred to as hydrophilic (literally, "water loving") which have the property of absorbing or releasing water vapor as the environment changes. One of the best of these hydrophilic materials is silica gel. It is probably most familiar as an additive to packaging because of its drying properties and its chemically inert nature. This chemical reacts quickly to changes in relative humidity. It can be bought "preset" to a specified RH in granular form, packets, or as compressed tiles. The placement of the gel can be planned into the exhibit, and thus remain unobtrusive or invisible to the public.

Other hydrophilic substances are available including some hydrated salts, such as zinc sulfate, sodium chloride, magnesium nitrate, magnesium chloride, and lithium chloride. The problems with these are their reactivity with objects if they come into contact with them, and the need for more continuous maintenance. Salts melt and recrystallize in the process of absorbing and

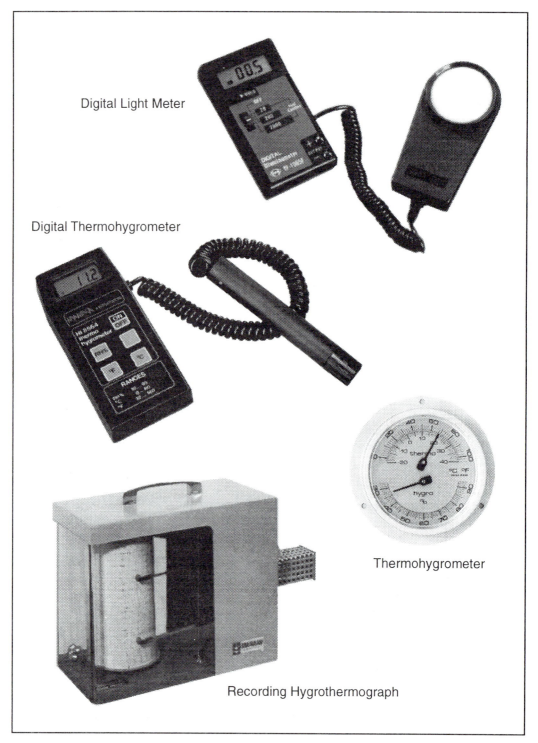

Digital Light Meter

Digital Thermohygrometer

Thermohygrometer

Recording Hygrothermograph

Figure 7.5 Environmental monitoring devices

releasing atmospheric water. This action leads to "creeping." That is, the crystals reform higher in the container with each cycle. They, therefore, "creep" up the sides of the bowl or pan. Creeping must be monitored to ensure that the crystals do not move into contact with the collection items.

Whether silica gel or salts are used, the case must be sealed tightly to allow the substance to do its work. If air passes freely from the macro-environment to the micro-environment, the effects of the buffering agent are quickly neutralized.

Monitoring micro-environments

Monitoring environments is an essential part of controlling them. There are several pieces of equipment that can greatly assist in monitoring. Thermometers, thermohygrometers, recording hygrothermographs, and psychrometers are all useful.

A "thermo-" prefix denotes temperature.
A "hygro-" prefix refers to humidity.
A "-meter" suffix means a gauge.
A "-graph" suffix indicates a recording device.

The thermohygrometer is an instrument that measures both temperature and relative humidity. It is available in several forms including some electronic types. Thermohygrometers are typically small because they have no means of recording changes. They are useful in reading conditions at the time of observation only. Another similar tool, that makes a record allowing monitoring to be continuous over days and weeks, is the recording hygrothermograph. Again, there are many varieties of this machine, even some that are relatively small and compact.

A third piece of equipment is the psychrometer. This device measures temperature and relative humidity in such a way as to give instantaneous readings. One of the chief uses of the psychrometer is in calibrating the hygrothermographs and thermohygrometers. The psychrometer utilizes two thermometers, one dry, the other wet, to determine the actual RH in the environment. The other two devices rely on bi-metal springs for temperature, and materials that react to humidity to derive their measurements. Sometimes these devices need adjusting or calibrating to match actual conditions.

When buying a thermohygrometer, it is best to choose one that can be recalibrated and that is small enough to be placed inside a case or vitrine. These are a useful means of monitoring micro-environments. Recording hygrothermographs tend to be larger due to the drive and recording mechanisms. They are placed in galleries on a pedestal or mounted on the wall in an unobtrusive location. Recording hygrothermographs should be used continuously to document the conditions under which collection objects are being presented.

Placement of temperature and humidity monitoring equipment is critical. It should be located so that it is in the same conditions as the objects. Thermohygrometers may be placed inside a case or vitrine as mentioned, and larger instruments should be placed at the same height and under the same general conditions as the objects. Placing an instrument close to the ceiling to keep it out of reach produces unreliable results since temperature and humidity levels vary widely throughout a vertical space. The same is true of placing the monitoring equipment on the floor. Locating a hygrothermograph near an open door or window will also produce unsatisfactory results.

Psychrometers come in two basic kinds: a sling-type that must be swung around to obtain a reading, and a motor-driven type. Though less expensive than motor-driven machines, the sling psychrometer has the disadvantage of needing more space to operate. However, both instruments are adequate for accurately determining the temperature and relative humidity of a given space.

□   □   □   □   □

Technical note: three

Humidity effects on materials

CONSTANT HIGH HUMIDITY: ABOVE 70 PERCENT RH

- *Mold and mildew form on surfaces of paper, parchment, leather, and organic materials.*
- *Changes in tension and/or expansion of dimensions of cellulose, protein, and bone objects, with softening of materials making handling dangerous.*
- *Corrosion of ferrous metals and of copper alloys (possible spreading of bronze disease).*
- *Movement of salts (efflorescence) within stone and ceramic materials; development of opacity in old glass (crizzling).*
- *Condensation on surfaces with resultant water damage when ambient temperature drops below the dew-point.*

CONSTANT LOW HUMIDITY: BELOW 35 PERCENT

- *Desiccation and embrittlement of cellulose, protein, and bone objects causing shrinkage and changes in tension, with difficulty in handling.*
- *Shrinkage and warping of wood and wooden structures, causing cracking and splitting.*
- *Movement of salts within porous objects.*
- *Drying out of adhesives and support layers.*

VARIATIONS IN HUMIDITY

Particularly damaging with rapid variations between low and high RH values (for example, at a rate of 5 percent RH in 1 hour, or greater). Seasonal slow drifts are less harmful to structures than abrupt changes.

- *Expansion and contraction of humidity sensitive materials with resulting warping, cleavage, splitting, loss of layers of support, and design elements.*
- *Movement of salts to surface, or interior, in ceramics and stone with disruptions to structures and design.*
- *Periodic condensation and moisture formations occur particularly at dew-point temperature with resulting water staining, rusting, or corrosion in the case of metals.*

(Please note: this information is common to the museum community. It is included without attribution.)

Technical note: four

Recommended RH levels for collections at normal temperatures

ARCHAEOLOGICAL SPECIMENS (NOT AT SITE)

40–60 percent for humidity-sensitive items (wood, leather, fibrous components). 20–30 percent (or less if corrosive products or salts are active) for stone, ceramics, metallic specimens, other inert materials.

ARMS, ARMOR, METALS

15–40 percent according to condition of metal and oxide formations. Wooden components need special protection.
Polished metals, for example, brasses and bronzes will tarnish at 15 percent or above.

ETHNOGRAPHIC BARK CLOTH, BASKETRY, MANILA, SISAL, MASKS, FEATHERS, LEATHER GARMENTS

40–60 percent according to specific reactivity.

BOTANICAL OBJECTS, DRIED PLANTS, SEEDS

40–60 percent.

CERAMIC, TILES, STONE

20–60 percent, depending on embedded salts present. Susceptible to freeze/thaw damage.

COINS, NUMISMATIC COLLECTIONS

15–40 percent, depending on corrosion products, oxides and patina formations, and their degree of stability.

COSTUMES, TEXTILES, RUGS, TAPESTRIES

30–50 percent. Silk and wool are more sensitive to moisture damage than cotton or linen. Painted textiles are most sensitive to RH changes. Synthetic fabrics are less reactive, but exhibit electrostatic properties at low RH values, and readily accumulate dust on surfaces.

FURNITURE

40–60 percent, depending essentially on wood content, grain, joining, and condition of surface or barrier coating; especially affected by seasonal RH drifts or cycles. Some woods are less sensitive than others owing to resin content or construction.

GLASS

40–60 percent. Crizzled glass needs narrower band of controlled RH (for example, 40 percent) to prevent advance of this condition. For other kinds of glass the RH is not too critical.

INSECTS, DRIED AND MOUNTED (AS IN ENTOMOLOGICAL COLLECTIONS)

40–60 percent.

IVORIES, BONE CARVINGS

50–60 percent, requiring more control than anatomical collections. Dimensional responses very slow, except when in thin sheets, as in ivory miniatures.

LACQUER WARE

50–60 percent. Japanese authorities recommend higher levels to 70 percent.

LEATHER, SKINS, BINDINGS

45–60 percent. Variable according to tanning process.

PARCHMENT, VELLUM

55–60 percent. Narrow control required because of great hygroscopicity.

PAPER

40–55 percent (some authorities recommend less).

STRETCHED PAPER

45–55 percent. Paper screens, oriental screens, drawings on stretched frames need narrow RH control.

PHOTOGRAPHS, FILMS (CINE, AUDIO, AND VIDEO MATERIALS)

30–45 percent. The gelatin is reactive, as is support paper; plastic film components less responsive.

PAINTINGS ON CANVAS

40–55 percent. Unlined paintings or paintings lined with hygroscopic adhesives are more reactive than those lined with wax or synthetic materials.

PAINTINGS ON WOOD, POLYCHROME SCULPTURES

45–60 percent depending on thickness, wood grain, ground, and method of joining sections. Some panel paintings need narrow RH levels to minimize warping. Massive wooden sculptures are particularly susceptible to seasonal drifts.

PAINTED, VARNISHED WOOD, VARIOUS

45–60 percent. In this category are musical instruments, models, decorative objects having painted and coated wood as the principal components.

PLASTIC MATERIALS

30–50 percent. In general, plastic materials, for example, acrylic supports, sculptures, castings, have slight humidity responses, but do warp when in thin sheets and exposed to varying conditions. Electrostatic properties at low RH levels with dust accumulations.

(Please note: this information is common to the museum community. It is included without attribution.)

Question from the field: twenty-two

Question: What type of micro-climate is used in the storage area and in exhibits? How do you control the micro-climate?

Response: The subject of micro-climates is discussed in this *Handbook*, pp. 124ff. However, before designing a climate-controlled area, it is important to determine when, or if, a carefully regulated environment is warranted and when careful planning will reduce the need. Not every situation calls for a micro-climate. One of the first concerns should be to check the environmental conditions carefully in both the storage area and the exhibition galleries. Direct exposure to the outside, including entry doors that allow external air directly into the gallery, may have a dramatic impact on the environment. Natural light, even when filtered, can heat the atmosphere and have an impact on objects.

Drafts from the heating and cooling system, open windows, fireplaces, chimneys, even the number and intensity of the lights in the galleries will alter the temperature and relative humidity. Unless the museum's atmosphere is carefully and continually monitored, the creation and maintenance of micro-climates may be counter-productive and harmful to collection objects.

The buffering of objects can often lessen the need for specialized environmental conditions in storage. As an example, sealed storage units will buffer objects against rapid changes in temperature and relative humidity. Objects can also be protected from temperature extremes by using boxes or other types of enclosures. To reduce the relative humidity of the air surrounding a particular object silica gel can be used. (Silica gel is a commonly available drying agent. It is an artificially prepared crystalline substance composed of silicon and oxygen.)

To meet the special requirements of certain objects, regulated environmental conditions may be necessary. Cooling can be ducted to storage units for objects needing low temperatures. Exhibit cases can be vented and the air circulated by small, high-speed fans. The relative humidity in cases, both storage and exhibits, can be decreased by silica gel or dehumidifiers. The use of preconditioned saturated solutions of certain salts or silica gel will increase the relative humidity.

The book *Conservation and Exhibitions* by Nathan Stolow provides good information on micro-climates and the use of saturated solutions of salts. On p. 243 is the following information on salt solutions and the resulting RH levels at room temperature:

Saturated solution of	RH
lithium chloride	12
magnesium chloride	34
magnesium nitrate	55
sodium bromide	59
sodium chloride	75[4]

☐ ☐ ☐ ☐ ☐

Question from the field: twenty-three

Question: Does noise affect the collections in storage as well as on exhibit?

Response: Noise itself is not a factor for concern. It is the vibrations resulting from the noise that can cause damage. As an example: automobile traffic around the museum can be distracting but not particularly harmful. It is the vibrations that are transmitted through the road surface and the ground that are problematic. They can cause museum collections to move, develop sympathetic vibrations, and come into contact with surrounding objects or surfaces.

A more severe example of noise-generated vibration is the high frequency sound waves coming from audio speakers. Vibrations of this level can cause damage to a museum building as well as to the collections.

Certain types of collections are much more susceptible to noise-related vibrations than others. Some mineral specimens are extremely delicate and are easily damaged by even slight vibrations. Glass, stone, ivory, jades, some fossil material, and paintings may be negatively affected by vibration.

Fragile objects require careful cushioning while in storage or on exhibit. They should be placed on a padded surface that will provide support and prevents contact with surrounding objects. It is preferable to store fragile objects in areas away from air-conditioning or heating ducts, primary passageways, and elevators.

□　□　□　□　□

Questions from the field: twenty-four

Question:　In our museum we have a large collection of prints, drawings, and other works on paper. How should we handle the material so it is not damaged? It seems that every time we take a print or drawing from storage it has faded, yellowed, or gotten dirty. What can we do?

Response:　Prints, drawings, and photographs are an important part of most fine art collections. Many museums have found works on paper to be affordable as well as interesting for exhibition and research. Unfortunately they are also easily damaged. Careful handling and storage is a major step in preserving paper objects.

Storage

- The best protection for prints, drawings, and other works on paper is to store them in complete darkness in properly designed, dust-proof storage cabinets or portfolios in environmentally controlled rooms with filtered air.

Handling

- The greatest damage is caused to prints, drawings and other works on paper by handling in an improper or careless manner. While "common-sense" habits are often assumed to provide basic guidelines, this is generally not the case. A few simple rules will eliminate hazards and protect fragile collection objects. Standards for handling paper items (prints, drawings, books, and other documents) are as follows:

  - Wear clean white gloves when handling objects.
  - Use two hands when lifting objects. This will prevent bending, creasing, tearing, or otherwise causing tension or undue stress of objects.
  - Unmatted prints or drawings should never be stacked directly to the backing board.
  - To ensure maximum protection for the art, prints and drawings should be matted. The second level of protection is to keep pieces in acid-free folders or envelopes.

133

- Care should be taken not to drag or slide anything across the surface of prints or drawings. Pastel drawings, etchings, and mezzotints are particularly vulnerable to surface damage.
- Never use pressure-sensitive tapes, gummed brown wrapping tape, rubber cement, synthetic glues, or heat-sealing mounting tissue on prints, drawings, books, or paper documents that are to be preserved.
- Matted prints and drawings should be protected with acid-free cover tissue in storage.
- Always lift mats with two hands from the outer edge. Never allow fingers to come in contact with the picture surface with or without gloves.
- For prints and drawings in mats or folders the best method for storage is in drawers or solander boxes. When stored in drawers, care should be taken not to stack excessively as the weight will damage the bottom pieces.
- Mail, ship, or otherwise transport loose prints or drawings packed in flat boxes or containers, never rolled.
- Works on or of paper should be marked with an accession number using a no. 2 (soft) pencil, and writing on the extreme edge of the margin for prints and drawings and on the edge of the beginning or end flyleaves of books. Care must always be taken not to damage picture or text surface. Never use library-type markings on spines or bindings.
- Books may be stored in plastic envelopes to protect them from dust or friction. Envelopes should be perforated to prevent the possibility of condensation and the build-up of harmful gasses.

Protection from light

- Direct light on the surface of prints, drawings, and other works on paper should be as low as possible and should in no case be more than 50 lux. Serious deterioration of paper will occur in two to four weeks of exposure to full sunlight.
- Light damage is multiplied by the time of exposure.
- Direct sunlight (daylight) and ultraviolet rays from all sources should be kept away from prints, drawings, and other works on paper. The best source of artificial lighting is tungsten incandescent bulbs. Fluorescent tubes should be coated with UV-absorbent lacquer or plastic film. (All light, even that with an insignificant amount of ultraviolet, bleaches and destroys paper.)
- Strong lighting on prints, drawings and other works on paper under glass is to be avoided even for very short periods of time.

Humidity and pollution

- The optimum relative humidity (RH) for prints, drawings, and other works on paper is between 40 and 55 percent. Lower humidity does not present an acute danger; however, paper kept at a relative humidity lower than 40 percent gradually loses its elasticity and flexibility. At a relative humidity over 65 percent there is a danger of damage from mold and bacteria.
- Dust and gaseous atmospheric pollutants should be kept away from prints, drawings, and other works on paper to the extent possible.

Mechanical damage

- Prints and drawings are usually mounted by hinging to the backing. Hinges are commercial, acid-free, linen tape, or strips of acid-free paper. Care must be taken to use adhesives that will not harden or cause discoloration. (An adhesive that fulfills these conditions is rice or wheat starch. It is first stirred to a thick paste with cold water, then hot water is added while stirring to reach the desired consistency. Another adhesive is carboxymethylcellulose prepared by adding the commercial powder to de-ionized water.) A small amount of thymol can be added to the mixture to inhibit mold growth in mold-sensitive material like rice paste. Most self-adhesive films and tapes contain plasticizers that may stain the paper. *Under no circumstances should prints or drawings be pasted or dry mounted to boards.*

- The board used for the mounting and backing should be all-rag or acid-free (neutral pH or pH balanced) board. Mat board or mounting (backing) materials containing wood pulp or alum and rosin sizing should not be used. They contain acidic compounds that will increase their acidity with age. When the acidic nature of the mounting and backing material is in doubt it can be checked with a pH testing pen or other testing method.

- For greater protection, insert colorless film between the over mat and the print or drawing. Protective films that decompose to release destructive substances, such as polyvinyl chloride (PVC) which gives off small amounts of hydrochloric acid, are unsuitable as are those that release plasticizers. Acid-free tissue is also used to protect the surface of the prints or drawings. However, protective coverings should *never* touch the surface of chalk, pastel, or charcoal drawings. Contact could cause smudging or rubbing that will damage the work. Pastels should be framed and protected by glazing, even in storage.

- Either glass or sheet acrylic (plexiglas) is suitable for glazing. Glass has the advantage of not carrying an electrostatic charge that will attract dust and lint. Sheet acrylic is lighter and some types filter out harmful ultraviolet rays. Sheet acrylic should not be used as glazing for pastels or charcoal works as the electrostatic nature of the material can lift the drawing unless it is well fixed. "Museum glass" is non-reflective glass that will reduce light glare and reflection; however, it restricts viewing and has a negative impact on color. Prints and drawings should be protected with mats to prevent the picture surface from coming into contact with the glazing material. Pastel and charcoal drawings should be at least 0.5–1 cm (0.20–0.394 inch) from the glazing. Museum-quality mat board is normally available in three thicknesses: 2-ply ($\frac{1}{32}$ inch thick); 4-ply ($\frac{1}{16}$ inch thick), and 8-ply ($\frac{1}{8}$ inch thick.)

□ □ □ □ □

Question from the field: twenty-five

Question: With limited funding, is it possible to have "safe" lighting in exhibits?

Response: The common thinking is that money solves all problems in exhibit conservation. Indeed, adequate funding is desirable and effective, but even with very limited resources, conservation can still be a priority and achievable.

The acrylic sheet material containing UF-3 (the ultraviolet filtering material) is expensive. However, the purchase of the tubes or sheets to cover or shield fluorescent lights will last a long time. A less expensive material is a thin acetate sheet that comes on a roll. It can be cut and fitted around fluorescent tubes. The useful life of the thin material is less than that of the tubes. It lasts about five years before becoming brittle.

As an alternative to filtering, reflecting light off a light-colored surface will prevent the ultraviolet from reaching collection objects.

Incandescent lighting produces heat. It is important to keep heat away from collection objects. In cased exhibits, however, the lights are inside with the objects. Separating the lights from the collections is the correct way to solve the heat problem. Glass or acrylic between the light source and the objects can accomplish this aim. Additionally, ventilating the space containing the lights will allow heat to escape.

Even with separation and ventilation, heat can build up in an enclosed exhibit. It is wise to check the temperature fluctuations in a case by putting a thermometer in the space. Over an 8-hour period, it will show whether the temperature rises and falls dramatically. If it does, ventilating is needed.

A final note: it is always advisable to prevent natural sunlight from reaching collection objects. Artificial lighting, though having properties harmful to collections, is usually safer than direct sunlight.

Question from the field: twenty-six

Question: In the museum where I work we have no specialized equipment to monitor objects on exhibit. I feel certain that some of the objects, particularly the paintings and textiles, are being hurt by the amount and type of light being used. I believe they are fading but our director does not think a problem exists. We do not have money to hire a conservator and even if we did I do not think I could convince the board to bring someone in to look at the objects. Is there something I can do to document the problem? I do not want to cause a problem, I just feel like something should be done.

Response: The problem you are describing is not unusual. Fading and discoloration are gradual and often go unnoticed until a great deal of damage is done. It is also not unusual to be told that paintings and textiles are exposed every day to light in people's homes and there is "nothing wrong with them there so why worry about it here [in the museum]?"

One thing to do is to borrow a photographer's light meter. With that device you can determine the level of light down to 5 foot-candles (50 lux). This will give you an idea of the level of light and allow you to compare the lighting you have against recommended illumination. This may not convince your director there is a problem as light damage, like temperature and relative humidity, is an abstract concept.

A simple fade test can be conducted using a "blue scale" or a similar device you make. Cover several pieces of 100 percent rag or buffered (museum) board with dark blue cotton fabric. It is best to make the test boards at least 3 by 12 inches (approximately 8 cm by 30 cm) but they can be smaller to make them less conspicuous. Reserve one board for a comparative test exposed to direct sunlight.

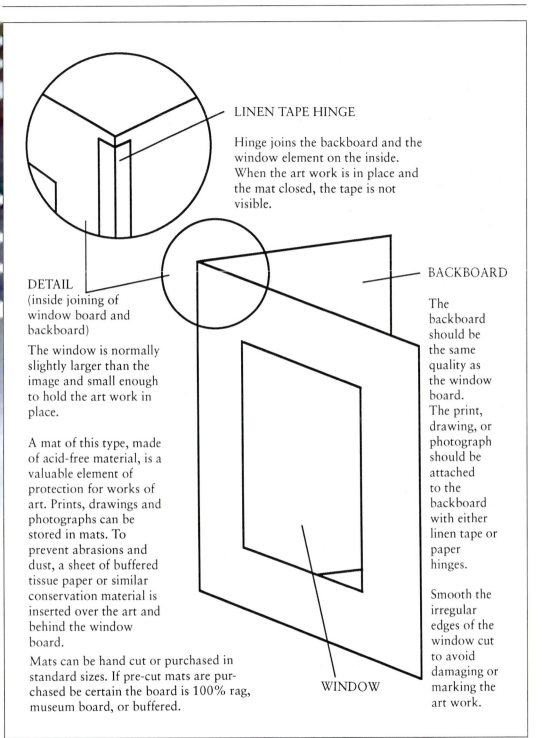

LINEN TAPE HINGE

Hinge joins the backboard and the window element on the inside. When the art work is in place and the mat closed, the tape is not visible.

DETAIL
(inside joining of window board and backboard)

The window is normally slightly larger than the image and small enough to hold the art work in place.

A mat of this type, made of acid-free material, is a valuable element of protection for works of art. Prints, drawings and photographs can be stored in mats. To prevent abrasions and dust, a sheet of buffered tissue paper or similar conservation material is inserted over the art and behind the window board.

Mats can be hand cut or purchased in standard sizes. If pre-cut mats are pur-chased be certain the board is 100% rag, museum board, or buffered.

BACKBOARD

The backboard should be the same quality as the window board. The print, drawing, or photograph should be attached to the backboard with either linen tape or paper hinges.

Smooth the irregular edges of the window cut to avoid damaging or marking the art work.

WINDOW

Figure 7.6 Single window mat for a print, drawing, or photograph

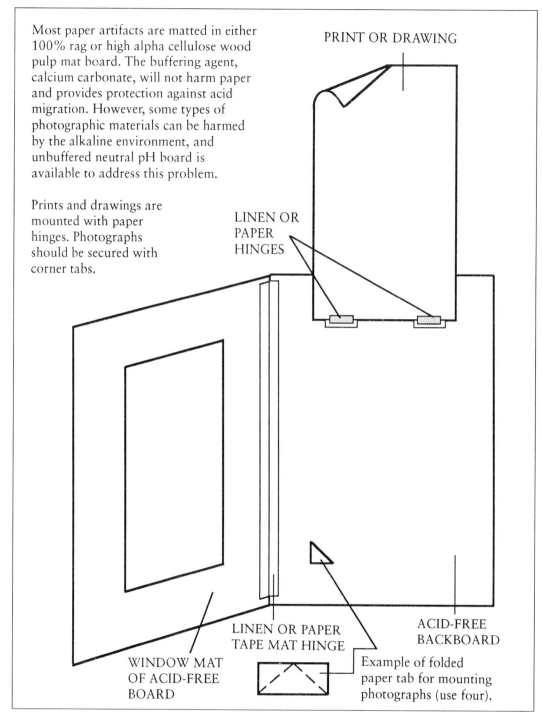

Most paper artifacts are matted in either 100% rag or high alpha cellulose wood pulp mat board. The buffering agent, calcium carbonate, will not harm paper and provides protection against acid migration. However, some types of photographic materials can be harmed by the alkaline environment, and unbuffered neutral pH board is available to address this problem.

Prints and drawings are mounted with paper hinges. Photographs should be secured with corner tabs.

PRINT OR DRAWING

LINEN OR PAPER HINGES

LINEN OR PAPER TAPE MAT HINGE

WINDOW MAT OF ACID-FREE BOARD

ACID-FREE BACKBOARD

Example of folded paper tab for mounting photographs (use four).

Figure 7.7 Single window mat with paper or linen mounting hinges for prints, drawings, or photographs

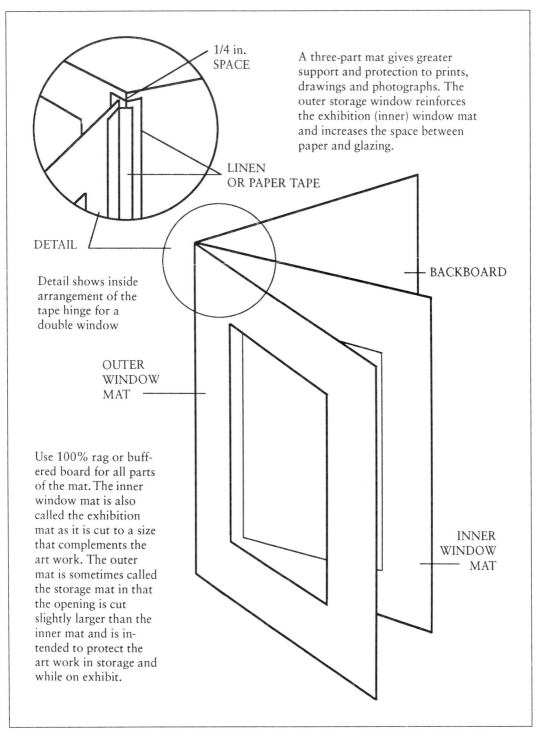

1/4 in. SPACE

A three-part mat gives greater support and protection to prints, drawings and photographs. The outer storage window reinforces the exhibition (inner) window mat and increases the space between paper and glazing.

LINEN OR PAPER TAPE

DETAIL

Detail shows inside arrangement of the tape hinge for a double window

BACKBOARD

OUTER WINDOW MAT

Use 100% rag or buffered board for all parts of the mat. The inner window mat is also called the exhibition mat as it is cut to a size that complements the art work. The outer mat is sometimes called the storage mat in that the opening is cut slightly larger than the inner mat and is intended to protect the art work in storage and while on exhibit.

INNER WINDOW MAT

Figure 7.8 Double window mat for works on paper

Those boards that are to be attached to the gallery walls, cover except for about 0.5 inch (1–1.5 cm) of fabric. Use a covering material that will not allow the light to penetrate. Attach the test boards to a wall in the gallery next to the paintings or textiles, in a place where visitors will not disturb them and where they will not distract from the exhibits. At pre-established intervals (every two or three days) move the covering material to expose an additional 0.5 inch (1–1.5 cm) of the blue fabric. Be consistent in the time of exposure and the amount of fabric exposed. Keep records of the date and time the cover material is moved. Leave the last inch (2 to 3 cm) of the blue fabric covered through the entire test as a reference. At the end of the test period the blue fabric will be faded in a progressive pattern if there is an excessive amount of light or UV exposure. The test board placed in direct sunlight can be used as a comparison to reinforce severity of the problem. Usually a thirty-day test will provide adequate information to document the presence of harmful conditions.

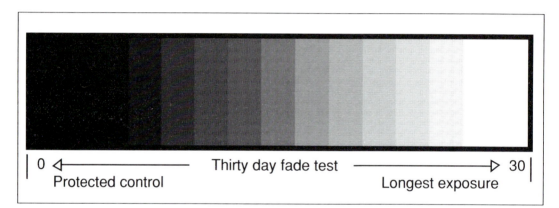

0 ◁————————— Thirty day fade test —————————▷ 30
Protected control   Longest exposure

Figure 7.9 Blue card fade pattern

This test will document the problem and demonstrate the need for preventive measures. The exhibited material may need to be rotated or protected from direct natural light. In some cases the gallery lights may be fitted with UV filters, and in extreme situations the material may require immediate conservation attention. Call a conservator if you have questions.

☐   ☐   ☐   ☐   ☐

Notes

1. Sterling, F. (1985) "Criteria for Human Exposure to Humidity in Occupied Buildings," paper for American Society of Heating, Refrigerating and Air Conditioning Engineers.
2. Witteborg, L. (1991) *Good Show!*, Washington, DC: Smithsonian Institution Traveling Exhibition Service, p. 79.
3. Stolow, N. (1986) "The Microclimate: A Localized Solution," in his *Conservation and Exhibitions*, London: Butterworth & Co., p. 1.
4. Stolow, *Conservation and Exhibitions*, p. 243.

Suggested reading

Brill, T. (1980) *Light – Its Interaction with Art and Antiquities*, New York and London: Plenum Press.

Guldbeck, P. (MacLeish, A., ed.) (1986) *The Care of Antiques and Historical Collections*, 2nd printing, Nashville, Tenn.: American Association for State and Local History.

Kühn, H. (1986) *Conservation and Restoration of Works of Art and Antiquities*, Vol. 1, London: Butterworth & Co.

Shelley, M. (1987) *The Care and Handling of Art Objects*, New York: Metropolitan Museum of Art.

Stolow, N. (1986) *Conservation and Exhibitions*, London: Butterworth & Co.

Thompson, G. (1978) *The Museum Environment*, London: Butterworth & Co.

Thompson, J. M. A. (ed.) (1984) *Manual of Curatorship, A Guide to Museum Practice*, 2nd edn 1992, London: Butterworth & Co.

Section III
Interpretation and communication

8

Museum exhibitions

At the beginning of exhibitry in western cultures, the objective was to present or display objects as a sign of wealth, cultural achievement, or intellectual enlightenment. In some cases, even the idea of education for the public was in the mind of the exhibitor.

In large part, however, museum exhibits were for the educated, knowledgeable, and elite in society. Interpretation has not always been a primary goal. Exhibits were created by directors, curators, technicians, and academicians. The need for trained exhibition designers was neither appreciated nor desirable. Designing exhibitions was subordinate to elementary display practices. Though some museum visionaries such as Vivant Denon and Charles Willson Peale saw the need for systematized organization of displays, and to a limited extent interpretation, open storage was the principle strategy for exhibitry.

Around the beginning of the twentieth century changes began to take place. As museums became more dependent upon public funding, attitudes shifted from acceptance of the former elitism, both social and academic, toward an expectation that public institutions ought to provide public service. Although altruism played a role in this evolution, the main factor was the recognition that museums depended upon the favor of the populace for their support and survival. Justifying the institution's existence became a strong motivation for developing public programs and exhibitions. This lead to two innovations in museology:

1. public accountability; and

2. the development of museum education.

> "The museum can help people only if they use it; they will use it only if they know about it and only if attention is given to interpretation of its possessions in terms they, the people, will understand."
>
> John Cotton Dana[1]

To the mission of museums, along with the primary one of collection care and management, was added public education – using collections to interpret, tell stories, and communicate. The field of museum education came into being. With it came the need for new ways to present and interpret collections, and professionals who knew how – museum educators.

Interpretation has become the watchword of the twentieth century. There are three basic definitions of the word "interpretation":

1. To translate, as into another language.

2. To explain, to put into a context.

3. To represent the meaning of something, as with interpretive dance.

Which of these is correct in the museological context? Translating the "language" of objects "in terms they, the people, will understand"[2] is certainly a function of museum interpretation. Placing things in context is important because "an organizing storyline against which the pieces can be understood facilitates learning" and "teaching methodologies – like museums – have as twin goals attraction to and retention of the subject matter."[3]

Two major movements arose during the twentieth century that have changed the public perception of museums[4] and have given exhibitions a new vocabulary:

1. blockbusters; and

2. interactivity or participation.

The term blockbuster pertains to the huge bombs used in the Second World War that had the capability of leveling a large section of a city. The adaptation of the term for exhibitions carries with it the imagery of a major event; an explosive and powerful exhibition. The advent of blockbuster exhibitions created a need to re-examine the movement of people through spaces like galleries due to the large numbers involved. If educational criteria were to be met at all, the public had to gain something intellectually as they moved through the galleries, often in a single file.

> "When museum education came of age, we began looking for new ways to communicate without having to write it all on the wall. We had to find new exhibition vocabularies that had little to do with numbered checklists."
>
> James W. Volkert[5]

Interactive or participatory exhibitions created demands upon space utilization in another way. Placement and context became important factors. In institutions like the Exploratorium in San Francisco, there is no fixed pattern to visitor traffic. People wander at will through the massive, warehouse-like structure examining exhibits on varied scientific subjects. The first considera-tion was to provide spaces and places for people to do things; to become actively involved in manipulating exhibits. This was a design issue. The second need was to give the diverse exhibits a context or framework to exist within. This presented an educational challenge.

With the development of these sorts of design and education puzzles came the realization that there needed to be people whose interests and expertise were providing the solutions. The role of the exhibit designer and the museum educator as separate but integrated functions within the museum profession arose from these issues.

Along with specialization and the educational thrust for museums the team approach to exhibition design has evolved, and the results are something more than mere displays of objects – they are highly directed, refined, and executed learning environments; true homes for the Muses.

Defining museum exhibitions

Why do people visit museums? The question has been asked countless times. What do people expect to find at museums? Visitors typically do *not* arrive at the museum doorstep wishing to:

1. read lengthy texts;

2. be lectured to by a teacher;

3. be amused, to find a place to spend a few hours. Society and commerce offer endless diversions elsewhere.

All the above may be true for some, but most people have a desire or need (if only subconsciously) for encountering something that will enrich their lives on a very personal level. Amusement is seldom a real goal. It is also unlikely that they want to become a captive audience. However, most visitors *do* have the desire to:

1. engage in experiences that will enrich life in personal ways;

2. look at things;

3. do things;

4. gain knowledge.

The main wish is to see the genuine object – the "real thing." This is the particular domain in which museums hold undisputed sway, and is their source of uniqueness among all other public institutions.

Public exhibitions

The places where people see the real thing are the exhibit galleries. The public side of a museum is its galleries, and the outward representation of the whole institution is its public exhibitions.

Museums are much like an iceberg – most of the mass lies below the surface, hidden away from public view. Since museums depend upon community approval to justify their existence in modern society, there is a real need to reveal the richness of the hidden depths. That is why, in the ICOM definition of museum, exhibitions are basic.

Without a great deal of impractical and undesirable exposure of the whole collection that would conflict with proper collection care and management, museums must rely heavily upon exhibitions and public programs to favorably represent the entire institution. Exhibitions are important for public relations and for justifying the museum to its supporting community. Exhibitions, then, are an extremely vital part of any museum's activities, perhaps second only to the care of collections.

Defining exhibitions

Exhibits are all around us. Frequently museum and commercial exhibits are synonymous in the public mind. For example, a display of Egyptian funeral objects might be seen as essentially the same thing as a window display of household appliances. Obviously, museum professionals do not believe that to be true.

What, then, is different about "museum" exhibits? How may they be distinguished from any other kinds of exhibits and displays?

Consider the roots of the word "exhibit." *Webster's New World Dictionary*[6] defines it this way:

> **ex•hib•it** (ig zib'it) *vt*. [M.E. *exhibiten*, Lt. *exhibitus*, pp. of *exhibere*, to hold forth, present, *ex-*, out + *habere*, to hold: see HABIT] 1. to present or expose to view; show; display . . . *n*. 1. a show; display; presentation 2. a thing exhibited; esp., an object or objects displayed publicly . . .
> -SYN. see PROOF, SHOW.

This is a general meaning of the word, but it does not clarify what it specifically means in a museum context. Every business is engaged in the kind of enterprise described by the dictionary. Department stores and discount stores, delicatessens and fast food restaurants, airlines and car dealerships, public service agencies and philanthropic institutions all "exhibit" their wares. Exhibits are everywhere: in store windows, at shopping malls, even two-dimensionally in the electronic media.

"Exhibiting" does not always imply anything apart from the act of showing something. A display of vacuum cleaners is, in the dictionary sense, an exhibit.

It is not merely the act of presenting that differentiates museum exhibits, but rather it is the intents or goals of the maker.

Supplying a suffix may help clarify the issue. Add "-ion" to "exhibit." The result, "exhibition," is more clearly related to museum exhibits. *Webster's*[7] defines exhibition as:

1. the act or fact of exhibiting

2. the thing or things exhibited

3. a public show or display, as of art, industrial products, athletic feats, etc.

Exhibition is a broader term than exhibit. It indicates a structured or formalized presentation with specific goals in mind and including the idea of public display.

1. Museum exhibitions are deliberate and structured in their intent and content.

2. Exhibition is a form of interpretation; a complete presentation including not only objects, but their contexts, meanings, histories, importance, and so forth.

According to Verhaar and Meeter; in their book, *Project Model Exhibitions:*[8]

> An exhibition is a means of communication aiming at large groups of the public with the purpose of conveying information, ideas and emotions relating to the material evidence of man and his surroundings with the aid of chiefly visual and dimensional methods.

The authors expand upon the word "exhibition" as meaning "all forms of presentation." By communication they mean the "transfer of information and ideas" with the intent to change opinions, increase knowledge, and alter behavior, as deemed desirable by the exhibit-makers. The term "visual," is not exclusive, but includes appeals to all the senses – vision simply being dominant.

The central issue is not so much how things are presented, but why – the purpose or intent. Commercial and public service exhibits always carry with them the purpose and motivations of their producers. Exhibiting wares for sale or services for hire have the goal of creating a desire to possess a product or use the service. The intent is to stimulate interest in what is offered, and to effectively change or strengthen feelings. Public service exhibits support the aim of promoting programs or ideologies. The intent is to change or modify attitudes, and to increase conformity within the society.

How do these intentions fit with the museological purpose of exhibitions? The goals are the same. Museum exhibitions also support the maker's purpose. Profit may not be the specific motivational factor, but museums have the intent to:

1. represent or "sell" the institution;

2. change attitudes;

3. modify behavior;

4. increase conformity in knowledge.

All are viable and reasonable goals for museums.

The main difference between commercial or public service exhibits and museum exhibition lies in the purpose or mission of the institution.

1. The term "commercial" defines exhibits for such enterprises. They are presented with commercial or business goals in mind.

2. "Public service" exhibit is also self-explanatory. That is the exhibits are used to perform public awareness and assistance aims.

3. If one considers that the word "museum" literally means "a place of the Muses" – that is, a place for study, reflection, and learning – then museum exhibitions are self-defining as well. The purpose is mainly educational in scope.

The museum's institutional motivation is to present objects and information in a manner conducive to meeting educational goals. Exhibitions fulfill, in part, the museum purpose:

1. By revealing collections, thus confirming public trust in the museum as caretaker of the societal record.

2. They also promote community interest in the museum by offering alternative leisure time activities where individuals or groups may have rewarding experiences.

3. Financially, exhibitions support the institution as well. They help the museum as a whole justify its existence, and its confident expectation for continued support.

4. Exhibitions provide proof of responsible fiduciary management and proper handling of collections. Donors, both public and private, are more likely to impart support to or bestow collections on a museum with an active and meaningful exhibition schedule. Potential donors are much more inclined to place their treasures where they will be cared for, and where they will be presented for the public good in a thoughtful and informative manner.

5. In general, a vigorous, well-presented public exhibition program affords an institution credibility.

To summarize:

1. Exhibitions are one of the primary means by which a museum represents itself to its supporting community.

2. Exhibitions are offered with the intent to perform the institutional mission of revealing the collections to public view, providing enlightening and educational experiences, and proving the public trust.

3. The specific goals of museum exhibitions involve the desire to change attitudes, modify behavior, and increase the availability of knowledge.

Exhibition as an interpretive medium

> "An exhibition is a means of communication aiming at large groups of the public with the purpose of conveying information, ideas and emotions relating to the material evidence of man and his surroundings with the aid of chiefly visual and dimensional methods."
>
> Jan Verhaar and Han Meeter[9]

The definition by Verhaar and Meeter states some key elements in a museum meaning of exhibition. However, exhibition is more than simply a process of presenting things. It is also a collective creative activity with an overall goal of communicating a message or messages – that is a medium or channel of expression.

The word "medium" applied to exhibitions invokes the same meaning as it does when applied to an artistic mode of expression. Just as paintings, sculptures, books, and weavings are mediums of expression, an exhibition may be viewed as a medium or method of communication.

A comparison may help to explain: an artist's experiences, ideas, attitudes, aspirations, skills, and knowledge are present in his or her mind. These supply the background resources from which he or she can draw. The paint, canvas, brushes, and easel are the physical resources required. By combining these elements along with an intent of self-expression, the artist produces a painting – a personal medium of communication. The viewer will observe the finished art work, filter its images through his or her own set of experiences and attitudes, and arrive at some conclusion. In essence what has occurred is transfer of information – visual, emotional, intellectual.

Thinking of an exhibition as a collective medium, similarities suggest themselves.

1. The museum staff's collective knowledge, experiences, and goals are the intellectual resources.

2. Varied materials and strategies are used to achieve educational and communication goals.

3. Two- and three-dimensional collection objects are the primary physical resources.

4. Collections are supplemented with structures, graphics, text, banners, colors, shapes, traffic flow, lighting, audio-visuals, demonstrations, docent lead tours, and other physical resources.

151

5. Definite messages are intended to be presented.

6. The visitor is expected to view the message, process it through his or her own particular set of experiences and opinions, and arrive at conclusions and a desire to learn more.

Exhibition is a collective creative activity with an overall goal to communicate a message or messages, either cognitive or affective, or both.

The idea of exhibitions as medium has with it some inherent warnings that museums are now beginning to recognize and admit:

1. The people making exhibits have their own views about any subject.

2. The people making exhibits choose what will be shown.

> "Museums have the authority to select, interpret, and present that which they decide has value or significance. Removed from their original contexts and functions, objects take on new meanings that are sometimes laden with unconscious interests. Some museum professionals lose sight of the fact that exhibition is by its very nature an interpretive act. The process of selecting and arranging objects is at bottom a fabrication and, as such, a statement about what the fabricators suppose an object to say."
>
> Lisa Roberts[10]

This being true, then museums are not necessarily places in which truth is a given, or in which all sides of the subject are discussed. This creates challenges for exhibitors, for example:

1. Presenting more than one point of view for a subject.

2. Informing visitors that the exhibition they are viewing is an interpretation made by other human beings based on their own feelings, biases, and opinions.

It has been suggested, strongly in some quarters, that exhibit team members should visibly put their signatures on an exhibition to make their roles clearly understood.

Exhibition equations

Presentation is the physical act of placing collections on public view

Presentation	(physical display)
+ Interpretation	(explanation and exposition)
= Communication	(the exhibitor's goal)

Communicating information and ideas is the intent of the exhibit maker.

How that is accomplished depends upon subject matter and available resources. Exhibits are often categorized by the sorts of objects or themes presented. Example: a presentation of paintings is considered an art exhibition; an array of animal specimens is a natural history exhibition, and so forth. However, the type of exhibit should not so much be determined by what is in it, as by what it is intended to accomplish.

Usually one associates museum exhibitions with collection objects or their representations as the primary focus for information. This is not true in all cases. Some museum exhibitions may incorporate no objects at all. These are usually instructional in content and intent. There are justifiable uses and reasons for this form of exhibitry, but in the main the uniqueness of museum exhibitions rests in their employment of the actual object.

Using this as a basis for categorizing exhibitions is more helpful in planning than simply relying upon their contents. Exhibits may range from being either purely object-oriented at one extreme, or largely concept-oriented at the other. That is to say either things or messages are dominant.

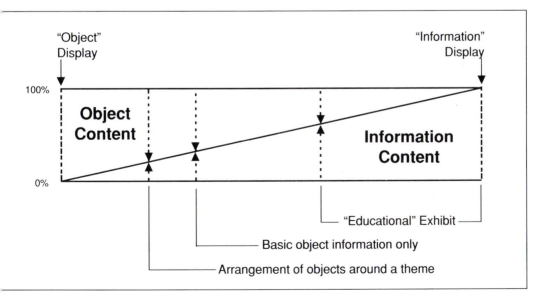

Figure 8.1 Exhibit content scale

The scale in Figure 8.1, adapted from diagram 9, in Verhaar and Meeter's, *Project Model Exhibitions*,[11] illustrates this idea.

1. At one end is an object display: a presentation of objects purely for the object's sake; no interpretive information is involved. This is an exhibit in its purest sense, not an exhibition. It is like showing off a collection of vases or ceramic animals on the living-room mantle. The intent is simply to attractively arrange the objects, relying upon the things to "speak" for themselves.

2. At the other extreme is the information display in which objects are either not present or of minimal importance. This kind of presentation depends upon text and graphics to get its message across, much like a book. The intent is to communicate an idea or ideas that the exhibitor has determined are in the viewer's best interest to know.

3. Along the diagram's diagonal line is where most exhibitions fall. The relative dominance of one aspect or the other determines whether an exhibition is more object-oriented or concept-oriented.

In an object-oriented exhibition, objects are central. Characteristics of this type are:

1. Educational information is limited or not presented at all. Relationships, values, and hidden or implied meanings are not examined to any significant degree.

2. The exhibit designer focuses on a direct aesthetic or scientific approach to display, such as arrangement by taxonomic order, or age, et cetera.

In a strongly concept-oriented exhibit, attention is focused on the message; the transfer of information. Characteristically:

1. The aim is to get the story across regardless of whether collections are available for interpretation or illustration.

2. Text, graphics, photographs, and other like materials comprise the majority of the exhibition content.

The middle ground, which is most often used in the museum setting, takes into account the dual mission of museums to collect objects and to use them to educate. Forms of this range of presentations are:

1. Thematic exhibitions, closer to the object-oriented end of the scale, use collections arranged around a theme with only basic information provided, such as a title sign and identification labels. For instance, in an exhibition featuring Picasso's works, they might be exhibited with only basic labeling, relying upon the artist's reputation and a written catalog to impart whatever interpretive details are deemed desirable.

2. Closer to the concept-oriented end, on the other hand, are "educational" exhibits. These combine about 60 percent information and 40 percent objects (see Figure 8.1).

It is important to note that there are no sharp lines of demarcation between the two ends of the scale and that none of the above are "right" or "wrong" as approaches to exhibitions. Their use should be determined by the goals and intents of the exhibitors.

Decisions made about content and the setting of goals is done in the planning phase. Things to consider are:

1. What is the exhibit intended to communicate?

2. What combination of objects and information will communicate this best?

These ought to be deliberate choices based on the goals of the exhibition and the planners' knowledge of the target audiences.

Since a museum's primary milieu is the "real thing," some think that all that is needed is to present objects and to let them speak for themselves. However, what do a painting, a bone, or a rock communicate alone without interpretation? On the other hand, is the story behind the object always the main point, or is emotional impact fundamental?

When the other element of the exhibit equation, interpretation, is minimized, leaving presentation dominant, the result is called "open storage." This form of exhibition hearkens back to older presentation techniques, though in some specific instances it still has validity today.

Most museums now recognize that communication can only be accomplished within a more interpretive framework than open storage. The educational mission of museum exhibitions has become the primary focus. The information behind an object – its provenance – needs to be related to the viewer through planned and structured interpretation.

The goals for communication vary from museum to museum, exhibition to exhibition, and community to community. However, some messages can be reasonably well identified as being common to most museum exhibit efforts.

1. Museums are places to encounter the actual objects – the "real things." The presentation of collections allows at least a near approach by the public to genuine objects. This has the effect of stimulating curiosity and interest. The value of being in the presence of da Vinci's *Mona Lisa* or the skeletal remains of a Tyrannosaurus Rex is immeasurable. Hopefully the result will be an interest and curiosity that will develop into life-long personal growth and enrichment.

2. Besides the rather intangible benefits afforded at a personal level, there are a wider range of advantages available. As an alternate educational environment for state funded schools, museums are invaluable and unparalleled. Coordination between exhibition objectives and school curricula can be an extremely beneficial partnership. Bringing subject matter to life in tangible ways is what museum exhibitions excel

at doing. A museum visit can do as much to stimulate a student's life-long interest in a subject as all the books he or she may ever read.

3. Museum exhibitions offer enjoyable ways of assimilating information, sometimes even of very great complexity. The fact of viewing the real thing is, in itself, intellectually pleasing for many people. The opportunity to view objects in a relaxed, comfortable environment where interaction between the viewer and the object, the student and the teacher or tour guide, or the pupils with their peers can occur leads to retention and personalizing of otherwise academic topics. It is much more enjoyable to view an actual pre-Columbian figure, than only to read about it in a book and look at a photograph. Combine the effect of doing both, and the result is lasting impressions and respect.

4. The entertainment value of exhibitions as a communication tool should not be overlooked. Communication occurring in a relaxed, enjoyable environment promotes a willingness to learn and to continue learning. The "gee whiz!" factor is part of the entertainment aspect. Things that are big, famous, genuine, or impressive in some sense, are readily, if not eagerly, examined by almost everyone. When inquiry takes place, guided by intelligent and sensitive interpretative labeling or docenting, then learning occurs without duress.

In discussing the communicative capability of museum exhibitions, one overriding objective emerges:

> The museum visitor should leave an exhibit with a sense of, "I am personally better – more knowledgeable, more interested and interesting – for having made the effort to go to the museum."

When museum exhibitions accomplish such a response, they are effective communication tools and are extremely important to the museum mission.

Evaluating the use of the exhibition medium

Whether to exhibit or not to exhibit is the point at which to begin the planning process. In thinking about an exhibit subject it is important to ask, "Is the exhibition medium the best or most appropriate means of expressing the intent of the exhibitor?" In some cases, exhibition is not the most effective medium. Abstract ideas and complex philosophical reasoning do not lend themselves well to exhibitions. The philosophies of Plato or Socrates would be difficult to translate into an exhibition.

However, seemingly difficult subjects, if properly linked to concrete ideas and images, can be very effective exhibition material. For example, "Why should we save the rain forests?" This question has deep philosophical content. It also has very practical conceptual elements. An exhibit on rain forests, global ecology, or related subjects can communicate splendidly and, in turn affect attitudes and behavior.

156

What this means is that it is best to analyze the strengths and weaknesses of the exhibition as a medium before deciding whether to continue. What are some of the strengths of exhibit presentation? They might be summarized by the following:

1. Genuine objects allow the visitor to encounter reality, to confront the direct source, and to experience the "real thing."

2. The visitor can assimilate the presented material at his or her own pace and way.

3. Exhibition is a multi-functional method of communication, allowing any number of activities to be added to the central presentation, thereby enhancing the overall experience through tours, programs, lectures and demonstrations.

What then are exhibitions' weaknesses? They can be stated thus:

1. Exhibitions tend to be superficial, object-oriented, and visual. That is, they primarily deal with the physical aspects of things, and even if interpretation is excellent, exhibitions do not afford a complete source of information.

2. Profound or highly abstract concepts cannot always be properly conveyed through exhibitions. Cinematography or books may be better mediums.

3. Exhibitions using collection items are often static. Conservation needs, resource availability, and personnel limitations can lead to the appearance of stagnation for long-term exhibitions.

4. The very freedom of movement or informal educational environment that characterizes exhibitions can create coherency problems, especially for highly directed storylines.

To summarize, exhibitions can be made to work for almost any subject, but reasonable and practical considerations about appropriateness, levels of commitment, and the value of the exhibit to the public should be thoroughly thought out before choosing that medium of communication.

Question from the field: twenty-seven

Question: How long should you leave a permanent collection on exhibit?

Response: There is no simple guide to the time an object may be on exhibit without sustaining possible damage. Some objects appear to withstand long periods on exhibition without visible damage while others may change rapidly.

Knowing the exact condition of the material is the first step in the care of the object on exhibition. Careful inspection is an important step in determining the condition of objects.

Once on exhibition the changes may be so gradual that without prior knowledge they remain undetected. Prior knowledge of the object's condition or level of stability will also alert the inspector to particular trouble areas. Condition reporting may be written and objects documented with photographs. Photographs provide an excellent reference with which to compare the object and reduce dependency on the observer's memory.

The two most effective ways to avoid damage to objects on exhibit are good record-keeping and regular monitoring. Good records will include the date the object was last exhibited, the object's conditions including previous conservation information, and other pertinent information. The data will help determine the appropriateness of placing the object on exhibit and the conditions to be watched while it is out of the storage area.

All members of a museum staff have a responsibility to observe and report the condition of objects on exhibit. Docents, security staff, exhibit personnel, curators, or conservators may notice a change or an alteration in the condition of an object. Good collection care is the responsibility of everyone working in a museum.

Question from the field: twenty-eight

Question: Suppose you are employed as a conservator for a structure that has two equal spaces. One space is an open courtyard and the other is an enclosed area destined to be a museum. The museum space has a controlled climate but is already filled to capacity. On the walls of the open courtyard are paintings that have been there for over 200 years.

Because of the pollution and increased moisture, the paintings are deteriorating. The architects conserving the structure say the paintings are important to the design of the building and want them to remain in place. They say any protective covering of the paintings will detract from the original structure.

The paintings as well as the building should be saved. What should be done?

Response: This is a complex problem. It reinforces the fact that conservation issues are often complex. It is not unusual for the protection of one element to interfere with the care of another. In reality there is no ready-made answer to the problem.

Continued exposure to the elements will eventually destroy the paintings. Even if a micro-environment was constructed around each art work, the adverse conditions will be only partially alleviated. As no physical barriers are allowable to protect the paintings, then the only immediate answer is to remove the paintings.

One solution is to reproduce the paintings using a photo process that will provide a two-dimensional representation of the three-dimensional surface. In this process, the brush strokes and painted surface are visible. The photo-image will also show the impact of time and signs of deterioration. By using a UV filtered laminate to protect the photo-images from both sun and rain, they will last for a time. To ensure continuity, several images can be made and the negatives preserved for future use. Conservation and proper storage of the original paintings will make them available for special occasions.

There is no perfect solution for this situation. Most visitors will expect to see the original paintings. Most will also understand the potential damage of these valuable historic objects due to continued exposure to the elements.

As a suggestion: Clearly state in all descriptive material that the paintings are copies. Make a written statement about the process used to produce the copies and the importance of preserving the original paintings. Schedule special times each year when the original pieces will be on exhibit in their original locations. In this way the pride of conserving the objects for future generations will be shared.

Question from the field: twenty-nine

Question: If a curator places a value on a piece as part of the loan process and the insurance company rejects the value, what do you do?

Response: If the object has been recently acquired and a certified appraisal from an outside appraiser is available, include a copy of that document as proof of the value. To determine the value of an object for insurance purposes, particularly for traveling exhibits, it is sometimes worthwhile to have the object appraised by more than one person. (As a suggestion, rather than rule, have three appraisals and use them to document the curator's determination.)

The real difficulty arises when dealing with artifacts, specimens, or samples from a museum collection that have no true "market value." These may include natural science specimens, archaeological artifacts, or mineral samples. However, the research value far exceeds any assessable dollar value. To address this issue, it is advisable to show a minimum value for insurance purposes on types of objects in a museum collection. With this documentation, it will be easier to verify the value assigned by a curator.

If the valuation is for loaning the object, include a statement in the loan agreement noting the lending institution's curator as the person to assign the insured value.

Notes

1. John Cotton Dana, cited in Alexander, E. (1983) *Museum Masters*, Nashville, Tenn.: American Association for State and Local History.
2. Lisa Roberts, cited in Volkert, J. (1991) "Monologue to Dialogue," *Museum News*, Vol. 70, No. 2, March/April, p. 47.
3. Chadbourne, C. (1991) "A Tool for Storytelling," *Museum News*, Vol. 70, No. 2, March/April, p. 41.
4. Lisa Roberts, cited in Volkert, "Monologue to Dialogue," p. 47.
5. ibid.
6. Guralnik, D. (ed.) (1974) *Webster's New World Dictionary of the American Language*, New York: William Collins and World Publishing Co., Inc.
7. ibid.
8. Verhaar, J. and Meeter, H. (1989) *Project Model Exhibitions*, Leiden: Reinwardt Academie, p. 26.
9. ibid.
10. Lisa Roberts, cited in Volkert, "Monologue to Dialogue," p. 47.
11. Veerhaar and Meeter *Project Model Exhibitions*, p. 26.

Suggested reading

Belcher, M. (1991) *Exhibitions in Museums*, Leicester: Leicester University Press.

Finn, D. (1985) *How to Visit a Museum*, New York: Harry Abrams, Inc.

Fondation de France/ICOM (1991) *Museums Without Barriers*, Paris: Fondation de France/ICOM in conjunction with Routledge.

Kanikow, R. (1987) *Exhibit Design*, New York: PBC International.

Karp, I., Kreamer, C., and Lavine, S. (eds) (1992) *Museums and Communities: The Politics of Public Culture*, Washington, DC: Smithsonian Institution Press.

Karp, I. and Lavine, S. (eds) (1991) *Exhibiting Cultures: The Poetics and Politics of Museum Display*, Washington, DC: Smithsonian Institution Press.

Klein, L. (1986) *Exhibits: Planning and Design*, New York: Madison Square Press.

Loomis, R. (1987) *Museum Visitor Evaluation: New Tool for Management*, Vol. 3, AASLH Management Series, Nashville, Tenn.: American Association for State and Local History.

Neal, A. (1969) *HELP! for the Small Museum, Handbook of Exhibit Ideas and Methods*, Boulder, Colo.: Pruett Publishing.

(1976) *Exhibits for the Small Museum*, Nashville, Tenn.: American Association for State and Local History.

Serrell, B. (1985) *Making Exhibit Labels*, Nashville, Tenn.: American Association for State and Local History.

9

Project management

There are a number of tasks to be performed in producing a museum exhibition. Someone must provide expertise about the subject. There must be someone to design the gallery, plan the educational parts, and oversee the process and resources. These jobs may be performed by one person or it may involve a team of people who are specialists in each task: a curator, a designer, an educator, and a project manager. If possible, others may be added to the process such as carpenters, writers, and record-keepers. By combining specialists in museum education, design, and management with the expertise of curators, it is more possible to present public-oriented exhibitions tailored to meet popular expectations and needs. However, these goals can be realized even with small staffs.

A useful way of creating exhibitions is to approach them as a type of project or enterprise with a definite product as the end result – the exhibition. The outlines and models presented are intended to suggest ways in which to think about exhibition development. The outline forms the ladder from the starting-point (having an idea) to the destination (the completed exhibition). It is the process of climbing the ladder that matters, and grasping the sequence of activities and tasks will help understand how to ascend the ladder.

Product cycle as a model

In commercial affairs, accomplishing tasks is a highly organized operation. The systematized approach used by businesses to manage their projects can be quite valuable if related to exhibition development. That is because any course of action with a product as its ultimate goal is a project.

All projects, regardless of how they begin or what they are intended to do, share common traits. The time it takes to plan, develop, and execute the project is limited. Projects have beginnings and ends, and in between are recognizable phases and stages based upon the different jobs to do. Throughout the project there are three types of activity that go on. They are:

1. Product-oriented activities – efforts concerned with objects and interpretation.

2. Management-oriented activities – tasks that focus on providing the resources and personnel.

3. Coordination activities – keeping every job moving toward the same goal.

All projects also have definite phases they go through. They begin with an idea, progress through a planning and implementing period, then end. As seen in the diagram in Figure 9.1, the project can be drawn as a series of events along a line of time. This is a project model.

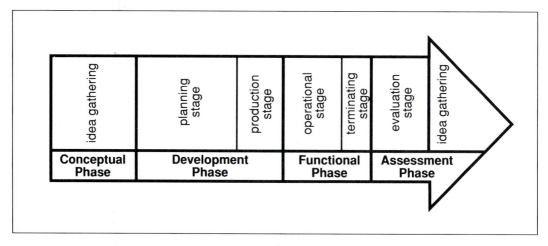

Figure 9.1 Exhibition project model

The progressive, sequential nature of a project or system life-cycle, as in Figure 9.1, works well in exhibition development. The phases and stages make it easier to identify tasks and to make a plan of action. As shown below, the phases and stages may be outlined to make types of activities and specific tasks more easily recognizable. By dividing the parts of the exhibition's development into tasks, the job becomes easier to plan.

Examining the phases of development will help in understanding the tasks and roles, and it will help identify times when decisions are needed.

Concept phase

Where do exhibits begin? There is no single answer. Exhibit ideas come from many sources. A museum should be like a leaky vessel or sponge within its community – ideas should seep in and be absorbed from all parts of the society. That means keeping one's eyes and ears open to possibilities and sifting through the ideas constantly, looking for ones that fulfill the criteria of public service and education.

Someone's experiences or travels, or even a new museum collection can excite a desire to create an exhibition. In some instances, the need to replace existing exhibits may prompt the search for new exhibit ideas. Gathering ideas from all sources will provide a museum with many possibilities. Enthusiasm for the exhibition must be channeled into a coordinated process, or it will become chaotic and frustrating; a mixture of conflicting messages and confused goals.

Sorting through the concepts can be done is several ways. One of the best is to have a "brainstorming" session. The museum staff and, when useful, representatives from the community can gather to discuss the ideas informally. By examining the museum's goals and talking about the various possibilities in a relaxed atmosphere, good concepts will gain support and new ideas will emerge. The result should be a slate of exhibition proposals that demonstrate sensitivity to public needs and expectations, yet adhere to institutional goals and standards.

From the slate of proposals, who decides on the ones to pursue, and what are the criteria for making such decisions? As the museum profession has grown and developed, two important ethical considerations have appeared: accountability and adherence. Accountability toward the public, and adherence to accepted international museological standards. These are clearly expressed in ICOM's booklet on ethics.

To apply ethical concerns to concrete matters, a museum needs to state its own individual ethics and goals. It is helpful to have a written mission statement and a good grasp of the community's needs. Also, establishing educational goals and a list of available resources is valuable. It is a good idea to have a written exhibit policy statement, and, of course, knowing your collection is essential.

Armed with these tools, an administrator can make decisions that meet museum needs. It is usually the role and responsibility of the museum director to make the final decision about which exhibitions to develop. In large museums, other staff members may be involved in decision making, but with the support documents mentioned, no matter whether the staff is small or large, the criteria will be clear.

Planning is not always easy. In fact, it is far easier to use an "ad hoc" approach to exhibit planning. That leads to being driven by the demand to fill space rather than creating exhibitions that answer to the concerns and expectations of the community. However, as with any organization, museums should be in the business of improving their operation. The efforts made to assemble the criteria-setting documents will be worth the labor.

The motivations for exhibitions should include a fundamental orientation toward public service. The personal likes and dislikes of directors or curators are not entirely adequate foundations for exhibitions. Even in museums where staffs are small and largely voluntary, the guidelines for decision making ought be clearly spelled out, and based on a sense of the community.

To become informed and remain current, the body of knowledge about a community requires time, skills, and energies usually not available to museum staffs. If such knowledge is not available, museums should enlist aid from the community to gain a basic idea of needs and expectations.

Development phase

The goal of the project is the product – the exhibition. The most visible tasks are those involved in working with the collections. However, other tasks are involved as well. They are not so obvious: management activities aimed at assessing and making resources available. Resources required are time, funding, quality control, information gathering, and coordination of efforts.

After the decision to develop an exhibition idea has been made, the director will make decisions about who to include and what disciplines and skills are required to get the job done. In small museums this decision may be simple: the director will do everything. Larger museums will probably use their own staffs or hire consultants to provide technical and academic expertise. Whichever is the case, the exhibition is ready to move into the planning stage.

The planning stage sets the standards – builds the framework – upon which the exhibition is built. Without spending sufficient time and effort at this point, the rest of the process is likely to be confusing at best, and, at worst, will result in a poorly executed exhibition lacking in content and coherence.

The exhibition planner or planners should look at community information to determine which audiences to target. Developing and writing down the exhibition goals will help identify the objectives needed to meet them. This results in a clear set of standards, useful in evaluating the effectiveness of the exhibition later.

Once exhibition goals and objectives are established, more concrete, object-oriented work such as researching the topics, writing the interpretive materials, designing the gallery, and creating educational and promotional plans may proceed.

During the planning stage, management activities are critical and are centered around budgeting: budgeting time, personnel, and funds. These are resources for realizing exhibition goals. There are usually more jobs than people or funds, which makes budgeting time a necessity for efficiently using available skills and energies.

Planning activities require someone to oversee and coordinate resources, sometimes called the project manager. That person's job is to facilitate communication, see that information and resources are available as needed, call meetings, assign tasks as required, and act as a mediator when necessary. In museums with one person or small staffs, this job is one of the many that falls to available personnel. The functions of the project manager are needed whether or not it is that person's sole responsibility.

Depending upon funding and the scope or complexity of the exhibition, special advisors may be consulted. Sometimes such advice is provided through a university, but some services may be provided locally, such as carpentry skills, or making signs and labels.

The end result of all the planning activities is a plan of action for producing the exhibition. The plan should include a timeline or a series of deadlines, the budget, the interpretive material, a conservation and maintenance schedule, drawings if needed, and the educational and promotional plans.

Next in the development phase is the production stage. Product-oriented activities in this stage are many. There is much to be done prior to installing collections in the exhibition. After the list of objects has been decided upon, a conservation assessment should be made to establish the level of care required for each object. Requirements concerning the types and degrees of support, the kinds of materials that are correct chemically and physically for the collection items, and the environmental conditions required (light levels, relative humidity, and temperature) should be written down. This can take the form of a care and maintenance instruction document, and can usually be prepared by the collection's caretaker or the curator.

When objects are borrowed for exhibitions, agreements for the loan must be carefully worked out. This may involve a detailed report about the borrower's facility including the size and experience of the staff, the kind of building the museum is in, the way collections are used, and so forth. Such a report informs the lender that proper care will be given to the loaned objects while they are outside its direct care.

Record-keeping activities are continuous, and documenting the conditions and movements of collections is an important duty. The locations of collection objects used in exhibitions must be recorded and updated, whether they move from room to room, or from city to city.

Based upon the research documents, interpretive materials such as text and labels are fitted to the audience needs and educational level. As the time nears to install the exhibition, label, text, and title copy must be produced.

Fabrication is the work of creating the graphics, building structures, and preparing mountings for the collection objects. It also involves preparing the gallery. For many exhibitions, special construction is needed, such as walls, cases, and vitrines.

For many smaller institutions, there may be little or no space for fabrication work. Much of the building and preparation must be done by private contractors in the community or ordered from suppliers. Often cabinetry, such as for cases and stands, must be contracted for, as may special mountings. Time and expense are major considerations. Pre-planning and ordering of supplies early to allow time for shipment is imperative.

While fabrication is going on, development of educational programs should be as well. This may include writing gallery guides, brochures, and training materials for tour guides and teachers. Training guides and arranging for lecturers, demonstrations, and the like are things to be done during this time.

In addition to these internal preparations, promotional plans should be put into action. Sending out information about the exhibition, writing press releases, issuing press packets, putting up posters, and coordinating with the media are tasks to be accomplished.

One of the main management tasks is budget control. Maintaining accurate accounts involving purchases for construction, conservation, publications, and bid letting is continuous. Constant supervision is essential in maintaining accountability for funds.

Another management concern, progress control, requires periodic checks to assess how the project is advancing. In some instances, especially if large projects are involved, progress reports might be needed as a control measure for administrators. Coupled with progress control is quality control. This should be done to ensure the exhibition will be as it was designed.

The many activities described above are in preparation for the main endeavor – installing the exhibition. During installation, display structures such as walls, panels, and the like are put in place, support materials are brought into the gallery, and the collection objects are placed on or into their mounts. Wayfinders, labeling, barriers, lighting, and all the other elements of the exhibition must be brought in and placed in the gallery.

Lighting is installed and checked to be sure it conforms to conservation standards, and, if available, monitoring equipment is placed in the gallery to check temperature and humidity. If such things are not available, then other reasonable actions should be taken. Keeping paintings and textiles out of direct sunlight, making sure objects do not become wet, periodically checking for insects and mildew, and the like are measures that can be accomplished in almost any circumstance.

Instructions should be distributed to the people responsible for overseeing the exhibition during its public life. As the exhibition nears completion, the security, custodial, and maintenance personnel need to be informed about problems to look for and how to report them. These people are the best eyes and ears a museum has while objects are on exhibit. The security staff should be shown areas and objects that may be vulnerable to vandalism, theft, or accidental damage. These should be few, but nearly every exhibition has some security concerns.

Periodic checks should be made to ensure that the instructions are clearly understood and complied with, and, where advisable, written instructions should be provided for operations such as the turning on and off of equipment, special conservation concerns, monitoring environmental equipment, and related activities.

The end result of all the activities described in the production stage is the opening of the exhibition to the public. This may be accompanied by special events such as lectures, demonstrations, and receptions. The successful completion of an exhibition is a time for celebration.

Functional phase

The functional phase is the time in an exhibition's life when it is available to the public and educational programs are offered. There are two main stages in this phase. First, the operational stage has to do with the day-to-day operation of the exhibition. Important activities include security, maintenance, housekeeping, and periodic examinations of the exhibitions. The main thing is to watch the collections for signs of deterioration or damage.

During this time, educational programs are presented and visitor surveys are conducted. Getting an idea of how well the exhibition is working is important. Interviewing visitors about their visit, having them answer questionnaires, and simply observing them in the gallery can provide a great deal of information about how well the goals of the exhibition are being fulfilled. Such information should be recorded for future reference.

Management tasks in this stage include settling accounts and providing maintenance costs. The objective of the product and management activities is to achieve the predetermined goals and to ensure that no undue deterioration of collections occurs.

Following the operational stage and bringing an end to the exhibition is the terminating stage. Activities involve closing the gallery to the public, dismantling the exhibition, and returning collection objects to their storage facilities or lending institutions. The gallery is cleared and necessary repairs are made in preparation for the next exhibition.

Condition reports must be compiled for the objects on loan, and then packing and transporting of those items is completed. The main management activity is the balancing of accounts and sales receipts, and assessing final costs for the exhibition in preparation for the evaluation report.

Evaluation phase

The final and an extremely important phase in exhibition development has to do with assessing the results. Evaluation is increasingly important to exhibit programs. It provides a means of determining whether or not the goals set early in the process were met. It also serves to point the way for future exhibitions, by suggesting ways to improve the process and the product.

The results of evaluating the process and the exhibition should be assembled into an evaluation report. Such a report will serve to document the exhibition, will give the museum an idea of how well or how poorly the process of development worked, and will demonstrate how well the exhibition performed in meeting the educational goals set for it. Evaluation inspires growth in both product and process, and will generate new ideas for future exhibition projects.

☐   ☐   ☐   ☐   ☐

Technical note: five

Stages of exhibition development

CONCEPT PHASE

Concept stage:
> *Product-oriented activities:*
>> sorting through ideas and deciding which to pursue.
>
> *Management activities:*
>> looking at the ideas in relation to museum and audience needs and the museum's mission;
>> selecting exhibit ideas to develop;
>> assessing available resources to do the project.
>
> *Results:*
>> creating the schedule of exhibits;
>> identifying potential resources.

DEVELOPMENTAL PHASE

Planning stage:
> *Product-oriented activities:*
>> setting goals for the exhibition;
>> deciding on the storyline;
>> designing the exhibition;
>> creating an educational plan;
>> creating a promotional plan (if needed).
>
> *Management activities:*
>> estimating costs;
>> looking for sources of funds or resources;
>> budgeting resources;
>> assigning tasks.
>
> *Results:*
>> a plan for making the exhibition;
>> a plan for educating with the exhibition.

Production stage:
> *Product-oriented activities:*
>> building the exhibit parts;
>> mounting and installing the objects in the exhibition;
>> developing the educational programs;
>> putting the promotional plan into action.

Management activities:
> *controlling the use of resources;*
> *keeping track of progress.*

Results:
> *presenting the exhibition to public;*
> *using the educational programs with the exhibition.*

FUNCTIONAL PHASE

Operational stage:
> *Product-oriented activities:*
>> *having the exhibition open on a regular basis;*
>> *presenting the educational programs;*
>> *doing visitor surveys;*
>> *doing maintenance on the exhibition;*
>> *providing security for the exhibition.*
> *Management activities:*
>> *settling accounts.*
> *Results:*
>> *achieving the exhibition goals;*
>> *preventing deterioration of collections.*

Terminating stage:
> *Product-oriented activities:*
>> *dismantling the exhibition;*
>> *returning objects to the collection storage.*
> *Management activities:*
>> *balancing accounts.*
> *Results:*
>> *the exhibition is closed;*
>> *the collections are cared for;*
>> *the gallery is cleared and repaired.*

EVALUATION PHASE

Evaluation stage:
> *Product-oriented activities:*
>> *assessing the exhibition;*
>> *assessing the process of making the exhibition.*
> *Management activities:*
>> *making an evaluation report.*
> *Results:*
>> *improving the product and the process*

□   □   □   □   □

Suggested reading

Alderson, W. and Low, S. (1987) *Interpretation of Historic Sites*, 2nd edn rev., Nashville, Tenn.: American Association for State and Local History.

Finn, D. (1985) *How to Visit a Museum*, New York: Harry Abrams, Inc.

Fondation de France/ICOM (1991) *Museums Without Barriers*, Paris: Fondation de France/ICOM in conjunction with Routledge.

Neal, A. (1969) *HELP! for the Small Museum, Handbook of Exhibit Ideas and Methods*, Boulder, Colo.: Pruett Publishing.

(1976) *Exhibits for the Small Museum*, Nashville, Tenn.: American Association for State and Local History.

Thompson, J. M. A. (ed.) (1984) *Manual of Curatorship, A Guide to Museum Practice*, 2nd edn 1992, London: Butterworth & Co.

Verhaar, J. and Meeter, H. (1987) *Project Model Exhibitions*, Leiden: Reinwardt Academie.

10

Interpretation

Interpretation is the process of making something understandable or of giving something a special meaning. By definition, the word "interpretation" has three principal meanings. They are:[1]

1. to explain or clarify;

2. to translate (as from one language to another);

3. to perform or present according to one's artistic understanding (as with interpretive dance).

The meanings most closely related to the museological use of interpretation are to offer an explanation about something, or to translate objects and knowledge into a "language" the visitor can understand. Perhaps the real key to understanding interpretation as it relates to the museum is found in the origin of the word. The root word *interpres*, comes from Latin and means a negotiator or a mediator between two parties. It is a goal of museums to be the mediators between collections and the public.

What is the purpose of emphasizing interpretation? The educational mission of museums is becoming increasingly important as is evident from ICOM's statements on the roles of education, exhibitions, and public access.[2] This is because most people find it difficult to understand why the arts of collecting and storing objects are relevant to their everyday lives, especially when economic and environmental stresses are taken into account. Presentation of public exhibitions and programs has become a museum's primary way of establishing accountability to the support community, and justifying the expectation for continued funding.

The process of interpreting requires an understanding of the ways ideas and information are communicated. A classic model of the interpretive pathway is illustrated in Figure 10.1.

As illustrated, the flow of interpretation is from sender to receiver, and back to the sender. An important aspect of the process is the way the path turns back on itself. Without this particular aspect of the process, the sender has no way of knowing whether the message has been received. The channels listed are only suggested. Many different channels may be devised.

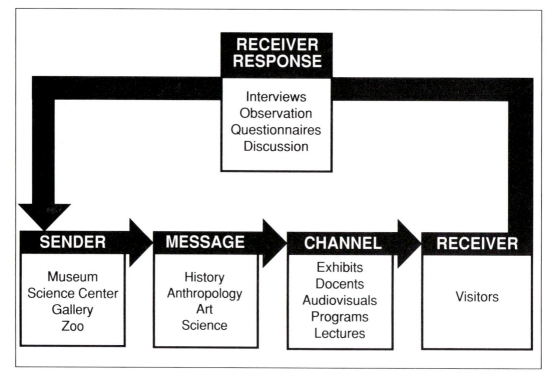

Figure 10.1 Interpretation loop

It is usually quite helpful to set down on paper the elements of the loop as suggested in the model. Such an exercise aids in clarifying the message or messages, identifying the audience, and assessing which channels are likely to be most appropriate. It is also very important to assess the successes and failures of exhibitions that are completed. The learning that occurs when such evaluation is done, greatly increases the chances of improving future exhibitions. An overarching goal for museum exhibitions should be the continual improvement of interpretive methods with a view to improving the value and enjoyment of the museum visit for the public.

People and museums

People are the only reason for museums to exist. Although it is an obvious point, that fact is frequently overlooked in the day-to-day process of operating a museum. It is always a danger to think of the museum as an end in itself, without the need to make it useful to the community. However, everything museological involves humans and an understanding of audience needs and expectations is fundamental to developing effective exhibitions.

Knowing who the audience is has become a major concern of museums. Of all the factors affecting decision making in museums, audience is the least understood and most perplexing. That is because people are themselves complex and unpredictable. Over time, we humans have gathered information about what makes us function – physically and psychologically. This knowledge can be valuable to the museum planner who wants to attract an audience, and then provide meaningful experiences. Much of what is known about human learning comes from the field of education, which in turn receives much of its information from the medical and psychological sciences. Using such knowledge in museums is appropriate since museums are educational institutions. An understanding of how people learn and their requirements for learning to be effective is of great value to exhibitors.

Targeting audiences

Anticipating visitor needs and tendencies begins with a clear idea of the museum audience. Museums should always be open to identifying and attracting new visitors. As a museum's knowledge of its community increases, and other factors such as population, educational levels, and economic conditions change, the institution needs to examine current visitorship with the intent to develop additional audiences. Knowledge of the community and institutional self-evaluation leads to focusing on groups of people that are linked by common attributes or interests: culture, leisure preferences, social affiliations, socio-economic levels, and so forth. Any such group is potentially a target audience, but committing precious museum resources to attracting new audiences should be carefully thought through. Methods valuable in evaluating these concerns include:

1. Examining the community as a whole by looking at existing population studies.

2. Interviews, questionnaires, seeking input from civic groups and leaders, and forming focus groups from the various community segments can be quite informative.

A decision to proceed with targeting a special group needs to be based upon the belief that a benefit can be derived by the audience, and that the target audience can effectively be reached.

Categorizing people, even in general terms, entails problems such as labeling, stereotyping, and unfair biasing. Museums are, or should be, one of the most egalitarian of institutions in a society, showing no preference or prejudice toward anyone, and serving the good of all. However, in determining where to allocate finite resources, some practical judgments may be required. By using objective criteria and admitting the likelihood of personal bias, it is possible to categorize in helpful ways.

Two models provide generalized overviews of populations and avoid subjective assessment. They are the Values-and-Lifestyles Segments (VALS) models (Figure 10.2.), and Maslow's Hierarchy of Human Needs (Figure 10.3).

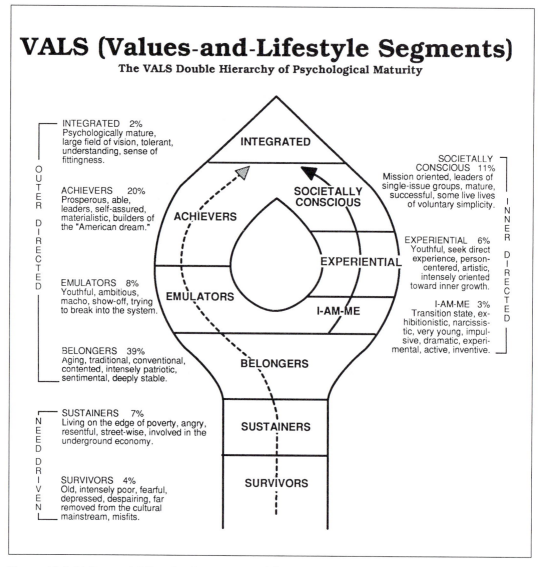

VALS (Values-and-Lifestyle Segments)

The VALS Double Hierarchy of Psychological Maturity

INTEGRATED 2%
Psychologically mature, large field of vision, tolerant, understanding, sense of fittingness.

ACHIEVERS 20%
Prosperous, able, leaders, self-assured, materialistic, builders of the "American dream."

EMULATORS 8%
Youthful, ambitious, macho, show-off, trying to break into the system.

BELONGERS 39%
Aging, traditional, conventional, contented, intensely patriotic, sentimental, deeply stable.

SUSTAINERS 7%
Living on the edge of poverty, angry, resentful, street-wise, involved in the underground economy.

SURVIVORS 4%
Old, intensely poor, fearful, depressed, despairing, far removed from the cultural mainstream, misfits.

SOCIETALLY CONSCIOUS 11%
Mission oriented, leaders of single-issue groups, mature, successful, some live lives of voluntary simplicity.

EXPERIENTIAL 6%
Youthful, seek direct experience, person-centered, artistic, intensely oriented toward inner growth.

I-AM-ME 3%
Transition state, exhibitionistic, narcissistic, very young, impulsive, dramatic, experimental, active, inventive.

OUTER DIRECTED

NEED DRIVEN

INNER DIRECTED

INTEGRATED
ACHIEVERS
SOCIETALLY CONSCIOUS
EXPERIENTIAL
EMULATORS
I-AM-ME
BELONGERS
SUSTAINERS
SURVIVORS

Figure 10.2 Values-and-Lifestyles Segments Model[3]

There are people in any population whose chief concern is the struggle to survive; to provide food, clothing, and shelter for them and their families. The VALS model identifies these segments as Sustainers and Survivors: those whose incomes are small, fixed, or irregular. The intensely poor, the homeless, and some elderly fit into these categories. There is an ethical and moral responsibility to make efforts to serve such audiences, but the approach must usually be made outside museum walls in the community at large, on the streets, in the state funded schools, through outreach programs, and so forth. Well-intended efforts to persuade people in desperate circumstances to spend time at the museum may lead to negative results rather than positive ones.

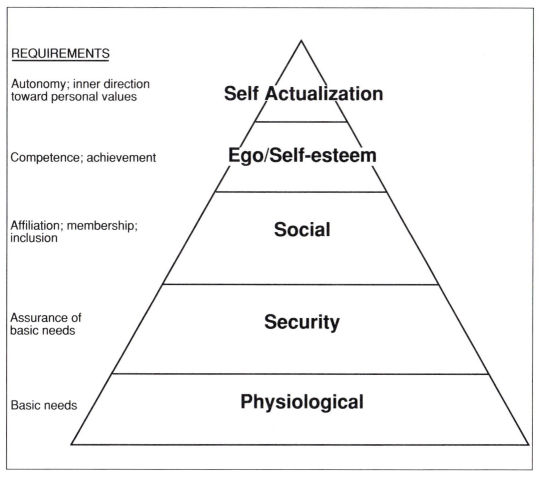

REQUIREMENTS

Autonomy; inner direction
toward personal values

Self Actualization

Competence; achievement

Ego/Self-esteem

Affiliation; membership;
inclusion

Social

Assurance of
basic needs

Security

Basic needs

Physiological

Figure 10.3 Maslow's Hierarchy of Human Needs[4]

Maslow's model illustrates that basic requirements for sustaining human life must be met before people will have the energy, will, or time to pursue cultural enrichment. History, art, or the sciences have little meaning when the struggle to survive fully occupies one's attention.

Special circumstances in some segments of the population may also suggest target audiences: persons with disabilities, those needing special attention, and elderly citizens. Such groups generally have their own concerns and problems. Things like transportation difficulties, the dislike for going places alone, the reluctance to venture out at night, physical and mental limitations, and a dislike of unfamiliar situations, are reasons for people to stay away from museums.

At the other end of the scale are those who regularly come to museums, and require little in the way of enticement. The reasons for their interest in museums are varied, but such visitors tend to be well educated and have ample resources, although great wealth is not necessarily a factor.

175

Between these extremes lies the museum's challenge: convincing the other audiences that the museum is worthwhile, enriching, and even fun as a leisure activity.

Museums are making efforts to serve all audiences. Tactile exhibits, "guided" tours, audio-visual devices, special activities, transportation options, providing exploration activities rather than sympathy, docents with sign language capabilities, emphasis on first-hand experience over books and words, and demonstrations all are ways to afford these special audiences effective museum exhibit experiences.

In targeting new audiences, one needs be sensitive to the negative aspects, and to meet special needs in positive, creative ways. This approach improves the visit for everyone.

Motivations

People have differing reasons for making choices from the varied leisure activities. They are searching for certain kinds of places, people, or activities that meet personal criteria. Since individuals differ, their criteria differ. However, studies have shown there are a few motivations common to most people. Marilyn Hood[5] lists six criteria by which adults make choices about the use of their leisure time. They are:

1. being with people, or social interaction;

2. doing something worthwhile;

3. feeling comfortable and at ease in one's surroundings;

4. having a challenge of new experiences;

5. having an opportunity to learn;

6. participating actively.

Social needs are probably predominant over the other criteria in choosing leisure activities. People generally enjoy the company of others when engaged in non-work-related activities. Family and friends are the chief sources of social interaction. Visitors to museums usually arrive with a companion or in a group, and prefer to share the visit experience with others.

Social interaction, an assessment of worthwhileness, a feeling of being challenged, and having the opportunity to learn are factors that the visitor has some responsibility in achieving. The educational criterion is more or less inherent in museums. However, the comfort that a visitor feels physically, emotionally, and intellectually is something the museum can impact. If a patron enters the museum and feels intimidated or frustrated, it is unlikely that he or she will enjoy the visit or return again.

The art of making people comfortable is an important aspect of exhibition planning and design. It is valuable to understand what comfort is, and how to produce it.

Comfort has been defined as freedom from stress. There are many factors that influence comfort in life: the time of year, the day of the week, one's socio-economic status, personal health, current events, the level of information available, the ease with which physical needs can be met, or feelings of adequacy or inadequacy. In short, anything in one's personal environment affects comfort.

Freedom from stress certainly includes the element of having physical needs met by providing restrooms, places to rest, signage for finding one's way around, and so on. Beyond physical comfort is another aspect: freedom from fear of failure or inadequacy. This relates more to the intellectual experience in museums.

In athletic leisure-time activities, physical exertion is common, expected, and even desirable. However, such stress does not deter people from engaging in games and contests. What is the difference between the stress caused by athletic exertion and that caused by one's work? In the workplace, failures to act or react pose threats to both physical and emotional well-being. In business, failure is not viewed as a positive result. In recreational activities, however, failure is not so critical. It is participation that is enjoyable rather than the result. If one fails to win a game, it may be disappointing but not especially stressful. There are always other games to play.

The same principle of comfort applies to other leisure activities as well. Hobbies have moments of failure, but fear of the results is not a factor in the experience. Applying the same logic to the museum means that visitors are not placed in situations where failure to understand is threatening. The patron should feel the same freedom to explore and experiment that they have in other leisure activities.

The museum learning environment

What kind of environment is a museum? How can a positive, comfortable environment be created in which learning can take place?

Museums have a history of being formal places where silence and decorum were desirable characteristics. For the scholar and the person seeking solitude and peace, that was ideal. For the average person looking for a quality leisure-time activity, such an atmosphere was repressive and stifling. In response to their current public-oriented mission, museums have become increasingly informal in their approach to presentation and exhibition. Normally, no compulsion is allowed, needed, or wanted in the interpretive learning process. Visitors may go and do as they wish within reason. They can learn at their own pace and in their own way. When no compulsion is present, formality and fear of failure are eliminated, giving the visitor an opportunity to have a comfortable museum experience. However, comfort does not mean that challenge is eliminated. Remember that one of Hood's criteria is the opportunity to be challenged. Presenting a comfortable, congenial atmosphere for the museum visitor in no way means presenting flaccid, static exhibitions.

The main challenge to exhibition designers is to provide an environment that the visitor not only feels comfortable in, but that he feels adequate to understand and meet the challenge of learning new things. The engendering of a sense of adequacy begins with understanding how people learn, that is, how they acquire knowledge and how they process information.

Psychology of learning applied to museum exhibitions

Learning is expressed in two modes: cognitive or rational learning, and affective or emotional learning. Most people prefer active, rather than passive information-gathering activities; they desire to do things rather than just read about or hear them. What does that mean to a museum exhibitor, remembering that the audience is not captive and is there because of choice?

Why do people learn more and more easily from experiencing something than from reading or being told about it? The key lies in the mechanisms of information-gathering. Humans have three main ways of acquiring information: through words (language either heard or read), through other senses (taste, touch, smell, hearing), and through images (visually). Of the three, vision is the dominant method. Eighty percent of the information entering our minds is gathered through vision.

The way humans are constructed points to the way we learn. Our eyes are on the front of the head, pointed forward, and aligned to produce binocular vision allowing depth perception. Peripheral vision is good and color vision is normal. Our other senses are less well developed although generally good.

The way we process information is largely visual as well. People manipulate new information by visualizing it in six basic operations:

1. Pattern seeking and recognition – looking for the familiar then adding information.

2. Rotation through space – visualizing an object as seen from different points of view in three dimensions.

3. Dynamic structures – mentally constructing the actions and reactions of objects moving through space.

4. Orthographic imagination – mentally constructing three-dimensional images from two-dimensional representations such as drawings.

5. X-ray thinking – visualizing space and object relationships based upon an imagined ability to see through the intervening objects.

6. Visual reasoning – visualizing action/reaction sequences.

By creating situations where one or more of these visualizing operations are involved, information is processed and assimilated more easily and completely.

Appealing to the other senses effectively reinforces what is gained through vision. Odors, coolness or warmth, surface textures, and sound are sensations that are associated with visual input and assist in memory formation. The more senses involved in learning the easier and more effectively information is committed to memory and retained; far more than by reading or hearing alone.

The above are aspects of the learning that with some degree of sensitivity, thought, and skill can be affected with an anticipated level of success. However, the one part of a visitor's psyche that is unpredictable is the mind set or world-view.

World-view, misconceptions, and naive notions

World-view is a personal, rationalized, cognitive structure or model of one's world. It is composed of how the person thinks of themself (self-image), and their preconceived ideas about the nature of reality. There are many factors that influence one's world-view. Virtually everything a person sees, hears, touches, smells, or tastes adds to their model of reality. Some predominant influences are a person's culture, religion, physiology, psychology, and socio-economic status.

Much of what a person is comes from what he or she thinks about themselves. Based upon one's self-image, a person's perceptions about the world around them evolves. The result is a model of how the world is, a cognitive structure, consisting of facts, concepts and propositions, theories and generalizations, and raw perceptual data. The world-view forms a filter or sieve through which information is shifted and fitted into the existing structure. The filtering occurs as a series of judgments and assessments. There are three such processes: evaluation or making value judgments, anticipating or making prejudgments, and interpreting or translating information into personal meaning.

The ability of exhibitions to educate is dramatically influenced by the perceptions of the visitor. No matter how clever or adroit in manipulating learning factors, the visitor's world-view will affect all perceptions. That requires recognizing community attitudes, codes, and mores to be a part of planning for successful exhibitions.

Every visitor who enters a museum carries a personalized set of preconceived data and expectations. Often these can be in the form of misconceptions or naive notions. Naive notions are not the result of a lack of intellect. Quite the contrary, they are usually the result of a logical progression of ideas, but with the wrong conclusions. The key to arresting attention and focusing on correcting misconceptions is to appeal to something familiar, then build upon it. If visitors see nothing familiar or have difficulty fitting new information into their world-view, they will be resistant or uncomfortable, effectively blocking the avenues of communication.

An answer to the unpredictability of visitor preconceptions is to preface the exhibition with something familiar, recognizable, friendly, and easily assimilated. Upon such a basis virtually any degree of abstraction or new information can be built, as long as it is presented in easily digestible portions. Pattern recognition centered on the cycles of life, everyday activities or objects, humorous situations, and human interests such as family relations, sibling rivalries, and gender roles, are the kinds of things that people immediately identify with and with which they feel comfortable.

Presenting objects without interpretation or in a scholarly manner using technical language will discourage most casual visitors. By providing a framework or context for the object, the visitor's own perceptions will help guide interpretation, and with some assistance from the museum will produce a reasonably correct one.

Recognition, whether brought to the museum by the visitors or gained from the last panel they viewed, triggers memories, leading to interest, and in turn stimulates curiosity and learning. Typically, facts are not remembered as isolated units, but when presented with familiar references, they add to the store of memory. To illustrate this point think of the last novel you read. Reconstruct the book's plot in your mind. Try to remember what happened in the second chapter. Finally, try to remember what occurred on page 100. Obviously, it is easier to remember the story plot than it is to recall specific details. Memories are stored in frameworks, patterns, and associations.

Right and left brains

The physiology and psychology of the human brain are other factors affecting the efficiency of learning and building memories. The human brain is in reality two brains linked by a communications network. The brain is divided into the right and left brains, and their functions are different and complementary. People learn in differing ways depending upon which side of the brain is dominant. Research indicates that memories are stored as complexes of information throughout the whole brain, but the tasks involved in processing information have been identified as being reasonably localized for some activities.

The left brain is normally dominant and is our cognitive learning center. Its job is to translate perceptions into logical, semantic, and phonetic images. The left brain communicates by logic-analytical processing, and it controls language and reasoning, reading, writing, counting, and digital communication. In cases of left-brain dysfunction, the results are distortions or incomplete memories. Such aberrations as the ability to recognize a person's face, but not being able to remember their name or relationship has been observed.

The right brain discerns complex patterns and structures. We refer to this as intuitive thinking. The right brain perceives the whole context (gestalt) from bits and pieces of information. Right-brain function often appears as leaps of intuition, rather than as a logical sequence of ideas. The right side operates with a holistic world-view. It responds to images, not verbal language, and is appealed to through jokes, pictures, sounds, smells, touch. The *pars pro toto* (the part stands for the whole) approach of presenting concepts works well with the right brain.[6] An object may be used to evoke images of a whole subject or area of study. The right brain is the affective learning center, responding more to feelings than logic. The right brain does not process negatives well. "Man plants tree," is easily visualized, but "man plants no tree," is confusing, and hard to visualize.[7]

Most formal education is organized around left-brain cognitive learning; dealing with definitions, descriptions of function, concrete concepts, reasons, and formulae. Although schools in western cultures are normally organized around cognitive learning, it has been found that coupling left-brain analysis capabilities with right-brain imaging and intuitive thinking promotes faster, more rewarding, and more effective learning. By aiming exhibition design at a holistic use of the brain, learning can be more effective than by using a single approach. Museums offer real objects – the ideal fuel for whole-brain learning. This is why museums are viable alternative and complementary learning environments for students.

Summary

By integrating the information about learning gained so far into an exhibit design methodology, the success of interpretive exhibitions can be greatly enhanced. Some suggestions for doing this are listed below:

1. Use strong visual images to arouse curiosity and hold attention.

2. Arrange objects in contextual settings; appeal to familiar elements as a basis for recognition and orientation.

3. Use sensory stimuli – sound, smell, touch, taste – to reinforce visual information. Interactive exhibits are very effective in this approach.

4. Associate didactic, cognitive elements, such as texts, labels, lectures, and tours, with visual information. Do not rely solely upon oral or written descriptions for interpretation.

5. Use visual language in written materials.

6. Appeal to those things that are the strengths of museums: amazement, wonder, awe, curiosity, the chance to look at and experience the real thing.

7. Appeal to curiosity. Museums offer answers to questions: how things work, why they were made, or how did this or that appear long ago? People see the museum as a place of answers.

8. Use human tendencies to attract attention. Studies have shown that:[8]

    a. larger objects produce longer viewing times;

    b. moving objects produces longer viewing times;

c. novel or special objects attract more attention;

d. certain qualities of objects are more intrinsically interesting (dangerous objects, baby animals, valuable objects).

Through an understanding of human learning and a continual effort to remain aware of community interests and structure, museums can be more effective in reaching and retaining wider audiences than has been possible in the past. Interpretation of collections for the public can only become more important to museums as long as accountability and education remain ethical responsibilities and functional obligations. It is the museum professional's responsibility to seek out and try new ways to make the museum experience one that is worthwhile and valuable to the greatest number of people.

Question from the field: thirty

Question: How do you choose the focus group within your community?

Response: A thorough knowledge of the community is essential. This comes from living in a community for a while. Another way is by talking with people who have lived there a long time. With such knowledge, it is relatively easy to identify subgroups within the community. They will have common interests, cultural associations, ethnic affiliations, and so on that link them into identifiable population segments.

Choosing which groups to focus upon is a matter of answering three questions.

- Does the museum have a responsibility to the focus group?
- Can the museum effectively meet the focus group's needs?
- Can the museum attract the group to the museum using available resources?

The answer to the first question should always be, "Yes." The answers to the other two are more difficult. Representatives of the museum must get acquainted with members of the focus group. This can be done on a one-to-one basis, initially. Later, it is usually effective to gather several members of the focus group into one place and discuss with them at least three topics:

- their needs and expectations,

- how they perceive the museum's role in the community, and

- how the museum can meet the focus group's needs.

Depending upon the insights gained, the museum staff can decide how to answer the last two questions. If the answers are yes, then the museum has a new focus group with which to work.

Question from the field: thirty-one

Question: What is a storyline and how is it developed?

Response: The storyline provides the framework – a verbal blueprint – around which to build the educational content of an exhibition. The storyline is a compound document consisting of:

1. the narrative,

2. an outline of the exhibition, and

3. a flowchart of information and/or a storyboard.

The narrative is the research documentation that is the source for the other elements of the storyline. Essentially, the narrative is everything the curator feels is important to say about the exhibit subject matter. This information will probably take the form of a scholarly paper or treatise. The narrative must precede the other parts of the storyline.

After the narrative is done, the outline of the exhibition follows. This document is, as the name implies, an outline of the salient points in the exhibition. Beginning with the title, it outlines the topics, sub-topics, and specific points within the exhibition. Details of the outline may include descriptions, images, and collection objects to support the story. Subdividing the topics may be done to the degree necessary to describe the content of the exhibition adequately. Below is an example of a portion of a relatively simple outline.

Ethnohistory of the people of the Southern Plains of North America

II.   Technology – subheading "Trends in Technologies"

a.   Making pots and baskets – text panel heading –

"Cooking and Storage"

i.   coil method of pot making

- examples of coil pots: 1975–245
- individual labels for objects   1945–31–3a
                                                                                          1983–107–25
- photographic sequence (seven photos) of Maria of San Ildefonso in the process of building a coil pot. Caption label for each photograph.
- short text explaining process of coil making.

ii.   basketry techniques

- examples of baskets: 1956–2
  individual labels for objects   1983–45–3c
- diagrammatic drawing of woman weaving a basket. Text explaining materials and methods.
- Three diagrams showing woven patterns traditionally used, with label.

An outline may also include suggestions about the general arrangement of information. It may address possible methods of illustrating topics such as audio-visuals. Including the educational programming requirements is important. Planning the exhibition for tours includes allowing space for the group to gather round a docent. Involving a demonstration means setting aside space for that activity. Any such needs should be at the designer's fingertips when that person begins planning the gallery. It is not the purpose of the outline to address the design or aesthetics of the exhibit directly. However, it may act as a guide for those concerns later.

The flowchart of information is an expansion of the outline. It illustrates how to arrange the information to aid visitor learning. A simple floorplan or a linear flowchart may suffice. However, using a floorplan means being careful to concentrate on the flow of information and not on the design of the gallery.

Optionally, a storyboard can make communication easier. A storyboard might consist of arranging cards on a wall or bulletin board corresponding to the outline. It might be sketches of the envisioned sections of the gallery, arranged in sequential order. The storyboard can be quite helpful in visualizing exhibition content and appearance. Having people outside the planning process "read" the storyboard can provide a pre-test of the plan. The storyboard provides an easily changeable model of the exhibit content.

☐　☐　☐　☐　☐

Notes

1. Guralnik, D. (ed.) (1974) *Webster's New World Dictionary*, 2nd college edn, Cleveland, Ohio: William Collins and World Publishing Co., Inc., p. 737.
2. International Council of Museums (1990) *Statutes: Code of Professional Ethics*, Paris: ICOM, p. 26.
3. Mitchell, A. (1983) *The Nine American Lifestyles*, New York: Warner Books.
4. Maslow, A. (1954) *Motivation and Personality*, New York: Harper & Row Publishers.
5. Hood, M. (1983) "Staying Away," *Museum News* 61, April, pp. 50–7.
6. Schouten, F. (1983) "Visitor Perception: The Right Approach," in Reinwardt Academie, *Exhibition Design as an Educational Tool*, Leiden: Reinwardt Academie, p. 44.
7. ibid.
8. Conroy, P. (1988) "Cheap Thrills and Quality Learning," in S. Bitgood, J. Roper Jr, and A. Benefield (eds) *Visitor Studies*, Jacksonville, Ala.: Center for Visitor Social Design, p. 189.

Suggested reading

Blatti, J. (ed.) (1987) *Past Meets Present, Essays about Historic Interpretation and Public Audiences*, Washington, DC: Smithsonian Institution Press.

Burstein, D. and Stasiowski, F. (1982) *Project Management for the Design Professional*, London: Whitney Library of Design, an imprint of Watson-Guptill Publications.

Karp, I. and Lavine, S. (eds.) (1991) *Exhibiting Cultures, The Poetics and Politics of Museum Display*, Washington, DC: Smithsonian Institution Press.

Loomis, R. (1987) *Museum Visitor Evaluation: New Tool for Management*, Vol. 3, AASLH Management Series, Nashville, Tenn.: American Association for State and Local History.

Merriman, N. (1991) *Beyond the Glass Case*, Leicester: Leicester University Press.

Serrell, B. (1985) *Making Exhibit Labels*, Nashville, Tenn.: American Association for State and Local History.

Witteborg, L. (1981) *Good Show! A Practical Guide for Temporary Exhibitions*, Washington, DC: Smithsonian Institution Traveling Exhibition Service.

11

Object interpretation

John Cotton Dana, the innovative founder of the Newark
Museum in 1909, expressed his social philosophy in these
words:

A good museum attracts, entertains, arouses curiosity,
leads to questioning and thus promotes learning. It is an
educational institution that is set up and kept in motion –
that it may help the members of the community to
become happier, wiser, and more effective human beings.
Much can be done toward a realization of these objectives
– with simple things – objects of nature and daily life – as
well as with objects of great beauty. A museum should
also reflect our industries – be stimulating and helpful to
our workers and promote interest in the products of our
own time. The Museum can help people only if they
use it; they will use it only if they know about it and
only if attention is given to the interpretation of its
possessions in terms they, the people, will understand.[1]

Understanding human motivations and learning requirements is fundamental to
developing exhibitions to serve audience needs. Anticipating visitor needs and
tendencies demands a clear idea of the group or groups being served by the
museum. The process of determining these groups is known as "targeting," and
the groups are normally referred to as "target audiences" or "focus groups."

Museums should always be open to identifying and attracting new audiences.
Factors such as demographics, educational levels, economic stresses, and
special interests within the museum's constituency change, and as the factors
change, so does the visitor and potential visitor. The museum staff must be
aware of the changes and make exhibition and programming decisions about
developing new audiences.

Once the new visitor is in the museum, the main challenge is to provide an
environment in which the person can feel comfortable and understand the

material being presented. If the visitor is not comfortable, i.e., free from environment-related stress, they are unlikely to benefit from the visit and probably will not return.

> "We will conserve only what we love. We will love only what we understand; we will only understand what we are taught."[2]

The most obvious approach to understanding by museum visitors is to present information by means of the verbal material included with the exhibit.

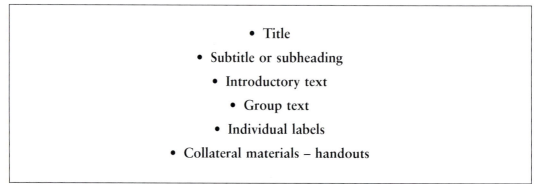

- Title
- Subtitle or subheading
- Introductory text
- Group text
- Individual labels
- Collateral materials – handouts

Figure 11.1 Levels of verbal information

The title panel's main function is to identify the exhibit. The text panel provides the primary educational resource for the exhibit. It explains and explores important aspects of the exhibit. The labels identify specific objects in the exhibit. They indicate which objects are being emphasized and they explain why the objects are important. The collateral materials such as hand-outs, gallery guides, educational brochures, programs, and catalogs are means of presenting information not included in the other communication methods.

Most exhibits have some form of introductory panel and object labels. Exhibits of this type are normally defined as "object-oriented." They are common in that they are ideally suited for certain kinds of specimens or artifacts. Exhibitions of art objects are a good example. The introductory panel may explain the subject of the exhibit or the artist represented. It may give some information about the style, location, time, or characteristics of the art work. The labels normally give only the name of the artist, the name of the art work, the medium, date, and possibly location where the work was executed. The object is thought to convey the message. Many art connoisseurs believe that the inclusion of too much information distracts from the work and interferes with the aesthetic appreciation of the object by the viewer.[3]

The title panel sets the mood for the exhibit and gives a general introduction. In designing the title there are at least six points that should be considered:

- **Size** – large and imposing, normally largest typesize.
- **Message length** – usually short, one–ten words.
- **Appearance** – attention-getting.
- **Content** – thematic in orientation – information level superficial.
- **Concept** – design over content.
- **Attitude** – mood setting to reflect exhibit content (comic, serious, controversial, elegant, etc.).

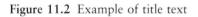

los Ojos de Oro

Figure 11.2 Example of title text

The subtitle is the second level of information relating to the exhibit. It refines the title by focusing on the exhibit content. The subtitle should be prepared with at least five points in mind:

- **Size** – large enough to read from a distance but smaller than the title, smaller typesize but still relatively large.
- **Message length** – no more than ten words.
- **Content** – informative.
- **Concept** – topic-oriented.
- **Attitude** – narrows the information to the exhibit content.

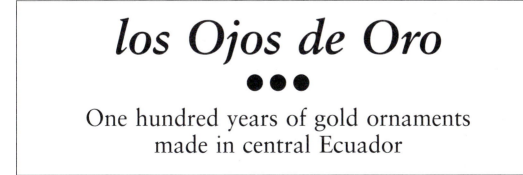

Figure 11.3 Example of title text with subtitle

The introductory text tells the visitor what the exhibit is about, how it is organized, and what to expect. In preparing the introductory text there are four factors to consider:

- **Message length** – the text can be fairly long, 50 to 200 words, but should be divided into easily read sections of not more than 75 words each. Type size should be large enough to be read from a distance.
- **Content** – explanatory, tells the rationale for the exhibit and explains the relationship of the objects.
- **Concept** – inclusive, explains the major concepts included in the exhibit to give the visitor a sense of the entire exhibit.
- **Attitude** – instructive, should be placed near the beginning of the exhibit to prepare the visitor for contents.

The next level of information is the group text. It has the important role of drawing the parts of the exhibit together. There are four points that should be considered when preparing the group text:

- **Message length** – 75 to 150 words, text size can be relatively small but larger than label copy.
- **Content** – informative and interpretive – explains association between groups of objects.
- **Concept** – unifying the parts of the exhibit.
- **Attitude** – focusing, requires a greater level of interest to read.

Individual labels are the specific text-providers of the exhibit. They give information about individual objects and identify names, dates, materials, and techniques relating to single exhibit items. In defining some objects such as photographs or forms of literal material, labels may be described as captions. In either case the text answers questions:

- **Message length** – short but adequate to give pertinent information. Type size can be small but adequate for persons with corrected vision to easily read.
- **Content** – restricted to factual information such as title, maker, medium or material, and date of execution.
- **Concept** – identification.
- **Attitude** – specific.

Visits to museums encourage learning that goes far beyond reading labels. People learn about themselves by interacting with exhibits and with one another. They ask questions and learn how to learn. Museums offer answers to questions the visitors bring with them (for example, how things work, why things are as they are, how things looked a long time ago, and what distant places look like).

- What the exhibit is about.
- What the exhibit has to do with the visitor.
- How the exhibit is organized.
- What the visitor is expected to learn from the exhibit.

Figure 11.4 Things the museum visitor needs to know and be told more than one time!

Effective object interpretation should be concerned with how people gather, process, and store information. Most people prefer active, rather than passive information gathering. People learn more from experiencing something than from simply reading about it. Human information gathering is 80 percent visual.

> "There is a truism in the museum field that people do not read labels. Casual observation of museum visitors will tend to confirm this. Nevertheless, it is not true of every visitor, nor is it true of every exhibition."[4]

Museums are not amusement centers, but institutions dedicated to the collecting, conserving, and interpreting of objects. By having an understanding of the functions of learning, museum personnel can design exhibits that accomplish pre-established objectives more effectively. At the same time, meeting needs and stimulating curiosity brings people to museums and gets them to return.

Too often we assume that museum visitors are a passive audience willing to be influenced by the objects or exhibits in the museum. In reality research has lead to the conclusions that:

- visitors do not read labels,
- visitors hardly look at objects,
- visitors do not change their views or attitudes, and
- visitors continue to show exit-oriented behavior.[5]

In preparing exhibits, museum personnel must not attempt to explain everything there is to know about the exhibited objects. Care must be taken to utilize the audience's recognition to lead them to new information. To do this it is important to know what makes an exhibit successful. At the same time, all museum workers should understand that a successful exhibit in one location may not be equally well received in another. Knowing the audience is the first rule for museum exhibits.

- Ask questions
- Stimulate the imagination
- Use familiar language
- Make comparisons - relate the familiar to the unfamiliar
- Give instructions - ask or tell visitors what to do
- Use quotes

Figure 11.5 Techniques for adding human interest to exhibits

Undoubtedly our best efforts fail from time to time, not because of our inability to collect or design exhibits, but because of misconceptions about our audience. This may also be one of the primary reasons people and nations fail in their efforts to define and maintain an identifiable national heritage. One of the most obvious complications arises with the realization that museum visiting is a "leisure-time" activity and that the majority of visitors constitute a relatively minor portion of the total audience potential.

"Museums and the cultural treasures they display, protect, and study, have become almost everywhere valuable tools in the application of national cultural policies."[6]

Each of us has a responsibility to preserve and disseminate information about the cultural properties of our countries and the characteristics of its people. The recognition and maintenance of cultural pluralism are important and meaningful roles for museums. As a community of international institutions, museums can foster the finest aspects of cultural pluralism. This challenge is immediate, complex, and of vital importance if museums are to provide the appropriate leadership to "promote a greater knowledge and understanding among people."[7]

Notes

1. John Cotton Dana, cited in E. Alexander (1983) *Museum Masters*, Nashville, Tenn.: Association of State for Local History, p. 396.
2. Craig, T. (1988) "Changing the Way People Think," *Museum News*, Vol. 67, No. 1, September/October, pp. 52–4.
3. Klein, L. (1986) *Exhibits: Planning and Design*, New York: Madison Square Press, p. 70.
4. ibid.
5. Schouten, F. (1983) "Visitor Perception: The Right Approach," in Reinwardt Academie, *Exhibit Design as an Educational Tool*, Reinwardt Studies in Museology, Leiden: Reinwardt Academy.
6. Abranches, H. (1984) "Museums and Cultural Identity," in A. Bochi and S. de Valence

(eds) *Proceedings of the 13th General Conference and 14th General Assembly of the International Council of Museums*, London, July 24–August 2, 1983, Paris: ICOM.

7.   International Council of Museums (1989), *Statutes*, Paris: ICOM.

Suggested reading

Alderson, W. and Low, S. (1987) *Interpretation of Historic Sites*, 2nd edn rev., Nashville, Tenn.: American Association for State and Local History.

Alexander, E. (1979) *Museums in Motion, An Introduction to the History and Functions of Museums*, 4th printing 1986, Nashville, Tenn.: American Association for State and Local History.

Loor, L. (1987) *El museo como instrumento de aprendizaje*, Cuenca: Banco Central del Ecuador.

Neal, A. (1969) *HELP! for the Small Museum, Handbook of Exhibit Ideas and Methods*, Boulder, Colo.: Pruett Publishing.

Serrell, B. (1985) *Making Exhibit Labels*, Nashville, Tenn.: American Association for State and Local History.

Verhaar, J. and Meeter, H. (1987) *Project Model Exhibitions*, Leiden: Reinwardt Academie.

Witteborg, L. (1981) *Good Show! A Practical Guide for Temporary Exhibitions*, Washington, DC: Smithsonian Institution Traveling Exhibition Service.

12

Museum education

> "The museum should take every opportunity to develop
> its role as an educational resource used by all sections of
> the population or specialized groups that the museum is
> intended to serve. Where appropriate in relation to the
> museum's programme and responsibilities, specialist staff
> with training and skills in museum education are likely to
> be required for this purpose. The museum has an
> important duty to attract new and wider audiences
> within all levels of the community, locality or group that
> the museum aims to serve, and should offer both the
> general community and specific individuals and groups
> within it opportunities to become actively involved in the
> museum and to support its aims and policies."[1]

Museums have changed and are continuing to change. They are adjusting to
meet the needs and requirements of the communities in which they are located.
Greater expectations from museum users have prompted museum personnel to
provide greater services. Often museum educational activities relate to children,
but the larger audiences, children and adults alike, require learning experiences.
Adults are seeking opportunities to learn with their families. It is the museum
educator's role to serve as an advocate for the museum's audiences and to assure
public access to the collections through carefully prepared and sensitively
presented educational programming.

> "Assume you were charged with the responsibility of designing and building a new and innovative educational classroom for students of all ages. You would want a space that is attractive, easily accessible, well designed for support activities, and comfortable for both teacher and students. You would want material to demonstrate the major points of the instructional program. You would want experts to assist with a variety of programming topics, and you would want books, objects, documents of various kinds, and exciting visual aids to excite and stimulate your students. The classroom you have designed is a museum."[2]

Museums are unique places for teaching a variety of subjects if the museum educator has established a philosophical framework that outlines the criteria to be followed during the development, implementation, and evaluation of museum education programs.[3] Organized activities and open-ended questions that encourage creative observation and thoughtful interactions are taking the place of simple lectures[4] A museum is a laboratory for teaching by qualified museum personnel and learning by the public. It should be an environment where all can learn at a level and pace appropriate to their needs.

To be the most effective, educational program planning should be systematic. Museums with a staff of one or 100 should establish educational priorities and develop an organized and progressive plan for addressing those priorities. Museum educational programs should view schoolteachers as allies in the education process but realize that the museum is a "special vehicle" for learning. It is unlike the traditional academic environment and therefore has special challenges and equally special rewards.

As with collection management, educational programming requires a statement of purpose that defines its reasons for existence if it is to be successful. A statement of this kind will establish the reasons for the educational program and the general concepts to be covered. It is the basic rationale for the education program. A clearly defined statement of purpose will guide the development of programs.[5] In developing the statement, care should be taken to ensure consistency with the museum's general statement of purpose. As the educational mission is just one element of the entire institution, it cannot be considered in isolation.[6]

In planning an effective educational program, it is normal to begin by determining the target audience. Museum education programs are often developed for specific age or interest groups. In this way the information is presented in the vocabulary, comprehension level, and social manner of the group. Education programs can be designed as self-guided tours (without a docent or guide), or guided tours (with a guide and prearranged script) depending on the program objectives. By contrast, general museum programming of exhibits and events is less focused and intended for the casual visitor.

Museums are open to individual exploration and because of their object-orientation the learning process can be, and usually is, enjoyable. For the same reason, self-paced learning, the materials, content, methods, and objectives of the museum educational program must be well organized and carefully planned. Every experience in the museum is an opportunity for viewers to gain new insight into the cultural and scientific environment in which they exist. However, it is important to realize that exposure to information does not necessarily result in transfer of information. The primary learning/teaching element of the museum is the object – in most other educational situations, the written or spoken word is the conveyor of information.

Objects, that are collected, cared for, and exhibited in the museum, are tangible evidence of humankind and their surroundings. Specimens present the natural world, asking the viewers to respond to that world of which they are a part. Works of art and artifacts present a variety of human reactions to and interactions with the world and with other people. Presented in an interdisciplinary and humanistic manner, these objects invite the viewer to explore, participate in, and gain a deeper understanding of the human experience.[7]

> "Every museum has an educational responsibility to the public it serves. Museums offer a unique encounter with objects and ideas for people of many ages, interests, capabilities and backgrounds. Museum education strengthens that encounter by building bridges between visitors' experiences and expectations and the experiences and ideas that emanate from a museum's collections."[8]

Despite the fact that most museums have a commitment to education, in some form, there is a level of confusion about the museum as an educational institution. The lack of comprehension exists not only in the minds of the general public but equally in the thinking of many museum personnel and academic educators. For the most part, museums are viewed as institutions of enrichment. They are considered to be centers of culture and "the finer things" intended to enhance and reinforce the quality of life. Museums can do much more for many more members of the community of humankind. Museums can "strengthen basic skills, basic knowledge, basic comprehension, and basic understanding."[9]

Museum educational programs can enhance the interaction among all segments of the visiting public by forming a connection between the audience and the objects collected, preserved, and interpreted in the museum.

"Although museums are plainly institutions of object-centered learning and there is interest among educators and administrators alike for formulating museum learning theory more clearly, there is no accepted philosophical framework."[10]

It seems that many museum educators, in formulating their contribution to the learning process, believe that the simple presence of the "real" object is adequate to transfer both knowledge and understanding. Often museum educational programs are conceived, developed, and presented as independent, totally unique activities. In reality, museum educational programs are most successful if they are integrated into the interests or needs of the anticipated audience – the "focus group." School children will gain more from museum education programs if the information being presented relates to classroom learning. Adults are more willing learners if the subject relates to a special interest or pertinent topic.

Selecting the method for transfer of information in the museum must be carefully and thoughtfully considered. There are at least three techniques or levels of transfer that apply to all audiences. The first is direct interaction. At this level the "students" are encouraged to say something about their interests and how they might respond to a particular situation or circumstance that has been carefully selected to complement the educational programming objectives. This association with the "students" immediate world will help them become less self-conscious and begin to think in a predetermined direction.[11]

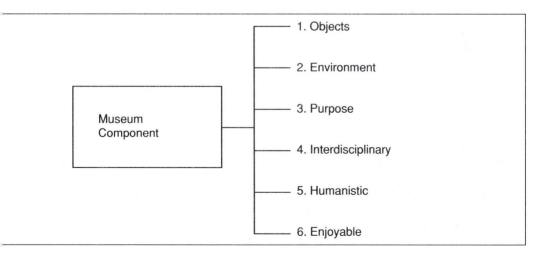

Figure 12.1 Museum component elements

The second method is to have the "students" view objects or exhibits and describe their feelings. They can be encouraged to compare what they see with their own environments or with their own reactions to object-stimulated emotions. This can be achieved by asking the "students" to describe, in their own words, what they see in an object or exhibition they are viewing.[12] In this way the "students" learn both to observe the objects in the exhibit and to experience the process of gaining information through observation.

The third technique is to connect the objects with the environment in which the "students" exist. By observation and discussion "students" can learn that the objects they view in the museum relate in a very direct way to their daily lives. The intent is to verify that although the museum houses wonderful and unique objects there is a correlation between the viewer and the objects that is very real and understandable.

> **"The whole point of education is to transmit culture, and museums can play an increasingly important role in this process. It is a mistake to think that preserving culture is distinct from transmitting it through education."**
> Frank Oppenheimer[13]

Effective museum education is a blend of at least three elements. The first is the preselected museum component; the second, the predetermined educational objective; and the third, the method for transferring the information.

An important first step for museums seeking to develop or expand their audience is to determine what potential visitors know about the objects housed in the museum and what they want to know. Once this information is gained it is possible to establish effective museum learning opportunities. The museum may have numerous objects about which there is general interest but without a clearly defined objective it is difficult to select those to be exhibited, the message they will present, and the method of delivering the message.

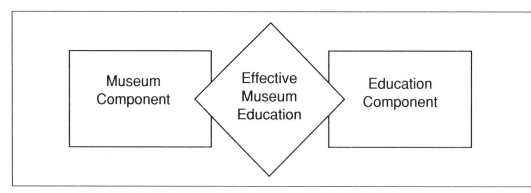

Figure 12.2 Effective museum education

> "Today most museums in the U.S. endeavor to narrate a coherent story through their collections, to stimulate the visitor toward exploration, discovery, wonder, and learning to 'see' by experiences; and to provide other enrichment and educational activities."[14]

A successful and effective museum educational program must identify and clearly state its purpose. This statement should be regarded as the reason for the educational program and its guiding philosophy.

The statement will form the foundation for the planning process and will establish goals and objectives. This step in the process is the difference between working toward a goal and just doing a job.

To complete the planning process there are a number of steps that should be addressed:

1. Goals – goals are the ends toward which effort is directed; they are the results the educational program wishes to achieve based on the statement of purpose.

2. Objectives – objectives may be considered as the translation of goals or purposes into definite, measurable targets with standards of performance.

3. Activity – encompasses the programming, planning, training, and preparation that needs to be done to achieve the stated objectives.

4. Plans – the plans should include the tactics and sequence of activities organized to achieve the established goals. This process identifies who will do what, when, and how.

5. Budget – a budget must be formed and approved to determine how much it will cost to execute the plan and achieve the goals.

6. Schedule – scheduling is an important factor in the educational programming process. Staff and volunteers must be available to present the programs, and consideration must be given to the times and/or locations that will best accommodate the target group.

7. Evaluation – program evaluation will provide useful information on two important parts of the educational program:

   a. It will provide the planners with an idea of whether the program as presented corresponded with the planning objectives.

   b. It will measure the extent to which the programs presented the anticipated information and serve as a guide for future programs of the same type.

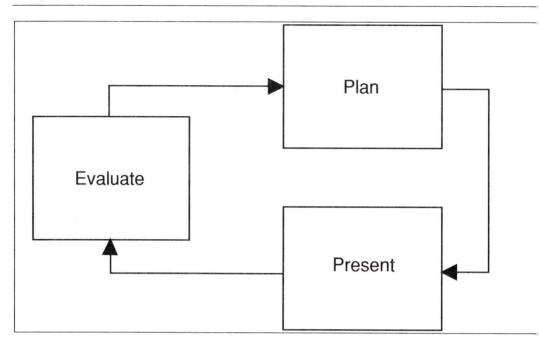

Figure 12.3 Educational programming sequence

In recent years, worldwide attention has been directed toward the enormous social and educational potential of museums. The diverse societies that occupy not only multicultural nations but the diversity represented in the world community is included in the collections of museums. Most museum workers agree that one of the primary tasks of any museum is to enlighten the people and to improve their condition. To provide this service is to enrich human society.

> **"Museums should seek to expand their audience base by actively extending into their communities with efforts and activities designed to build new audiences."**[15]

Objects in museum collections are the things of which a culture is composed. They are the measures of human existence and the thread that binds the elements of personal and national identity. Education is an activity with only relative meaning. It requires the perspective of association with real objects and ideas to have acceptable meaning. Knowledge, as a product of the educational process, is certain only when renewed, reinforced, and expanded. Museums, as repositories of unique collections, are the ideal laboratories for social, scientific, and cultural exchange.

There are some initiatives that are fundamental to museums such as promotion of critical thinking, enhancement of open-mindedness, and the sensitizing of visitors to objects. There are also values that are more temporal and limited and these may change to meet social needs. These values should advocate ethical and intellectual reasoning for the benefit of society.

There are a number of steps that can be taken to reinforce and expand the museum audience base. First, museums can support and promote special interest groups in the community. These groups can nurture the development of a wide array of creative programming endeavors to serve both the schools and other public institutions. They can also provide the basis for a dialog concerning the cultural diversity of the region. Support for these groups can be offered by a wide variety of activities, including thematic educational programming or "focus" tours.

Second, museum administrators and educators can promote multicultural education and the importance of cultural expression through exhibits and programming. A method of initiating this process is an assessment of the museum's potential constituency. The objective of the assessment is to identify the needs, interests, and expectations of the visitor pool. Using this information, the museum can establish its exhibits and programming goals. "No matter what the visitor's level of capability, there is the potential for learning, for expanding horizons."[16]

Resolution No. I,
Museums: Generators of Culture
15th General Conference of ICOM
Recognizing the potential contribution of museums,
To education,
- **by increasing the awareness of cultural heritage,**
- **by transmitting the essence of the evolving culture to new generations,**
- **by raising the awareness of other cultures;**[17]

A third means of expanding the audience base for museums is cultural conservation, renewal, or transfer. Special interest groups seek to reclaim or preserve personal identity through the conservation of objects of social or cultural significance. Cultural heritage, manifested in specific objects, can serve as a focal point for community participation in museum exhibits and educational programs. Great community interest can be stimulated to support the process of transferring meaningful information to the next generation. While the impact of the specific information may be on an individual basis, programming makes the process possible and creates a responsive audience.

A guiding premise of museums should be a commitment to education and public service for diverse audiences. Museums are an implement of democratization, a center of pride for a community, and a focal point for initiating positive change. Museum educational programs address a broad array of topics from sanitation and health care to national history and world geography. As centers of learning, museums have a responsibility to serve the public and represent the pluralistic society in which they exist.

> - Education is a constant process of re-evaluation and adjustment.
> - Education is long term.
> - Education correctly administered results in knowledge.

Few museums have completely satisfactory educational programs. Almost all are experimenting with different organizational structures, different methods, and different techniques that affect their educational role. Collaboration is a guiding logic for the future of museum education in that museums cannot operate in isolation. The collaborative effort must involve not only museum personnel but public administrators, educators for private and public schools, actual and potential museum visitors, and others in the community that can offer insight into the possibilities of educational adaptation and implementation in the museum environment. Cross-fertilization of ideas will stimulate the thinking process, generate a feeling of inclusiveness, and provide the basis for information exchange.

Every museum has a responsibility to preserve and disseminate information about the cultural or scientific properties of the community it serves. Assuming the underlying logic for most museums is education, then the responsibility is complex and impacts on almost every aspect of the intellectual and social life of the community. Museums are the ideal workshop for social and cultural investigation. They are places where information can be exchanged without intimidation and where cultural and personal pride can be reinforced. Through proper programming, museums can provide an environment for all people to have an enjoyable learning opportunity and experience the excitement of intellectual exploration.

> "every country must preserve and disseminate the cultural properties that constitute the particular characteristics of its people. . . ."[18]

□ □ □ □ □

Question from the field: thirty-two

Question: There is talk of traveling exhibits and "museum mobiles." The idea that if the people do not come to a museum then the museum has to go to the people sounds good – but does that not diminish the responsibility to collection care?

Response: Although care of collections is a primary responsibility of all museums, the notion of the "institution in the service of society and of its development," as described in the ICOM *Statutes*, is also of major importance. The sharing of the information, enjoyment, and inspiration associated with the objects housed in a museum is one way to serve and develop society. It is equally true that some museums are formed around the information rather than the object.

> An example of the information-based museum may be found in India where the government has given great attention to museums as educational institutions and agents of social development.

Taking the museum to the people need not include objects that will be endangered. Information can be presented using a variety of methods that will stimulate interest in a museum and the collections.

☐ ☐ ☐ ☐ ☐

Question from the field: thirty-three

Question: What is the best way to pack collection objects for travel?

Response: Each museum object has specialized packing and shipping requirements. There is no one way that meets the needs of all objects and all shipping situations. The packaging and transportation field have advanced rapidly along with the other areas of museum practice during the past twenty to twenty-five years. These developments have come about due to the needs of the transportation industry. Electronics, specialized equipment, and super-sensitive or fragile materials all require sophisticated packing and shipping techniques. Museum collections have benefited from this development. However, preparing museum objects for shipment and delivering them safely across country or around the world continues to be a complex process requiring skill, knowledge, and special training.

When possible, a qualified packing firm, experienced in dealing with museum objects, should be contracted to pack exhibits for travel.

☐ ☐ ☐ ☐ ☐

Notes

1. International Council of Museums (1990) "Educational and Community Role of the Museum," *Code of Professional Ethics*, Paris: ICOM, p. 26.
2. Grove, R. *Some Problems in Museum Education*, Washington, DC: Smithsonian Institution Press, p. 79.

3. Berry, N. and Mayer, S. (eds) (1989) *Museum Education: History, Theory, and Practice*, Washington, DC: National Art Education Association, p. 90.
4. Pitman-Gelles, B. (1981) *Museums, Magic and Children*, Washington DC: Association of Science–Technology Centers, p. 47.
5. ibid.: p. 17.
6. ibid.: p. 18.
7. Berry and Mayer (eds), *Museum Education*, p. 90.
8. American Association of Museums (1989) "Introduction," in *Professional Standards for Museum Educators*, Washington, DC: American Association of Museums.
9. Bloom, J. and Powell, E. (eds) (1984) *Museums for a New Century*, Washington, DC: American Association of Museums, p. 57.
10. ibid.: p. 57.
11. Pitman-Gelles, *Museums, Magic and Children*, p. 51.
12. ibid.
13. Bloom and Powell (eds) (1984) *Museums for a New Century*, p. 57.
14. Glaser, J. (1986) *USA Museums in Context*, Washington, DC: Smithsonian Institution Press, p. 20.
15. American Association of Museums (1989) "Audience Diversity," in *Professional Standards for Museum Educators*, p. 2.
16. Pitman, B. *et al.* (1992) *Excellence and Equity: Education and the Public Dimension of Museums*, Washington, DC: American Association of Museums, p. 14.
17. International Council of Museums (1989) *Museums: Generators of Culture*, report and comments, Paris: ICOM, p. 69.
18. Solana, F. (1981) "Inaugural Address," *Proceedings of the 12th General Conference of ICOM*, Paris: ICOM, pp. 17–21.

Suggested reading

Bloom, J. and Powell, E. (eds) (1984) *Museums for a New Century, A Report of the Commission on Museums for a New Century*, Washington, DC: American Association of Museums.

Burcaw, G. E. (1975) *Introduction to Museum Work*, 2nd edn 1983, Nashville, Tenn.: American Association for State and Local History.

Hooper-Greenhill, E. (1991) *Museum and Gallery Education*, Leicester: Leicester University Press.

(1992) *Museums and the Shaping of Knowledge*, London: Routledge.

Kavanagh, G. (ed.) (1991) *Museum Languages*, Leicester: Leicester University Press.

Pearce, S. (ed.) (1990) *Objects of Knowledge*, London: Athlone Press Ltd.

Reinwardt Academie (1983) *Exhibition Design as an Educational Tool*, Leiden: Reinwardt Academie.

Section IV
Professionalism
and ethics

13

Professionalism and museums

Starting about 1957 the words "museum professional" and "museum profession" came into common usage. Prior to that time, the idea of professionalism and museums appears not to have been a commonly accepted notion. In 1960, the Dutch museologist, H. Daifuku, wrote in an article "Museums and Research," printed in *The Organization of Museums: Practical Advice*,[1] that "the idea that museum work is a profession has gradually become widespread."

Museums and their activities are playing a larger role every day in global socio-cultural activities and, with proper direction and stimulation, they will have greater prominence in the world of tomorrow. While growth and expansion of museums on a worldwide scale are a certainty,[2] without a concerted effort there is reason to doubt their positive impact on either humankind or the ecosystem. A decisive factor in support of an affirmative response to these challenges will be the ethical attitudes and practices of this and future generations of museum personnel. To achieve and maintain high ethical standards in the museum, a common agenda of accepted practices must be established, circulated, endorsed, and applied.

A mutual ground for museum workers has been established on an international scale: the International Council of Museums (ICOM); and while it is international in concept it is not designed to minimize or exclude nationalistic motivations and interests. Each member or member institution has an opportunity to participate in the organization and to pursue self-designated directions according to personal motivation or as established by home-country national committees. A unified concern for museum standards, whether training, conservation, or documentation, is not intended to standardize activities. ICOM, through its committee structure, serves as a forum to advocate norms of acceptable museum practice. These practices serve as the foundation and ethics of the museum profession.

The ICOM *Statutes* explain that the primary aims of ICOM shall be:

(a) To define, support and aid museums and the museum institution; to establish, support, and reinforce the museum profession.

(b) To organize co-operation and mutual assistance between museums and between the members of the museum profession in the different countries.

(c) To emphasize the importance of the role played by museums and the museum profession within each community and in the promotion of a greater knowledge and understanding among peoples.[3]

Recognition and endorsement of professionalism are not abstract concepts that apply only to those who decide to join the "club." Global attention is focused on the cultural, historical, and scientific heritage of the world community and museums can serve a pivotal role in stimulating a new sociological awareness and encouraging more coherent thinking and a broader vision of humankind. Museums are the laboratories for these exchanges. The responsibility is great, perhaps overwhelming to the museum worker operating without the benefit of a support group – a professional organization.

Profession is defined as:

> A calling requiring specialized knowledge and often long and intensive preparation, including instruction in skills and methods as well as in the scientific, historical, or scholarly principles underlying such skills and methods, maintaining by force of organization or concerted opinion, high standards of achievement and conduct, and committing its members to continued study and to a kind of work which has for its prime purpose the rendering of a public service.[4]

The assumption of professional status carries with it a number of defined and presumptive responsibilities that must be embraced not only by those who join willingly but those who, by virtue of personal history, find themselves incumbent in the field. All museum workers, regardless of their status (i.e., paid staff, faculty, board member, or volunteer), have a responsibility to support and perpetuate a fundamental standard of quality. At the same time the museum profession must prepare, inform, and educate those persons so they may be knowledgeable of the appropriate standards. This interaction is a shared ethical responsibility and consistent with the recommendation of the ICOM 16th General Assembly: "[that] training programmes be developed which ensure an understanding of all aspects of the museum operation, having regard to the rapid development of new technologies and the increasing number of skills involved."[5]

Products of museum professionalization are greater collections care, better understanding of fiduciary responsibility, code of ethics, standardization of museum practices, greater attention of constituency needs, accreditation, and improved salaries for museum workers – to name a few. Higher standards within the museum profession have increased expectations. Levels of training and accrued knowledge that were acceptable a few years ago are no longer deemed adequate; and to support this growth the amount of published information has grown markedly in the last decade. There is a "new" standard for the profession to be used to measure the success rate of persons in and entering the field.

> Gaining status through work.

Diversity and proliferation have given new or different attitudes toward collections. Traditional norms have been circumvented – often with a focus on new collections and, in some cases, new museums, that do not fit extant patterns or processes.

In theory the museum workforce recognizes its ethical duty to care for collections and maintain them for future generations. There is little doubt that the material record of human culture and the natural world should be preserved. However, to achieve this goal a proactive program of collection management and care must be assimilated into the operational procedures of every museum. Reliance on past practices will not fulfill the desired goal. A reasonable balance must be gained that allows for both preservation and exhibition of collections. Stephen Weil notes, "Preservation serves the future at the expense of the present. Exhibitions serve the present at the expense of the future."[6] To meet the changing criteria is an ongoing process that requires continual training. Failure to grow in competency is not static, it is regressive and has a negative impact on the individual worker, the institution, and the entire profession. Neither museums nor museum personnel can afford the luxury of inertia.

In the book *Professionalising the Muses*, Piet Pouw addresses the evolution of professionalism in Dutch museums. He writes:

"professionalism was hardly the order of the day in the cultural sector. It was dominated by the enthusiasts, the committee, and those for whom working in the arts was a hobby. Most museum workers were technical specialists, or graduates who could not get a job elsewhere or were unhappy as school teachers."

Dr Pouw states, "At that time there was no clear sense of belonging to a profession. . . ." "The turning point," according to Pouw, "came in the early seventies, when museums were transformed from stuffy, inward-looking places into open and welcoming ones which had to justify their existence both to visitors and to the government." "This change," he states, "inevitably led to professionalisation."[7]

Ethical museum practice must emanate from those working in museums and must serve as the signal banner for the profession. In this way the ethics as well as the practice will be dynamic and evolve in response to new developments and orientations. "Professional ethics is the off-shoot of general moral norms adopted by members of the same profession, who may be identified as a group."[8]

The supposition among most like-thinkers is that there is an obvious need for a code of ethics within the museum field that will establish basic standards of conduct and moral judgment by which museum professionals can act and be evaluated. Also usually endorsed is the belief that ethical action must be more than applied logic or common sense; it must be founded on acquired knowledge and established museum practices. Furthermore, as a code of professional ethics must address a broad agenda that will allow for growth and change, it is the assigned responsibility of each museum and museum worker to train and retrain according to the evolving requirements of the profession.

Ethical theories focus on principles rather than conclusions and on reasoning rather than outcomes. They explain how things ought to be and provide justification for actions. Ethical theory is not concerned with only the right and wrong of an issue, but more with the 'why' through explaining the principles involved. While it is the ethical obligation of all museums to comply fully with the law,[9] in some cases legal and ethical concerns may not be mutually inclusive. A readily available logic for an action is the maintenance of legality or acting within the "letter of the law." The same act may be beyond all accepted museum ethics. When the two are in conflict, the law must be obeyed but ethical practices must be the guide where legal boundaries are limited or ambiguous.

In the quest for the highest possible level of achievement in the museum setting, skill development and intellectual growth are imperative. To create an environment where the museum professional can flourish is an important challenge to all institutions. The traditional strength of the museums has been described in terms of the collections without recognition of the fact that knowledgeable curatorial, educational, and presentation (exhibit) staff are essential to transform collections into substantive exhibits and programs. The idea of the museum not as a collection of objects but as a collection of professionals dedicated to using and interpreting the objects for the purposes for which they were brought together is an ethical element of proper stewardship. Research and scientific work in museums are in the public interest.[10] Museum human resources also require adequate care and training to guarantee the correct and appropriate response to collection and constituency needs.

The addition to the knowledge base of any subject is achieved through research and intellectual exchange. The sharing of that knowledge requires communication at all levels of the museum workforce. The proper utilization of knowledge necessitates applications under controlled conditions. All three of these elements: research, communication, and application are essential to meeting the "minimum requirement to practice as a member of the museum profession."[11]

> This ethical duty is precisely stated in the ICOM *Code of Professional Ethics*:
>
> Members of the museum profession require appropriate academic, technical and professional training in order to fulfill their important role in relation to the operation of the museum and the care for the heritage, and the governing body should recognize the need for, and value of, a properly qualified and trained staff, and offer adequate opportunities for further training and re-training in order to maintain an adequate and effective workforce.[12]

Undoubtedly there are differing ethical concerns within specific elements of the museum personnel. However, it is most appropriate to recognize the underlying principles of continual training as it equates to professional practice. Every museum must include in its policy a commitment, both ideological and financial, to hire appropriately trained personnel and to provide opportunities for retraining incumbent staff.

The presumption of the museum as a "resting place for well-meaning amateurs" ended long ago. The museum profession demands a workforce with greater skills and better training. The stated ethical responsibility of the museum profession relates to the outward manifestation of defined and accepted practices. By maintaining professionalism, museum workers will be better equipped to define and meet institutional needs, and gain the backing of parent or support organizations and regional or national governmental entities.

The modern museum can no longer be a warehouse of antiques and relics where things are indiscriminately amassed. Ethical, realistically sound, decisions must be made concerning the collection of "new" items.

> At the 14th General Conference of ICOM, Nicolai Ivanov of the Soviet Union stated:
>
> "There is a need to improve substantially the museums' material and technical base by giving them the full possibility to fulfill their role as the principal custodians of historical and cultural relics and the guarantors that those relics are preserved and used effectively."[13]

Every exhibit presented, every educational program prepared and, in many ways, most objects collected, reflect the cultural assumptions and intellectual resources of the people making the decisions. Credibility is assigned to selected objects or notions and withheld from others. The whole question of moral and ethical responsibility in the presentation of people, history, ideological concepts, and scientific specimens and theories is a fascinating and highly significant aspect of every museum's and museum worker's agenda.

The maintenance of cultural pluralism is an important and meaningful role for museums. They must represent cultural diversity in their collections and their exhibits. As a community of international institutions, museums exemplify cultural pluralism. However, endorsement of global ideals does not always extend into the inner workings of the museums. Staff and boards often do not represent the full diversity of the constituency served. Assumptions of ethnic representation are often well meaning but usually inadequate. The challenge to meet the requirements of cultural pluralism is immediate, complex, and of vital importance if museums are to provide the appropriate leadership to "promote a greater knowledge and under-standing among people."[14]

☐   ☐   ☐   ☐   ☐

Question from the field: thirty-four

Question: One of our projects in archaeology is to create a reference collection of bones of native fauna. We use this material to make comparative studies with old fauna. This comparison has contributed to a better understanding of the environment and societies from the past. To get these samples, we process native animals, removing the tissue and retaining the bones. We record the bones carefully and store them in good containers. We also record ethnographic information we get from the inhabitants of the area where the animals are collected. Some of the animals are dead when they are found, but the majority we buy from the people who hunt them. It is this matter that worries us.

Our collection is serving researchers at the national level and is an incentive for study of zooarchaeology. The collection is also important in that we no longer have to depend on analysis from the USA or Europe where scientists are unfamiliar with our fauna.

The collection is housed at a research center at an archaeological site. It is available for use by any researcher. The problem is that the existence of this program is being questioned because the hunters are killing animals that are becoming extinct.

Is our research project justified?

What options are there to the process we are using?

Response: Undoubtedly the collection you are building is of extreme importance not only to your organization but to scholars worldwide and for generations. The question of whether the project is valid and worthwhile is easily answered. It is certainly a viable project. It is not the project but the method of collecting the specimens that is of concern. The idea of a museum intentionally seeking and destroying animals on the verge of extinction creates a very negative impression. ICOM has addressed this issue in the *Code of Professional Ethics.*

210

> "So far as biological and geological material is concerned, a museum should not acquire by any direct or indirect means any specimen that has been collected, sold or otherwise transferred in contravention of any national or international wildlife protection or natural history conservation law or treaty of the museum's own country or any other country except with the express consent of an appropriate outside legal or governmental authority."
>
> ICOM, *Code of Professional Ethics*, section 3. "Acquisitions to Museum Collections," paragraph 3.2, p. 28.

The second element that gives a negative impression is the payment to the hunters. The act of paying people to commit a wrongful act against nature is completely contrary to the ideas of conservation and ecological responsibility. Many institutions have a policy against paying for specimens for this reason.

> "Field exploration, collecting and excavation by museum workers present ethical problems that are both complex and critical. All planning for field studies and field collecting must be preceded by investigation, disclosure and consultation with both the proper authorities and any interested museums or academic institutions in the country or area of the proposed study sufficient to ascertain if the proposed activity is both legal and justifiable on the academic and scientific grounds. Any field program must be executed in such a way that all participants act legally and responsibly in acquiring specimens and data, and that they discourage by all practical means unethical, illegal and destructive practices."
>
> ICOM, *Code of Professional Ethics*, section 3. "Acquisitions to Museum Collections," paragraph 3.3, p. 28.

Suggestions for dealing with this situation:

1. Know the national and international laws on the gathering and possession of endangered animals.

2. Review your institution's policy on the taking of animals. Determine, define, and document the policy approved by the institutional decision-making body.

3. If a national policy on the taking of endangered species does not exist, take an active role in encouraging its formation. Design a method of regulating the animal collection

activities of your institution. Issue your own documentation describing the size, gender, age, and other specifics of the animals to be taken and the controls that must be observed. Describe, in plain language, the planned use of the animal.

4. Be honest and forthright in your actions. Explain to the inquiring public about the animal-related activities and their importance of the collections. Avoid all appearance of unwarranted or irresponsible action.

5. Maintain careful records and make good, well documented, use of the collection.

From a professional point of view, the collection process that involves payment to persons not restricted by professional standards is asking for trouble. If the animals are important to the collection, get the appropriate permits, mount a controlled collecting activity, and complete the research collection. Address a scientific matter in a traditional and accepted scientific method. Museums have collected material using field methods for years with the work executed under the direction and supervision of curators.

Notes

1. Daifuku, H. (1960) "Museums and Research," in *The Organization of Museums: Practical Advice*, Paris: UNESCO, *Museums and Monuments* IX, ch. IV, pp. 68–72.
2. Naisbitt, J. and Aburdene, P. (1990) "Renaissance in the Arts," in their *Megatrends 2000: Ten New Directions for the 1990's*, New York: William Morrow & Company, Inc., section 2, pp. 62–3; 71–2.
3. International Council of Museums (1990) "Aims of ICOM," *Statutes – Code of Professional Ethics*, Paris: ICOM, p. 4, section III.
4. *Third New International Dictionary, Webster's* (1966) (Philip Gove editor in chief), Springfield, Mass.: G. & C. Merrian Co.
5. International Council of Museums (1989) "Recommendation 2," Resolution 89/2, *Museums: Generators of Culture: Report and Comments from the 15th General Conference of ICOM* in The Hague, Paris: ICOM.
6. Weil, S. (1985) "Introduction," in his *Beauty and the Beasts*, Washington, DC: Smithsonian Institution Press, pp. xiii–xiv.
7. Pouw, P. (1989) "Museum Training in the Netherlands," in P. van Mensch (ed.) *Professionalising the Muses*, Amsterdam: AHA Books.
8. van Mensch, P. (1989) "Museum Ethics," in his *Professionalising the Muses*, p. 97.
9. International Council of Museums (1987) "Institutional Ethics, 2.11 Legal Obligation," *Statutes*, Paris: ICOM, p. 19, section II.
10. Dillon Ripley (1970) "Museums in Today's Changing World," in H. Evelyn (ed.) *Training of Museum Personnel*, London: ICOM address at ICOM meeting, September 27, 1968.
11. International Council of Museums (1990) "Preamble," *Statutes*, p. 15.
12. International Council of Museums (1990) "Institutional Ethics," *Statutes* p. 18.
13. Ivanov, Nicolai (1989) "The Tasks of Soviet Museums in Preserving the Cultural Heritage," in A. Bochi and S. de Valence (eds) *ICOM '86. Proceedings of the 14th General Conference and 15th General Assembly of the International Council of Museums*, Paris: UNESCO, p. 35.
14. International Council of Museums (1990) "Preamble (c)," *Statutes*, p. 15.

Suggested reading

Alexander, E. (1983) *Museum Masters, Their Museums and Their Influence*, Nashville, Tenn.: American Association for State and Local History.

Bloom, J. and Powell, E. (eds) (1984) *Museums for a New Century, A Report of the Commission on Museums for a New Century*, Washington, DC: American Association of Museums.

Burcaw, G. E. (1975) *Introduction to Museum Work*, 2nd edn 1983, Nashville, Tenn.: American Association for State and Local History.

Evelyn, H. (ed.) (1970) *Training of Museum Personnel*, London: ICOM.

Finley, D. E. (1973) *A Standard of Excellence, Andrew W. Mellon Founds the National Gallery of Art at Washington, DC*, Washington, DC: Smithsonian Institution Press.

International Council of Museums (1990) *Statutes*, Paris: ICOM.

Kavanagh, G. (ed.) (1991) *The Museums Profession*, Leicester: Leicester University Press.

van Mensch, P. (ed.) (1989) *Professionalising the Muses*, Amsterdam: AHA Books.

14

Museums and patrimony

In recent years, global attention has been directed toward the considerable social and educational potential of museums. There is a need for museums and collections to represent the diverse societies that occupy not only multicultural nations but the diversity represented by the world community. Museums as establishments of "culture" have drawn criticism from those who view culture as the tool of authority and museums as instruments of cultural homogeneity. One segment of the museum community is seeking to place collections and repositories in the neighborhoods of our nations. Another group is advocating a global perspective of humankind in relation to the natural, social, and cultural environments.

> "Museums are central to our culture, to our sense of ourselves, and to the future of our country. We [museums] are agents of change and represent one of a diminishing number of institutions in which it is acceptable – encouraged, in fact – to think, to debate, and to disagree."[1]

We live in a time when the world's cultural and natural heritage is rapidly diminishing in scope and diversity. Every day is a new starting point from which growth is essential. Museums are evolving at a previously unequaled rate. Just over 100 years ago, museums were curiosities. Today they are a part of almost every community and a benchmark of every nation in the world. Imagine a society without a record of its past. Visualize a people without images or objects to describe their history or to tell future generations of their beliefs, dreams, or achievements. Think also of a land where no music is played or sung, no dances are danced, and where art, history, and science are shared with no one. Imagine a land where all external cultural influences are restricted.

Music is silent until played or sung. Art is but a personally significant gesture if executed in a void and shared with no one. Scientific collections are rocks, bones, and hides without the benefit of human interaction. These "things" make a culture unique. They are truly significant to the maintenance of personal and national identity. Education is an activity with only relative meaning that requires the perspective of association. Knowledge is certain only when constantly renewed, reinforced, and expanded. It is a process that presupposes precedence.

> "All citizens have the right to share in the enjoyment of cultural riches as well as to share in their creation. Culture is an indispensable element of the quality of life. . . ."[2]

Most realize that cultural and economic developments do not advance at an even pace. Many nations, with a high level of cultural attainment, cannot support the level of museological achievement they desire. It is equally true that the cultural institutions of many wealthy countries are struggling with concerns that include inequity of access, censorship, pollution, and fiscal instability. Less than perfect circumstances should not lead to a deterioration of what we are as cultural entities. They should lead to new forms of expressions of what we have always been.

The proliferation of collections and museums is not limited to one people, society, or country. If it was, the phenomenon might be described as socio-logical or simple national egotism. However, many societies are experiencing the same growth.[3] World organizations have given new attention to national treasures and have established new and demanding norms for the care and maintenance of culturally significant materials.

> "Museums and the cultural treasures they display, protect, and study, have become almost everywhere valuable tools in the application of national cultural policies."[4]

Each museum worker has a responsibility to preserve and distribute information about the cultural properties of our countries and the charac-teristics of its people. When we measure this duty against the rapid modernization of the world we experience a condition of massive cultural change. The loss of important sites, linguistic integrity, ways of life, traditions, and the supportive environment that has maintained and protected the natural beauty and uniqueness of our lands is inexcusable. Museums must strive to preserve the diversity of human culture as that diversity rapidly disappears. The uniqueness of each of our cultures is of extreme importance to this and future generations.

215

The need to preserve the cultural and historical objects of a community, state, or nation is not directly linked to economic development or prosperity. The inclination to collect, preserve, research, and exhibit is equally pervasive in all lands and among all people. Economic factors not withstanding, the obviousness of museum and collection proliferation has drawn attention. The defined intention of museum and collection diversification, decentralization, and democratization certainly fits within the museum logic supported by most active participants in ICOM.

The museum workforce recognizes its duty to transfer to future generations the material record of human culture and the natural world.[5] To achieve this goal the operational procedures of every museum must include new initiatives for collection management, care, and utilization. These initiatives must emanate from those working in museums and must serve as a directive to the profession. In this way the ethic as well as the practice will be dynamic and evolve in response to new developments, needs, and orientations.

> "Professional ethics is the off-shoot of general moral norms adopted by members of the same profession, who may be identified."[6]

Most of the public and many museum staff members still perceive museums as facilities for the collecting, preserving, and exhibiting of objects (in some cases only collecting and exhibiting). The associated research and the resulting educational activities, or even the basic act of visitor enjoyment, is given little thought.[7] It is incorrect to assume that the practices of the past will always satisfy the needs of the future.

Exhibits, educational programs, and collections reflect the cultural bias and intellectual decision-making of the museum personnel. The question of moral and ethical responsibility in the presentation of people, history, concepts, and scientific information and theory is a significant aspect of every museum's agenda. There is an assumed role of responsibility for museums as "trusted guardians"[8] in the service of the public. The conceptual world of humanity (i.e., the public) is infinite and beyond most human perception. Museums give that world substance.

> "The contemporary museum strives to be a forum where the genius of the times and the spirit of the people find expression."[9]

Museums have a primary role in the conservation of culture through the preservation of cultural heritage. This responsibility is manifest at all levels – local through international. To accomplish this goal, there is a new standard for the profession to be used to measure the achievements of the museum community. Diversity and proliferation have given new and different attitudes toward collections and their use.

As a community of international institutions, museums can foster the finest aspects of cultural and social awareness. They must move from preoccupation with self to a greater awareness of the human species and the environment in which we exist. This challenge is complex and of vital importance if museums are to provide the appropriate leadership to "promote a greater knowledge and understanding among people."[10]

Consider the possibility that each of us is directly linked to the patrimony of our nations. Visualize a pyramid and at one point is a segment of humanity representing one element of the society of any country. They strive to survive and to provide for their individual needs and those of their immediate families. By the nature of their existence, they try to maintain a state of anonymity. To affect self-value and to counter this state of non-being, they evoke their heritage. They seek persons of their same linguistic background. They frequent places where they are comfortable among their cultural peers, and they exhibit the trappings and attire of their individual history. They seek personal identity through the preservation of group identity. Heritage is a shield against an anonymous existence over which they have little control.

Later, as those individuals enter the business and professional part of their society, they seek a sameness with their colleagues. They adopt the uniforms of their workplaces and seek the identity of the working environment. To achieve this change, they dismiss their heritage for a borrowed presence. They redirect their patrimonial allegiance. Later still, as these individuals situate themselves in secure positions, whether social, financial, or intellectual, they re-embrace their cultural heritage, often at an extreme and with a false measure of endorsement.

In the international community, we might consider any number of countries having a high degree of national pride with the people sustaining the practices, customs, and habits of their ancestors. In the normal pattern of growth, a segment of society will put aside the implements of the past and emulate a more prosperous society. In their desire for success they wish to be like the successful. This can include a preference for different dress, social customs, religion, and language. Success is very seductive, but once achieved the rewards carry little intellectual or emotional satisfaction. So, the successful nation tries to regain a sense of identity by seeking its origins – patrimony.

Succinctly, the base of the pyramid exemplifies patrimonial identification by need. The second level represents patrimonial redirection for acceptance. The third level depicts patrimonial endorsement by preference.

The theory of cultural change also identifies the strata of influence as they apply to support of the cultural heritage. Those at the base of the pyramid normally have no political, financial, or social authority. Those in the middle control a large portion of a nation's tangible wealth, but this group is dedicated to increasing its level of financial and social influence. Those at the top may have the money, influence, or social status to aid in the collection, preservation, and interpretation of cultural heritage. However, very often their recollection of past circumstances is obscured by sentiment, self-recrimination, and personal pride.

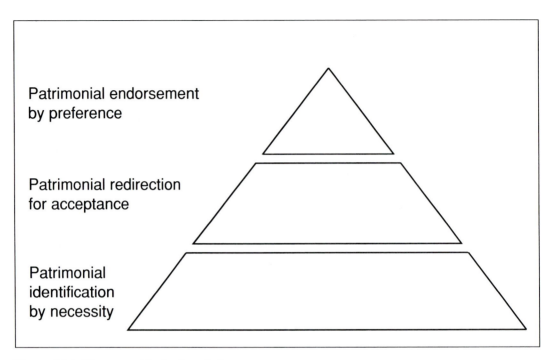

Figure 14.1 The pyramid of cultural change

This impression of cultural change is of particular interest when considering the various nations of the world, the origin of their people, and the level of care given cultural material. To the affluent individual handmade items of indigenous origin are "folk arts and crafts." To the working person, handmade items are a necessity of life.

A truly significant aspect of this concept is that there are persons at all levels of cultural change in all nations all the time. It is the preponderance of persons at a given level that creates the national identity. Obviously this concept appears to draw a direct correlation between cultural heritage and financial stability, but as with most broad-based theories the relationship is relative and self-modifying. The process of change may alter cultural heritage further by developing new forms in response to cultural, ethnic, and historical diversity.[11]

There are many nations temporarily fixed in each of the strata. Most of our countries, regardless of their level of economic development, are in either the first or second levels. Also significant is that people and objects are often identified according to their cultural affiliation rather than modern nationality.

The museum community has the responsibility to intervene in the social development process and stimulate the cultural identity of the nation.

Undoubtedly, museums can play an incisive role in the formation of a national consciousness, in national unity, and in economic and social development.

There are some initiatives that are basic to museums such as promotion of critical thinking, enhancement of open-mindedness, and the sensitizing of visitors to objects. There are also values that are more temporal and limited that may change to meet social needs. These values should advocate ethical and intellectual reasoning for the benefit of society – into this latter attitude must fall a concern for globalization. Ethnic and cultural diversity cannot be a shallow expression evoked as a popular response to the changing requirements of society.

As stated in *Museums for a New Century*: "For museums the act of collecting is more than an institutional expression of a human trait. It is our society's cumulative effort to save ourselves, our history, our natural surroundings, our technological and creative endeavors."[12] Certainly this concept can relate to all of us and all of our homelands.

Nowhere is it stated that all the answers are in place about the ways museums may serve the individuals of our lands or nations. In truth, there are only relative patterns (models) to provide a framework for tomorrow's museums in the service of future generations. We aspire to vision, truth, and perfection. We seek to collect, document, house, preserve, and interpret the greatest treasures of the world within our fragile walls. Fantastically, we are successful from time to time.

> "every country must preserve and disseminate the cultural properties that constitute the particular characteristics of its peoples. . . ."[13]

Remember, museums are made for people – people are not made for museums. The responsibility for service lies with the museum. As museum professionals we have no greater responsibility than to generate the ethical and moral climate necessary to strengthen the foundations of the society in which we live.

> "the maintenance of professional standards, critical as that may be, cannot be substituted for a sense of community service if a museum is long to survive."[14]

☐　　☐　　☐　　☐　　☐

Question from the field: thirty-five

Question: Do you believe in traveling exhibitions? Of particular concern are those at the international level where there is a possibility of damage to the objects caused by the moving process.

Response: Exchange between museums is an important part of cultural cross-fertilization. On the international level it is also a method of sharing important objects and information without depriving the country of origin. Traveling exhibits allow the broader community of museums, scholars, and the interested public the opportunity to view and study significant and often unique objects and specimens. Undoubtedly the movement of museum objects involves a certain level of risk. One of the primary obligations of the lending museum is to reduce those risks by working with conservators, packers, and shippers. For this reason careful attention must be given to all details of the shipping process. Intelligent use of available skills is the answer to moving valuable objects – not isolation.

The condition report is of primary importance in determining the level and extent of change that takes place in objects on loan or included in traveling exhibitions. The object should be photographed, giving special attention to possible problem areas. A detailed description of the object should be written, detailing the appearance of the object and noting all exceptional or unusual conditions including the exact measurements. The descriptive material must include diagrams, drawings, and details about the object that will allow the borrowing and lending institutions to make a comparative analysis of the object.

The first comparison is made when the object reaches the borrowing institution. The lender should request an evaluation in writing at that time based on the condition report. A second comparative evaluation is appropriate at a pre-established time during the loan period. The timing for this evaluation will depend on the nature of the loan object and the duration of the loan. The borrowing institution should make a condition review at the time the loan object is prepared for return to the lender. The final evaluation is made by the lending institution upon the return of the object. All the review material is maintained in one folder or book, and kept in a location accessible to curators, registrar, and conservator. A report of individual object alteration is also included in the object folder.

Careful documentation of objects on loan or included in traveling exhibitions serves many purposes. Three of the more important are:

1. The record provides a complete schedule and description of the times, locations, and conditions of the loan or travel of individual objects.

2. The record notes changes or alterations the object underwent during the loan or travel.

3. The record provides documentary evidence for determining which objects can withstand travel and which may or may not be considered for future loans or traveling exhibitions.

Notes

1. Southern, K. (1989) "Exhibitions are Our Forum for Debating Change," *Museum News*, Vol. 68, No. 8, November/December, p. 104.
2. Solana, F. (1981) in A. Bochi and S. de Valence (eds) *Proceedings of the 12th General Conference and 13th General Assembly of the International Council of Museums*, Mexico City, October 25–November 4, Paris: ICOM, pp. 17–21.
3. *Museum News* Staff (1988) "Museums: A Global View," *Museum News*, Vol. 67, No. 1, September/October, pp. 22–47.
4. Abranches, H. (1984) "Museums and Cultural Identity," in A. Bochi and S. de Valence (eds) *Proceedings of the 13th General Conference and 14th General Assembly of the International Council of Museums*, London, July 24–August 2, 1983 Paris: ICOM.
5. Bloom, J. and Powell, E. (eds) (1984) *Museums for a New Century*, Washington, DC: American Association of Museums.
6. van Mensch, P. (1989) "Museum Ethics," in his *Professionalising the Muses*, Amsterdam: AHA Books, p. 97.
7. Edson, G. (1990) "Museums and Collection Proliferation and the Impact on Training of Museum Personnel," an unpublished paper presented at the 15th General Conference of the International Council of Museums, The Netherlands.
8. Bloom and Powell (eds), *Museums for a New Century*, p. 23.
9. Solana, *Proceedings*, p. 17–21.
10. International Council of Museums (1990) "Preamble (c)," *Statutes – Code of Professional Ethics*, Paris: ICOM, p. 15.
11. Schensul, J. (1990) "Organizing Cultural Diversity Through the Arts," *Education and Urban Society*, California.
12. Bloom and Powell (eds) *Museums for a New Century*.
13. Solana, *Proceedings*, pp. 17–21.
14. Weil, S. (1986) "Questioning Some Premises," *Museum News*, Vol. 65, No. 5, pp. 20–7.

Suggested reading

Burcaw, G. E. (1975) *Introduction to Museum Work*, 2nd edn 1983, Nashville, Tenn.: American Association for State and Local History.

Finlay, I. (1977) *Priceless Heritage: The Future of Museums*, London: Faber & Faber.

International Council of Museums (1990) *Statutes*, Paris: ICOM.

Karp, I. and Lavine, S. (eds) (1991) *Exhibiting Cultures: The Poetics and Politics of Museum Display*, Washington, DC: Smithsonian Institution Press.

Malaro, M. (1985) *A Legal Primer on Managing Museum Collections*, 2nd edn 1987, Washington, DC: Smithsonian Institution Press.

Messenger, P. (ed.) (1989) *The Ethics of Collecting Cultural Property*, Albuquerque, NM: University of New Mexico Press.

15

Code of ethics – registrars

This material is included as an example of a code of ethics developed and adopted by a discipline area within the museum. It is intended for use as a reference. It is reprinted with permission from *Museum News*, February, 1983, the American Association of Museums. All rights reserved.

Description of the position

- Individuals with the title or function of registrar have a varied range of responsibilities and activities. In this document the basic description of the position as defined in the glossary of Museum Registration Methods is adopted: "an individual with broad responsibilities in the development and enforcement of policies and procedures pertaining to the acquisition, management and disposition of collections. Records pertaining to the objects for which the institution has assumed responsibility are maintained by the registrar. Usually, the registrar also handles arrangements for accessions, loans, packing, shipping, storage, customs and insurance as it relates to museum material."
- Registrars are usually specialists in the areas of information management, risk management and logistics. The primary concerns of registrars are creating and maintaining accurate records pertaining to objects, including those documents that provide legal protection for their museums; arranging insurance coverage for objects; and handling, transporting and control of objects.

The registrar, the records and the objects

- Registrars' obligations to their museums' collections, to loaned objects and to the associated records are paramount.

Management, maintenance and preservation of the records

- The records and documents that form a body of information pertaining to the collections and loaned objects are the responsibility of registrars and are the cornerstone of the registrarial function.

222

- The records comprise legal documents establishing ownership or loan status of objects: records of accession, location, donor or vendor, exhibition and publication. They may also include photographs, licenses and permits, exhibition bond notices and historical records. Frequently, curators keep research files on the objects in their domain. Registrars must maintain records that are meticulously complete, honest, orderly, retrievable and current. Records must be stored in an archivally and technologically sound and secure manner, both to ensure their preservation and to prevent access to unauthorized persons. The expertise of legal counsel and archivists should be sought without hesitation.
- Registrars must protect their museums and the objects in them against the risk of liability through the use of valid documents such as gift, sales, loan and custody forms and receipts; by implementing all aspects of insurance coverage for owned and borrowed objects on premises or in transit according to the terms of their insurance policy or indemnity; and by complying with pertinent laws and regulations governing such things as import and export or other movement of objects, or rights and reproductions of objects.
- Registrars, through the records maintained, are accountable for the objects in the custody of their museums and must be able to provide current information on each object, its location, status, and condition.

Management, maintenance and conservation of the objects

- In maintenance and physical care of the collections, registrars must work in close cooperation with curators, conservators, collections managers and other museum staff, and must be guided by their museums' collections management policies. In management of loans, registrars also work in cooperation with exhibitions, technical and security staff, and they must adhere to and enforce the lenders' conditions of loan.
- In some museums it is not registrars but curators or collections managers who have responsibility for the physical care of collections in storage. Whichever is the case, the best and most secure environment possible should be ensured for the storage and preservation of objects. The condition of the collections should be reviewed periodically and expertise of conservators should be sought without hesitation.
- Objects in movement are the responsibility of registrars. As risk managers, registrars are responsible for determining and arranging for the correct methods of handling, packing, transporting and couriering objects. They must also consider borrowers' capabilities and facilities. Registrars identify potential risks and complications and act to reduce or eliminate them.
- Registrars share the responsibilities for loaned objects in the custody of their museums. They are responsible for their safe movement, temporary storage and correct disposition. Registrars always must treat loaned objects of whatever value, quality or type with the same care and respect given to objects in their museums' collections.

- Registrars must complete condition reports in an honest and timely manner, be familiar with the terms of their insurance coverage and ensure that insurance reporting is accurate. In filing an insurance claim all relevant circumstances of loss or damage must be disclosed, even if it appears that the museum is at fault.

Acquisition and disposal

- Registrars must adhere to the acquisition and disposal policies of their museums; if no written policies exist, then registrars should encourage and assist in their formulation. In the absence of written museum policies registrars should develop written procedures for use by their departments to ensure compliance with traditional but oral museum policies. Registrars should obtain the approval of their directors before implementing such procedures, and strive to ensure that the policies and procedures are complied with at all levels within their museums.
- Objects for acquisition or disposal are proposed, usually by curators, to the relevant museum committees for approval. Registrars' roles in acquisition are generally in an advisory capacity concerning the feasibility of storage, the risk of movement to the object under consideration and certain legal aspects of the transaction. Prior to using an accession number reflecting the date and/or order in which the object was added to the collection, registrars are responsible for obtaining documentation of the decision to acquire the object, the document transferring title of an object to the museum, and the receipt of delivery of an object. Registrars should be aware of, and not contribute to, the violation of tax, wildlife, import and other laws and regulations governing acquisition of objects by their museums and other institutions with which they are involved.
- Registrars should ensure that at least one appraisal of an object is acquired and institute insurance coverage if applicable according to museum policy. In order to prevent their use as an appraisal for tax or other purposes, these appraisals should not be made available to the donor or vendor of an object. Appraisals for tax purposes are the responsibility of the donor, who can be informed whether an object is accepted for the collection, for sale or for use by the museum.
- Registrars' roles in deaccessions and disposals are primarily those of monitoring and documenting procedures. Registrars also should bring to the attention of the curator any object in irreparable condition or one jeopardizing the safety of the rest of the collections. Registrars should verify the museum's legal right to dispose of an object, and inform the curator and other appropriate museum staff of any restrictions attached to an object that may bear on its disposition. When restrictions are attached to an object, legal counsel should be sought so the museum might be relieved of those restrictions by appropriate negotiation or legal procedure.
- Once all the proper approvals have been granted, registrars must amend all the related records to show the date of deaccession, the authority for it and the method of disposal. Records may also show the disposition of any funds

realized through sale or any exchange acquired as a result of the deaccession. Donor credit for, and use of funds realized through, the sale of an object must comply with the policies of the museum.

Availability of collections and records

- Museums hold and safeguard their collections for posterity, although they must allow reasonable public access to them on a nondiscriminatory basis. However, registrars must act according to the policies of their museums.
- Registrars, along with curators and conservators, must ensure that objects from the collections are examined and viewed in a manner not detrimental to an object. They must also ascertain that a borrowing institution's facilities are acceptable when considering a loan request, so that an object will not be placed in jeopardy.
- The records constitute part of a museum's accountability to the public. However, registrars must ensure by proper supervision that sensitive or confidential material in their museums' records is not accessible to unauthorized persons. When in doubt, registrars should consult their supervisors or their museums' legal counsel.

Truth in presentation

- Registrars are responsible for creating and maintaining accurate records and updating them in light of new research, and for ensuring that the records reflect the facts insofar as they are known.

The Registrar as staff member

General deportment

- Registrars are visible to the public, the profession, commercial representatives and government agents in situations ranging from collecting objects from donors and lenders in their homes or museums to negotiating with customs inspectors in cargo sheds. Registrars must behave in a dignified and ethical manner and gain the respect of others by not creating embarrassments either to their museum or their profession. Because of their access to confidential matters and information, it is incumbent upon registrars to be discreet and circumspect in all their communications or actions in an effort to preserve the integrity of their museum.
- In all activities and statements, registrars must make it clear whether they are speaking for their museums, their professional association or themselves. They must be aware that any museum-related action may reflect upon their museums, be attributed to it or reflect upon the integrity of the profession as a whole.

Conflict of interest

- Registrars must be governed by their museums' policies on conflict of interest and other ethical matters.
- Registrars should be loyal to their museums and not abuse their official position or contacts within the museum community, nor act so as to impair in any way the performance of their official duties, compete with their museums, or bring discredit or embarrassment to any museum or the profession in any activity, museum-related or not.

Responsibility to the collections and other museum property

- Registrars and their staff must never receive or purchase for their own or another individual's collections or purposes, even at public auction, objects deaccessioned from their museums' collections. The registrars' volunteers and interns should be guided by the codes governing their supervisors.
- Registrars should never put to personal use objects in their museums' custody and they should guard information that would enable others to do so. Registrars must never abuse their access to information and to other museum assets by using them to personal advantage. Registrars must be particularly vigilant concerning their knowledge of museum security procedures.
- Because of their experience and responsibility as risk managers, registrars are often regarded as authorities in the care and transport of valuable or problematical objects. They must guard against giving the impression that their museums endorse the services of any specific vendor or supplier.
- When recommending the services of conservators, appraisers, packers, shippers, customs brokers or others, whenever possible registrars should offer the names of three qualified vendors to avoid favoritism in commendations.

Personal collecting and dealing

- Registrars must be governed by the policies of their museums which usually are designed for curators and directors. If at the time of their employment their personal collections are similar to those of their museums', registrars should submit an inventory of their collections to the appropriate official and update this inventory in a timely manner. As to objects they acquire after they are employed, registrars may be required to give the museum the opportunity to purchase such objects at their acquisition cost for an appropriate period of time. In no case should registrars compete with their museums in any personal collecting activity. They should never act as dealers or for dealers.

Outside employment and consulting

- In any situation where registrars work for another organization, an individual or themselves on their own time, such work should not interfere with the performance of the registrars' duties for their museums. The nature of the employment should be disclosed to and cleared by their director and should conform to their museums' relevant personnel policy.

Gifts, favors, discounts and dispensations

- Registrars often use the services of commercial companies. They must not accept gifts of more than a trifling nature, such as unsolicited advertising or promotional material, so that their judgment will not be impaired when selecting a vendor. Such selections should be made upon merit and not for personal reasons or obligations.
- Registrars must not accept personal discounts from vendors who do business with their museums. Registrars must also avoid any appearance of being influenced by gifts or dispensations provided by vendors of services.

Teaching, lecturing, writing and other creative activities

- Registrars should teach, lecture, write and perform related professional activities for the benefit of others in the profession or those aspiring to such a position. They should also contribute to the general public understanding of museum registration.
- Registrars should enhance their own knowledge in all registration matters, ensuring that they are up to date with current methods of records management, object care and handling, packing, transporting, insurance, personnel and financial management, as well as changes in the laws affecting museums and their collections.
- Registrars should obtain the approval of their director and conform to their museums' policies on questions of use of official time, royalties and other remuneration for such activities.

Field studies and collecting

- Because legal and ethical problems can arise more frequently in fieldwork, registrars must be particularly zealous in completing accurate and timely records. Registrars must monitor compliance with local, state, national and international laws, as well as with their museums' acquisitions policies. They must also be sensitive to ethnic and religious beliefs.

The registrar and museum management policy

Professionalism

- Although the governing board of the museum is ultimately responsible for the museum, the director is the chief executive officer.

- Registrars must carry out their duties according to established guidelines and under the directions of their supervisors, who may be the director, the assistant director or curator of collections, or an administrative manager. In no case should they take direction from members of the governing board, who should confine their directives to the chief executive officer of the museums. If guidelines or delegations of authority are unclear, registrars should seek written clarification.
- Registrars should not be required to reverse, alter or suppress their professional judgment to conform to a management decision.
- When a disagreement arises between the registrar and the director or other supervisor, the registrar should consider documenting the difference of opinion, but should also conform to the grievance procedures of the museums. Only when asked to falsify records or in some way compromise legal or ethical standards should the registrar consider writing a report to the governing board of the museum, and then only with the full knowledge of the museum director.

Interpersonal relationships and intermuseum cooperation

- While registrars must strive for excellence in registration methods, they should understand the professional role within the total context of their museums and should act cooperatively and constructively with colleagues in the furtherance of their museums' goals and purposes. It is important for registrars to obtain the respect and trust of colleagues in their own and other museums.
- Intermuseum cooperation may take the form of providing safe storage for duplicate sets of collections records, of providing the services of conservation or preparation of objects for transport, of consolidation of shipment or safe storage for traveling exhibitions between sites. Such cooperation may also take the form of providing professional help and temporary storage of objects or records in the event of fire, flood or other disaster. When objects or records are taken into their museums' custody, registrars should ensure that valid documentation of the terms and duration of the custody arrangements is provided.

□   □   □   □   □

Suggested reading

Alexander, E. (1979) *Museums in Motion, An Introduction to the History and Functions of Museums*, 4th printing 1986, Nashville, Tenn.: American Association for State and Local History.

Beibel, D. (1978) *Registration Methods for the Small Museum*, Nashville, Tenn.; American Association for State and Local History.

Burcaw, G. E. (1975) *Introduction to Museum Work*, 2nd edn 1983, Nashville, Tenn.: American Association for State and Local History.

Dudley, D., Wilkinson, I., *et al.* (1981) *Museum Registration Methods*, 3rd edn rev., Washington, DC: American Association of Museums.

International Council of Museums (1990) *Statutes*, Paris: ICOM.

Kavanagh, G. (ed.) (1991) *The Museums Profession*, Leicester: Leicester University Press.

Malaro, M. (1985) *A Legal Primer on Managing Museum Collections*, 2nd edn 1987, Washington, DC: Smithsonian Institution Press.

Thompson, J. M. A. (ed.) (1984) *Manual of Curatorship, A Guide to Museum Practice*, 2nd edn 1992, London: Butterworth & Co.

16

Code of ethics – curators

This material is included as an example of a code of ethics developed and adopted by a discipline area within the museum. It is intended for use as a reference. It is reprinted with permission from *Museum News*, February, 1985, the American Association of Museums. All rights reserved.

A Curator is typically a specialist in a field related to the collection in his or her care and is responsible for the overall well-being and scope of that collection, including acquisition and disposal, preservation and access, interpretation and exhibition, and research and publication.

The curator and the collection

Management, maintenance and conservation

- Curators are authorities concerning the collection under their care. As such, they should develop and preserve thorough, up-to-date, easily comprehensible information about those collections.
- They should work in cooperation with the registrar, collections manager, conservator and other staff to ensure that the collections and related documentation are well maintained. In small museums where other collections staff are not employed, the curator must assume responsibility for record keeping and the condition of objects.

Acquisition and disposal

- Curators usually initiate or initially approve the acquisition and disposal of objects under their care.
- Curators must adhere to the acquisition and disposal policies of their institution. If written policies do not exist, curators should urge that such documents be developed.
- Curators must be cognizant of all laws (international, national and local) affecting the acquisition of objects in their areas of responsibility.

To avoid acquiring illegally exported or improperly collected specimens, curators can consult UNESCO Convention, the Archaeological Resources Protection Act, the American Indian Religious Freedom Act, state and federal wildlife laws and regulations, and the guidelines of their professional societies. The provenance of all objects should be known and recorded.

- Curators should review the objects in their collections periodically to assess their continued relevance to the museum's purposes and to evaluate their physical care.
- Curators should not overstock or under supply the collection.

Although the authority and final decision for deaccessioning always rest with the board of trustees or other governing authority (hereafter designated as the board), curators must offer guidance, based on their expertise, in order that the institution not suffer legally, financially, scientifically or esthetically through disposal of objects from collections.

- Curators must not prepare appraisals for objects to be deaccessioned. For an accurate indication of an object's value, outside appraisals must be sought.
- Curators must never purchase, even at public auction, objects deaccessioned from their own institution's collections.

Appraisals

- Curators may prepare appraisals only for internal use at their institution (e.g., insurance valuations for loans) and, with the approval of the curator's museum, for other nonprofit institutions.

Commercial use

- In collaboration with the conservator, curators should carefully evaluate proposals to replicate collections objects for commercial use. The safety of the original object must not be threatened, and inaccurate copies and inappropriate uses must be forbidden. To the extent possible, an object should be marked as a copy in as permanent a manner as possible.

Availability of collections

- A delicate balance may exist between object preservation and object access. Curators and conservators should confer to determine the needs and allowable access for each object.
- Whenever possible, legitimate requests for information and/or the examination of objects should be honored. This access shall include loans to responsible institutions as well as use within the owner institution.

231

Truth in presentation

- Curators are responsible for the accuracy of their research and interpretation and for the content of written descriptions and documentation of the collections under their jurisdiction, whether prepared by themselves or by others.
- Curators have a responsibility to an object's creator(s) and should present the creator's perspective and the object's cultural context as accurately and as sensitively as is possible.

Human remains and sacred objects

- Curators who have human remains or sacred objects in their collection must be aware of the peoples intimately involved or associated with these materials.
- Curators must be willing to exchange ideas with cultural representatives concerning the acquisition, exhibition, interpretation, storage or possible return of culturally sensitive objects.

The curator as staff member

General deportment

- In all activities and statements, curators must make it clear whether they are acting or speaking for their institution, their professional associations or themselves. They must not represent, or appear to represent, their institution or their associations without a mandate to do so.

Conflict of interest

- Curators owe loyalty to their museum. Activities that conflict with this loyalty or cause curators to favor outside or personal interests over those of their institutions must be avoided. Critical areas where curators must avoid conflicts of interest with their institutions are: personal collecting, dealing, gifts and outside consulting or employment. In all such areas, the open and frank disclosure by the curator of all private holdings and transactions is essential.

Personal collecting

- Curators in one discipline may be encouraged to establish personal collections in their specialty, while curators in other fields may be discouraged from doing so. Some art curators are expected to acquire museum-quality works for their own collections; archeologists, ethnographers, and natural scientists are generally restricted in such activities in order to preserve scientific data.
- Curators who collect privately must adhere to the following guidelines.

- Curators must follow the personal collecting policies adopted by their institution. If a written document does not exist, curators should urge that a policy be developed. Collections acquired before employment, family inheritances, and collections outside the museum's field of interest are generally exempt from such policy restrictions.
- At the time of employment, curators who collect should provide their institution with an inventory of their collection. This inventory should be updated periodically.
- Curators must never compete with their museum for an object. Curators must give their institution first option to acquire an object that they have purchased before adding it to their personal collection.
- Curators should not store personal collections on museum property or research or conserve their personal collections on museum time without the permission of their institution.
- If curators lend objects for an exhibition in their museum, they should lend them anonymously. Similarly, illustrations of works in curators' collections should be credited anonymously in the museum's publications.
- If curators decide to dispose of part or all of their personal collection, they should offer it first to their museum as a gift or at fair market value. If their museum chooses not to purchase the collection, curators should first consider sale at public auction rather than to a dealer. All such transactions should be documented.
- A curator should not negotiate personally with a dealer with whom the curator also does business on behalf of the museum.
- Neither relatives nor friends should engage in a transaction, on behalf of the curator, that is not in compliance with the above stated principles. Curators should also urge members of their immediate family to comply with these restraints and constrictions in their personal transactions.

Dealing

- There is a distinct difference between dealing (buying and selling for personal profit) and occasional sales to upgrade a personal collection. To avoid conflicting loyalties, curators must not become involved in dealing.
- A curator must not act as a dealer, be employed by a dealer or retain an interest in a dealership.

Gifts, favors, discounts and dispensations

- Curators should accept gifts only for their institution. Gifts accepted by a curator may bias that curator in favor of the donor. A gift relevant to the museum's collection should not be accepted by a curator for personal use.
- A donor may genuinely wish to give a gift directly to a curator. When a close personal relationship exists in addition to a professional one, the curator may accept the gift but must submit a record of the transaction to the museum.

- Curators must not accept personal discounts from a dealer if their museum also does business with that dealer.
- Curators who are artists must not use their position to advance their own work. To do so is equivalent to granting themselves special favors.

Outside employment and consulting

- Outside employment includes any situation where curators work for an organization, an individual or themselves on their own time and are privately paid.
- Curators should conform to their museum's personnel policy concerning outside employment.
- Curators should not undertake outside employment without prior clearance by the director of their museum.
- Curators should not allow outside employment to interfere with the full and conscientious performance of their museum duties.
- Curators should conform to the conflict of interest guidelines when undertaking outside employment.
- Curators should not draw upon any of their institution's resources when involved in outside employment, except with that institution's approval.

Teaching, lecturing, and writing

- Teaching, lecturing, writing, and professional consulting have the potential to increase a curator's knowledge and abilities and contribute to public understanding.
- Before engaging in any of these activities, curators should obtain clearance from the appropriate representative of their own institution.
- Curators should urge their institutions to prepare a written policy that deals directly with the disposition of lecture fees, royalties, and ownership of copyrights. In current museum practice, curators are eligible for personal remuneration if these (materials) have been prepared and/or presented on their own time; if prepared on museum time, any payment is at the discretion of the institution.

Field study and collecting

- Curators who collect in the field for their institutions are subject to the restraints and constriction outlined under "Acquisition and Disposal."
- Curators who collect, on their own time, for their personal collections ("Sunday" collectors) must exercise extraordinary discretion and follow the guidelines described in "Conflict of Interest," "Personal Collecting," "Dealing" and "Gifts."

The curator and museum management policy

Professionalism

- The director of the institution is the chief executive and must at all times serve as the conduit between the board and the curatorial staff. A curator may meet with the board or any individual member concerning museum management only with the full knowledge and approval of the director.
- Curators must carry out their assigned duties and functions according to the guidelines stated by the director.
- Curators must make every effort to operate within the institutional framework. No curator should bypass normal administrative channels until those channels have been fully explored.
- In rare instances in which a curator believes that the director is acting in an unethical manner, the curator must inform the director before discussing the problem with the board.

Interpersonal Relations

- Curators employed by the same institution should work in full support and cooperation with each other.
- Curators must also be mindful of the need for cooperative relationships with curators in other museums.

Ownership of scholarly material

- Curators hired to research and interpret the collection in their care sometimes regard the notes and associated materials that result from this work as their personal property, regardless of the museum's ownership of the actual collections objects. If the scholarly activity is a personal project, done exclusively on personal time and not within the scope of assigned responsibilities, it seems clear that the ownership is personal. If the work is within the scope of employment and fully funded by the institution, it is more likely to be the property of the museum. Curators must urge their own institutions to formulate policies on this issue.

A final word

- Throughout this document, the need for awareness of the law, adherence to written museum policies, knowledge of and concern for the collections and sensitivity to the public's interest in them, propriety in all one's dealings and open and frank disclosure of private holdings and transactions has been stressed.
- An ethics code for curators is difficult to formulate because curators in one discipline may be called upon to perform duties that curators in another

discipline would find, at worst, unethical and, at best, inappropriate. Like *Museum Ethics*, this code offers a set of guidelines. Curators are also urged to familiarize themselves with *Museum Ethics*, to consult codes of ethics that deal specifically with their own disciplines and to adhere to policies of their own institutions.

□   □   □   □   □

Question from the field: thirty-six

Question: Suppose you are a curator working for a museum and doing archaeological work. During your fieldwork you discover several small artifacts of major research value. These objects are very important to your personal research. During the two years following the find you write on the objects and publish papers. The information is well received by the academic community. Due, in part, to the acceptance of these papers, you are offered a position at a university. It is a very prestigious position at a salary far above the one you are making at the museum. You decide to take the position and leave your current employment taking the artifacts with you. The museum demands them back and states that the original field notes are their property as well and that they must be returned.

To continue your research you need the material. You feel that the artifacts are important because you wrote about them. They have little actual (i.e., monetary value) and you are willing to pay if the museum will accept a fair market value. You feel the field notes are personal property as you wrote them. The museum wants everything returned.

Who is right?

Response: This is a problem that has plagued many museums, particularly in the past when record-keeping was less organized. Curators and academics working in museums considered the material to be their discovery and subsequently their personal property for research and publication. It was a question of presumed ownership. Many important collections have lost their research value because the original field notes have been removed or misplaced.

The museum owns the material if the fieldwork was done under its general authority and/or if the curator or project was funded by or due to the museum's involvement. The artifactual material belongs to the museum and the related field notes should stay with the objects.

The curator would be wise to request access to the material or have the new employer seek a loan of the material for research purposes. The field notes can be photocopied assuming the museum will honor the request.

Problems of this nature should be addressed in the museum's policy and procedures. All museum employees should receive a copy of the policy and procedures manual for their information and protection.

Suggested reading

Alexander, E. (1979) *Museums in Motion, An Introduction to the History and Functions of Museums*, 4th printing 1986, Nashville, Tenn.: American Association for State and Local History.

Burcaw, G. E. (1975) *Introduction to Museum Work*, 2nd edn 1983, Nashville, Tenn.: American Association for State and Local History.

International Council of Museums (1990) *Statutes*, Paris: ICOM.

Kavanagh, G. (ed.) (1991) *The Museums Profession*, Leicester: Leicester University Press.

Malaro, M. (1985) *A Legal Primer on Managing Museum Collections*, 2nd edn 1987, Washington, DC: Smithsonian Institution Press.

Messenger, P. (ed.) (1989) *The Ethics of Collecting Cultural Property*, Albuquerque, NM: New Mexico University Press.

Thompson, J. M. A. (ed.) (1984) *Manual of Curatorship, A Guide to Museum Practice*, 2nd edn 1992, London: Butterworth & Co.

17

ICOM Code of Professional Ethics

The *Code of Professional Ethics* reproduced here is published with the permission of the International Council of Museums, Elisabeth des Portes, Secretary General.

I. Preamble

The ICOM *Code of Professional Ethics* was adopted unanimously by the 15th General Assembly of ICOM meeting in Buenos Aires, Argentina on 4 November 1986.

It provides a general statement of professional ethics, respect for which is regarded as a minimum requirement to practise as a member of the museum profession. In many cases it will be possible to develop and strengthen the *Code* to meet particular national or specialized requirements and ICOM wishes to encourage this. A copy of such developments of the *Code* should be sent to the Secretary General of ICOM, Maison de l'Unesco, 1 Rue Miollis, 75732 Paris Cedex 15, France.

For the purposes of Articles 5 and 16(c) of the ICOM *Statutes*, this *Code is* deemed to be the statement of professional ethics referred to therein.

1. Definitions

1.1. *The International Council of Museums (ICOM)*

ICOM is defined in Article 6 of its *Statutes* as "the international, non-governmental, and professional organization representing museums and the museum profession. In this capacity it maintains close consultative and co-operative relations with Unesco, ICOMOS, and ICCROM, and with other national, regional, or international, inter-governmental or non-governmental organizations, with the authorities responsible for museums and with specialists of other disciplines."

The primary aims of ICOM, as defined in Article 7 of the *Statutes* are:

"(a) To define, support and aid museums and the museum institution; to establish, support and reinforce the museum profession.

(b) To organize co-operation and mutual assistance between museums and between members of the museum profession in the different countries.

(c) To emphasize the importance of the role played by museums and the museum profession within each community and in the promotion of a greater knowledge and understanding among peoples."

1.2. *Museum*

A Museum is defined in Article 3 of the *Statutes* of the International Council of Museums as "a non-profitmaking, permanent institution in the service of society and of its development, and open to the public, which acquires, conserves, researches, communicates, and exhibits, for the purposes of study, education and enjoyment, material evidence of man and his environment."

In addition to museums designated as such, ICOM recognizes (under Article 4 of the *Statutes*) that the following comply with the ICOM definition:

"(a) Conservation institutes and exhibition galleries permanently maintained by libraries and archive centres.

(b) Natural, archaeological, and ethnographical monuments and sites and historical monuments and sites of a museum nature, for their acquisition, conservation and communication activities.

(c) Institutions displaying live specimens such as botanic and zoological gardens, aquaria, vivaria, etc.

(d) Nature reserves.

(e) Science centres and planetariums."

1.3. *The Museum Profession*

ICOM defines the museum profession under Article 5 of the *Statutes* as consisting of all of the personnel of museums or institutions as detailed under para. 1.1 above who have received a specialized technical or academic training or who possess an equivalent practical experience, and who respect a fundamental code of professional ethics.

1.4. *Governing Body*

The government and control of museums in terms of policy, finance and administration etc., varies greatly from one country to another, and often from one museum to another within a country according to the legal and other national or local provisions of the particular country or institution.

In the case of many national museums the Director, Curator or other professional head of the museum may be appointed by, and directly responsible to, a Minister or a Government Department, whilst most local government museums are similarly governed and controlled by the appropriate local authority. In many other cases the government and control of the museum is vested in some form of independent body, such as a board of trustees, a society, a non-profit company, or even an individual.

For the purposes of this *Code* the term "Governing Body" has been used throughout to signify the superior authority concerned with the policy, finance and administration of the museum. This may be an individual Minister or official, a Ministry, a local authority, a Board of Trustees, a Society, the Director of the museum or any other individual or body. Directors, Curators or other professional heads of the museum are responsible for the proper care and management of the museum.

II. Institutional Ethics

2. Basic Principles for Museum Governance

2.1. *Minimum Standards for Museums*

The governing body or other controlling authority of a museum has an ethical duty to maintain, and if possible enhance, all aspects of the museum, its collections and its services. Above all, it is the responsibility of each governing body to ensure that all of the collections in their care are adequately housed, conserved and documented.

The minimum standards in terms of finance, premises, staffing and services will vary according to the size and responsibilities of each museum. In some countries such minimum standards may be defined by law or other government regulation and in others guidance on and assessment of minimum standards is available in the form of "Museum Accreditation" or similar schemes. Where such guidance is not available locally, it can usually be obtained from appropriate national and international organizations and experts, either directly or through the National Committee or appropriate International Committee of ICOM.

2.2. *Constitution*

Each museum should have a written constitution or other document setting out clearly its legal status and permanent, non-profit nature, drawn up in accordance with appropriate national laws in relation to museums, the cultural heritage, and non-profit institutions. The governing body or other controlling authority of a museum should prepare and publicize a clear statement of the aims, objectives and policies of the museum, and of the role and composition of the governing body itself.

2.3. *Finance*

The governing body holds the ultimate financial responsibility for the museum and for the protecting and nurturing of its various assets: the collections and related documentation, the premises, facilities and equipment, the financial assets, and the staff. It is obliged to develop and define the purposes and related policies of the institution, and to ensure that all of the museum's assets are properly and effectively used for museum purposes. Sufficient funds must be available on a regular basis, either from public or private sources, to enable the governing body to carry out and develop the work of the museum. Proper accounting procedures must be adopted and maintained in accordance with the relevant national laws and professional accountancy standards.

2.4. *Premises*

The board has specially strong obligations to provide accommodation giving a suitable environment for the physical security and preservation of the collections. Premises must be adequate for the museum to fulfil within its stated policy its basic functions of collection, research, storage, conservation, education and display, including staff accommodation, and should comply with all appropriate national legislation in relation to public and staff safety. Proper standards of protection should be provided against such hazards as theft, fire, flood, vandalism and deterioration, throughout the year, day and night. The special needs of disabled people should be provided for, as far as practicable, in planning and managing both buildings and facilities.

2.5. *Personnel*

The governing body has a special obligation to ensure that the museum has staff sufficient in both number and kind to ensure that the museum is able to meet its responsibilities. The size of the staff, and its nature (whether paid or unpaid, permanent or temporary), will depend on the size of the museum, its collections and its responsibilities. However, proper arrangements should be made for the museum to meet its obligations in relation to the care of the collections, public access and services, research, and security.

The governing body has particularly important obligations in relation to the appointment of the director of the museum, and whenever the possibility of terminating the employment of the director arises, to ensure that any such action is taken only in accordance with appropriate procedures under the legal or other constitutional arrangements and policies of the museum, and that any such staff changes are made in a professional and ethical manner, and in accordance with what is judged to be the best interests of the museum, rather than any personal or external factor or prejudice. It should also ensure that the same principles are applied in relation to any appointment, promotion, dismissal or demotion of the personnel of the museum by the director or any other senior member of staff with staffing responsibilities.

The governing body should recognize the diverse nature of the museum profession, and the wide range of specializations that it now encompasses, including conservator/restorers, scientists, museum education service personnel, registrars and computer specialists, security service managers, etc. It should ensure that the museum both makes appropriate use of such specialists where required and that such specialized personnel are properly recognized as full members of the professional staff in all respects.

Members of the museum profession require appropriate academic, technical and professional training in order to fulfil their important role in relation to the operation of the museum and the care for the heritage, and the governing body should recognize the need for, and value of, a properly qualified and trained staff, and offer adequate opportunities for further training and re-training in order to maintain an adequate and effective workforce.

A governing body should never require a member of the museum staff to act in a way that could reasonably be judged to conflict with the provisions of this *Code of Ethics*, or any national law or national code of professional ethics.

The Director or other chief professional officer of a museum should be directly responsible to, and have direct access to, the governing body in which trusteeship of the collections is vested.

2.6. *Educational and Community Role of the Museum*

By definition a museum is an institution in the service of society and of its development, and is generally open to the public (even though this may be a restricted public in the case of certain very specialized museums, such as certain academic or medical museums, for example).

The museum should take every opportunity to develop its role as an educational resource used by all sections of the population or specialized groups that the museum is intended to serve. Where appropriate in relation to the museum's programme and responsibilities, specialist staff with training and skills in museum education are likely to be required for this purpose.

The museum has an important duty to attract new and wider audiences within all levels of the community, locality or group that the museum aims to serve, and should offer both the general community and specific individuals and groups within it opportunities to become actively involved in the museum and to support its aims and policies.

2.7. *Public Access*

The general public (or specialized group served, in the case of museums with a limited public role), should have access to the displays during reasonable hours and for regular periods. The museum should also offer the public reasonable access to members of staff by appointment or other arrangement, and full access to information about the collections, subject to any necessary restrictions for reasons of confidentiality or security as discussed in para. 7.3 below.

2.8. *Displays, Exhibitions and Special Activities*

Subject to the primary duty of the museum to preserve unimpaired for the future the significant material that comprises the museum collections, it is the responsibility of the museum to use the collections for the creation and dissemination of new knowledge, through research, educational work, permanent displays, temporary exhibitions and other special activities. These should be in accordance with the stated policy and educational purpose of the museum, and should not compromise either the quality or the proper care of the collections. The museum should seek to ensure that information in displays and exhibitions is honest and objective and does not perpetuate myths or stereotypes.

2.9. *Commercial Support and Sponsorship*

Where it is the policy of the museum to seek and accept financial or other support from commercial or industrial organizations, or from other outside sources, great care is needed to define clearly the agreed relationship between the museum and the sponsor. Commercial support and sponsorship may involve ethical problems and the museum must ensure that the standards and objectives of the museum are not compromised by such a relationship.

2.10. *Museum Shops and Commercial Activities*

Museum Shops and any other commercial activities of the museum, and any publicity relating to these, should be in accordance with a clear policy, should be relevant to the collections and the basic educational purpose of the museum, and must not compromise the quality of those collections. In the case of the manufacture and sale of replicas, reproductions or other commercial items adapted from an object in a museum's collection, all aspects of the commercial venture must be carried out in a manner that will not discredit either the integrity of the museum or the intrinsic value of the original object. Great care must be taken to identify permanently such objects for what they are, and to ensure accuracy and high quality in their manufacture. All items offered for sale should represent good value for money and should comply with all relevant national legislation.

2.11. *Legal Obligations*

It is an important responsibility of each governing body to ensure that the museum complies fully with all legal obligations, whether in relation to national, regional or local law, international law or treaty obligations, and to any legally binding trusts or conditions relating to any aspect of the museum collections or facilities.

3. Acquisitions to Museum Collections

3.1. *Collecting Policies*

Each museum authority should adopt and publish a written statement of its collecting policy. This policy should be reviewed from time to time, and at least once every five years. Objects acquired should be relevant to the purpose and activities of the museum, and be accompanied by evidence of a valid legal title. Any conditions or limitations relating to an acquisition should be clearly described in an instrument of conveyance or other written documentation. Museums should not, except in very exceptional circumstances, acquire material that the museum is unlikely to be able to catalogue, conserve, store or exhibit, as appropriate, in a proper manner. Acquisitions outside the current stated policy of the museum should only be made in very exceptional circumstances, and then only after proper consideration by the governing body of the museum itself, having regard to the interests of the objects under consideration, the national or other cultural heritage and the special interests of other museums.

3.2. *Acquisition of Illicit Material*

The illicit trade in objects destined for public and private collections encourages the destruction of historic sites, local ethnic cultures, theft at both national and international levels, places at risk endangered species of flora and fauna, and contravenes the spirit of national and international patrimony. Museums should recognize the relationship between the marketplace and the initial and often destructive taking of an object for the commercial market, and must recognize that it is highly unethical for a museum to support in any way, whether directly or indirectly, that illicit market.

A museum should not acquire, whether by purchase, gift, bequest or exchange, any object unless the governing body and responsible officer are satisfied that the museum can acquire a valid title to the specimen or object in question and that in particular it has not been acquired in, or exported from, its country of origin and/or any intermediate country in which it may have been legally owned (including the museum's own country), in violation of that country's laws.

So far as biological and geological material is concerned, a museum should not acquire by any direct or indirect means any specimen that has been collected, sold or otherwise transferred in contravention of any national or international wildlife protection or natural history conservation law or treaty of the museum's own country or any other country except with the express consent of an appropriate outside legal or governmental authority.

So far as excavated material is concerned, in addition to the safeguards set out above, the museum should not acquire by purchase objects in any case where the governing body or responsible officer has reasonable cause to believe that their recovery involved the recent unscientific or intentional destruction or damage of ancient monuments or archaeological sites, or involved a failure to disclose the finds to the owner or occupier of the land, or to the proper legal or governmental authorities.

If appropriate and feasible, the same tests as are outlined in the above four paragraphs should be applied in determining whether or not to accept loans for exhibition or other purposes.

3.3. *Field Study and Collecting*

Museums should assume a position of leadership in the effort to halt the continuing degradation of the world's natural history, archaeological, ethnographic, historic and artistic resources. Each museum should develop policies that allow it to conduct its activities within appropriate national and international laws and treaty obligations, and with a reasonable certainty that its approach is consistent with the spirit and intent of both national and international efforts to protect and enhance the cultural heritage.

Field exploration, collecting and excavation by museum workers present ethical problems that are both complex and critical. All planning for field

244

studies and field collecting must be preceded by investigation, disclosure and consultation with both the proper authorities and any interested museums or academic institutions in the country or area of the proposed study sufficient to ascertain if the proposed activity is both legal and justifiable on academic and scientific grounds. Any field programme must be executed in such a way that all participants act legally and responsibly in acquiring specimens and data, and that they discourage by all practical means unethical, illegal and destructive practices.

3.4. Co-operation between Museums in Collecting Policies

Each museum should recognize the need for co-operation and consultation between all museums with similar or overlapping interests and collecting policies, and should seek to consult with such other institutions both on specific acquisitions where a conflict of interest is thought possible and, more generally, on defining areas of specialization. Museums should respect the boundaries of the recognized collecting areas of other museums and should avoid acquiring material with special local connections or of special local interest from the collecting area of another museum without due notification of intent.

3.5. Conditional Acquisitions and other Special Factors

Gifts, bequests and loans should only be accepted if they conform to the stated collecting and exhibition policies of the museum. Offers that are subject to special conditions may have to be rejected if the conditions proposed are judged to be contrary to the long-term interests of the museum and its public.

3.6. Loans to Museums

Both individual loans of objects and the mounting or borrowing of loan exhibitions can have an important role in enhancing the interest and quality of a museum and its services. However, the ethical principles outlined in paras. 3.1 to 3.5 above must apply to the consideration of proposed loans and loan exhibitions as to the acceptance or rejection of items offered to the permanent collections: loans should not be accepted nor exhibitions mounted if they do not have a valid educational, scientific or academic purpose.

3.7. Conflicts of Interest

The collecting policy or regulations of the museum should include provisions to ensure that no person involved in the policy or management of the museum, such as a trustee or other member of a governing body, or a member of the museum staff, may compete with the museum for objects or may take advantage of privileged information received because of his or her position, and that should a conflict of interest develop between the needs of the individual and the museum, those of the museum will prevail. Special care is also required in considering any offer of an item either for sale or as a tax-benefit gift, from members of governing bodies, members of staff, or the families or close associates of these.

4. Disposal of Collections

4.1. General Presumption of Permanence of Collections

By definition one of the key functions of almost every kind of museum is to acquire objects and keep them for posterity. Consequently there must always be a strong presumption against the disposal of specimens to which a museum has assumed formal title. Any form of disposal, whether by donation, exchange, sale or destruction requires the exercise of a high order of curatorial judgement and should be approved by the governing body only after full expert and legal advice has been taken.

Special considerations may apply in the case of certain kinds of specialized institutions such as "living" or "working" museums, and some teaching and other educational museums, together with museums and other institutions displaying living specimens, such as botanical and zoological gardens and aquaria, which may find it necessary to regard at least part of their collections as "fungible" (i.e. replaceable and renewable). However, even here there is a clear ethical obligation to ensure that the activities of the institution are not detrimental to the long-term survival of examples of the material studied, displayed or used.

4.2. Legal or other Powers of Disposal

The laws relating to the protection and permanence of museum collections, and to the power of museums to dispose of items from their collection vary greatly from country to country, and often from one museum to another within the same country. In some cases no disposals of any kind are permitted, except in the case of items that have been seriously damaged by natural or accidental deterioration. Elsewhere, there may be no explicit restriction on disposals under general law.

Where the museum has legal powers permitting disposals, or has acquired objects subject to conditions of disposal, the legal or other requirements and procedures must be fully complied with. Even where legal powers of disposal exist, a museum may not be completely free to dispose of items acquired: where financial assistance has been obtained from an outside source (e.g. public or private grants, donations from a Friends of the Museum organization, or private benefactor), disposal would normally require the consent of all parties who had contributed to the original purchase.

Where the original acquisition was subject to mandatory restrictions these must be observed unless it can be clearly shown that adherence to such restrictions is impossible or substantially detrimental to the institution. Even in these circumstances the museum can only be relieved from such restrictions through appropriate legal procedures.

4.3. De-accessioning Policies and Procedures

Where a museum has the necessary legal powers to dispose of an object the decision to sell or otherwise dispose of material from the collections should only be taken after due consideration, and such material should be offered first, by exchange, gift or private treaty sale, to other museums before sale by public auction or other means is considered. A decision to dispose of a specimen or work of art, whether by exchange, sale or destruction (in the case of an item too badly damaged or deteriorated to be restorable) should be the responsibility of the governing body of the museum, not of the curator of the collection concerned acting alone. Full records should be kept of all such decisions and the objects involved, and proper arrangements made for the preservation and/or transfer, as appropriate, of the documentation relating to the object concerned, including photographic records where practicable.

Neither members of staff, nor members of the governing bodies, or members of their families or close associates, should ever be permitted to purchase objects that have been de-accessioned from a collection. Similarly, no such person should be permitted to appropriate in any other way items from the museum collections, even temporarily, to any personal collection or for any kind of personal use.

4.4. Return and Restitution of Cultural Property

If a museum should come into possession of an object that can be demonstrated to have been exported or otherwise transferred in violation of the principles of the Unesco *Convention on the Means of Prohibiting and Preventing the Illicit Import, Export and Transfer of Ownership of Cultural Property* (1970) and the country of origin seeks its return and demonstrates that it is part of the country's cultural heritage, the museum should, if legally free to do so, take responsible steps to co-operate in the return of the object to the country of origin.

In the case of requests for the return of cultural property to the country of origin, museums should be prepared to initiate dialogues with an open-minded attitude on the basis of scientific and professional principles (in preference to action at a governmental or political level). The possibility of developing bi-lateral or multilateral co-operation schemes to assist museums in countries which are considered to have lost a significant part of their cultural heritage in the development of adequate museums and museum resources should be explored.

Museums should also respect fully the terms of the *Convention for the Protection of Cultural Property in the Event of Armed Conflict* (The Hague Convention, 1954), and in support of this *Convention*, should in particular abstain from purchasing or otherwise appropriating or acquiring cultural objects from any occupied country, as these will in most cases have been illegally exported or illicitly removed.

4.5. Income from Disposal of Collections

Any moneys received by a governing body from the disposal of specimens or works of art should be applied solely for the purchase of additions to the museum collections.

III. Professional Conduct

5. General Principles

5.1. *Ethical Obligations of Members of the Museum Profession*

Employment by a museum, whether publicly or privately supported, is a public trust involving great responsibility. In all activities museum employees must act with integrity and in accordance with the most stringent ethical principles as well as the highest standards of objectivity.

An essential element of membership of a profession is the implication of both rights and obligations. Although the conduct of a professional in any area is ordinarily regulated by the basic rules of moral behaviour which govern human relationships, every occupation involves standards, as well as particular duties, responsibilities and opportunities that from time to time create the need for a statement of guiding principles. The museum professional should understand two guiding principles: first, that museums are the object of a public trust whose value to the community is in direct proportion to the quality of service rendered and, secondly, that intellectual ability and professional knowledge are not, in themselves, sufficient, but must be inspired by a high standard of ethical conduct.

The Director and other professional staff owe their primary professional and academic allegiance to their museum and should at all times act in accordance with the approved policies of the museum. The Director or other principal museum officer should be aware of, and bring to the notice of the governing body of the museum whenever appropriate, the terms of the ICOM *Code of Professional Ethics* and of any relevant national or regional Codes or policy statements on Museum Ethics, and should urge the governing body to comply with these. Members of the museum profession should also comply fully with the ICOM *Code* and any other Codes or statements on Museum Ethics whenever exercising the functions of the governing body under delegated powers.

5.2. *Personal Conduct*

Loyalty to colleagues and to the employing museum is an important professional responsibility, but the ultimate loyalty must be to fundamental ethical principles and to the profession as a whole.

Applicants for any professional post should divulge frankly and in confidence all information relevant to the consideration of their applications, and if appointed should recognize that museum work is normally regarded as a full-time vocation. Even where the terms of employment do not prohibit outside employment or business interests, the Director and other senior staff should not undertake other paid employment or accept outside commissions without the express consent of the governing body of the museum. In tendering resignations from their posts, members of the professional staff, and above all the Director, should consider carefully the needs of the museum at the time. A professional person, having recently accepted a new appointment, should consider seriously their professional commitment to their present post before applying for a new post elsewhere.

5.3. *Private Interests*

While every member of any profession is entitled to a measure of personal independence, consistent with professional and staff responsibilities, in the eyes of the public no private business or professional interest of a member of the museum profession can be wholly separated from that of the professional's institution or other official affiliation, despite disclaimers that may be offered. Any museum-related activity by the individual may reflect on the institution or be attributed to it. The professional must be concerned not only with the true personal motivations and interests, but also with the way in which such actions might be construed by the outside observer. Museum employees and others in a close relationship with them must not accept gifts, favours, loans or other dispensations or things of value that may be offered to them in connection with their duties for the museum (see also para. 8.4 below).

6. Personal Responsibility to the Collections

6.1. *Acquisitions to Museum Collections*

The Director and professional staff should take all possible steps to ensure that a written collecting policy is adopted by the governing body of the museum, and is thereafter reviewed and revised as appropriate at regular intervals. This policy, as formally adopted and revised by the governing body, should form the basis of all professional decisions and recommendations in relation to acquisitions.

Negotiations concerning the acquisition of museum items from members of the general public must be conducted with scrupulous fairness to the seller or donor. No object should be deliberately or misleadingly identified or valued, to the benefit of the museum and to the detriment of the donor, owner or previous owners, in order to acquire it for the museum collections nor should be taken nor retained on loan with the deliberate intention of improperly procuring it for the collections.

6.2. *Care of Collections*

It is an important professional responsibility to ensure that all items accepted temporarily or permanently by the museum are properly and fully documented to facilitate provenance, identification, condition and treatment. All objects accepted by the museum should be properly conserved, protected, and maintained.

Careful attention should be paid to the means of ensuring the best possible security as a protection against theft in display, working or storage areas, against accidental damage when handling objects, and against damage or theft in transit. Where it is the national or local policy to use commercial insurance arrangements, the staff should ensure that the insurance cover is adequate, especially for objects in transit and loan items, or other objects, which are not owned by the museum but which are its current responsibility.

Members of the museum profession should not delegate important curatorial, conservation, or other professional responsibilities to persons who lack the appropriate knowledge and skill, or who are inadequately supervised, in the case of trainees or approved volunteers, where such persons are allowed to assist in the care of the collections. There is also a clear duty to consult professional colleagues within or outside the museum if at any time the expertise available in a particular museum or department is insufficient to ensure the welfare of items in the collections under its care.

6.3. *Conservation and Restoration of Collections*

One of the essential ethical obligations of each member of the museum profession is to ensure the proper care and conservation of both existing and newly-acquired collections and individual items for which the member of the profession and the employing institutions are responsible, and to ensure that as far as is reasonable the collections are passed on to future generations in as good and safe a condition as practicable having regard to current knowledge and resources.

In attempting to achieve this high ideal, special attention should be paid to the growing body of knowledge about preventative conservation methods and techniques, including the provision of suitable environmental protection against the known natural or artificial causes of deterioration of museum specimens and works of art.

There are often difficult decisions to be made in relation to the degree of replacement or restoration of lost or damaged parts of a specimen or work of art that may be ethically acceptable in particular circumstances.

Such decisions call for proper co-operation between all with a specialized responsibility for the obect, including both the curator and the conservator or restorer, and should not be decided unilaterally by one or the other acting alone.

The ethical issues involved in conservation and restoration work of many kinds are a major study in themselves, and those with special responsibilities in this area, whether as director, curator, conservator or restorer, have an important responsibility to ensure that they are familiar with these ethical issues, and with appropriate professional opinion, as expressed in some detailed ethical statements and codes produced by the conservator/restorer professional bodies.[1]

6.4. *Documentation of Collections*

The proper recording and documentation of both new acquisitions and existing collections in accordance with appropriate standards and the internal rules and conventions of the museum is a most important professional responsibility. It is particularly important that such documentation should include details of the source of each object and the conditions of acceptance of it by the museum. In addition specimen data should be kept in a secure environment and be supported by adequate systems providing easy retrieval of the data by both the staff and by other bona fide users.

6.5. *De-accessioning and Disposals from the Collections*

No item from the collections of a museum should be disposed of except in accordance with the ethical principles summarized in the Institutional Ethics section of this *Code*, paras. 4.1 to 4.4 above, and the detailed rules and procedures applying in the museum in question.

6.6. *Welfare of Live Animals*

Where museums and related institutions maintain for exhibition or research purposes live populations of animals, the health and well-being of any such creatures must be a foremost ethical consideration. It is essential that a veterinary surgeon be available for advice and for regular inspection of the animals and their living conditions. The museum should prepare a safety code for the protection of staff and visitors which has been approved by an expert in the veterinary field, and all staff must follow it in detail.

6.7. *Human Remains and Material of Ritual Significance*

Where a museum maintains and/or is developing collections of human remains and sacred objects these should be securely housed and carefully maintained as archival collections in scholarly institutions, and should always be available to qualified researchers and educators, but not to the morbidly curious. Research on such objects and their housing and care must be accomplished in a manner acceptable not only to fellow professionals but to those of various beliefs, including in particular members of the community, ethnic or religious groups concerned. Although it is occasionally necessary to use human remains and other sensitive material in interpretative exhibits, this must be done with tact and with respect for the feelings for human dignity held by all peoples.

6.8. *Private Collections*

The acquiring, collecting and owning of objects of a kind collected by a museum by a member of the museum profession for a personal collection may not in itself be unethical, and may be regarded as a valuable way of enhancing professional knowledge and judgement. However, serious dangers are implicit when members of the profession collect for themselves privately objects similar to those which they and others collect for their museums. In particular, no member of the museum profession should compete with their institution either in the acquisition of objects or in any personal collecting activity. Extreme care must be taken to ensure that no conflict of interest arises.

In some countries and many individual museums, members of the museum profession are not permitted to have private collections of any kind, and such rules must be respected. Even where there are no such restrictions, on appointment, a member of the museum profession with a private collection should provide the governing body with a description of it, and a statement of the collecting policy being pursued, and any consequent agreement between the curator and the governing body concerning the private collection must be scrupulously kept. (See also para. 8.4 below.)

251

7. Personal Responsibility to the Public

7.1. *Upholding Professional Standards*

In the interests of the public as well as the profession, members of the museum profession should observe accepted standards and laws, uphold the dignity and honour of their profession and accept its self-imposed disciplines. They should do their part to safeguard the public against illegal or unethical professional conduct, and should use appropriate opportunities to inform and educate the public in the aims, purposes and aspirations of the profession in order to develop a better public understanding of the purposes and responsibilities of museums and of the profession.

7.2. *Relations with the General Public*

Members of the museum profession should deal with the public efficiently and courteously at all times, and should in particular deal promptly with all correspondence and enquiries. Subject to the requirements of confidentiality in a particular case, they should share their expertise in all professional fields in dealing with enquiries, subject to due acknowledgement, from both the general public and specialist enquirers, allowing bona fide researchers properly controlled but, so far as possible, full access to any material or documentation in their care, even when this is the subject of personal research or special field of interest.

7.3. *Confidentiality*

Members of the museum profession must protect all confidential information relating to the source of material owned by or loaned to the museum, as well as information concerning the security arrangements of the museum, or the security arrangements of private collections or any place visited in the course of official duties. Confidentiality must also be respected in relation to any item brought to the museum for identification and, without specific authority from the owner, information on such an item should not be passed to another museum, to a dealer, or to any other person (subject to any legal obligation to assist the police or other proper authorities in investigating possible stolen or illicitly acquired or transferred property).

There is a special responsibility to respect the personal confidences contained in oral history or other personal material. Investigators using recording devices such as cameras or tape recorders or the technique of oral interviewing should take special care to protect their data, and persons investigated, photographed or interviewed should have the right to remain anonymous if they so choose. This right should be respected where it has been specifically promised. Where there is no clear understanding to the contrary, the primary responsibility of the investigator is to ensure that no information is revealed that might harm the informant or his or her community. Subjects under study should understand the capacities of cameras, tape recorders and other machines used, and should be free to accept or reject their use.

8. Personal Responsibility to Colleagues and the Profession

8.1. *Professional Relationships*

Relationships between members of the museum profession should always be courteous, both in public and in private. Differences of opinion should not be expressed in a personalized fashion. Notwithstanding this general rule, members of the profession may properly object to proposals or practices which may have a damaging effect on a museum or museums, or the profession.

8.2. *Professional Co-operation*

Members of the museum profession have an obligation, subject to due acknowledgement, to share their knowledge and experience with their colleagues and with scholars and students in relevant fields. They should show their appreciation and respect to those from whom they have learned and should present without thought of personal gain such advancements in techniques and experience which may be of benefit to others.

The training of personnel in the specialized activities involved in museum work is of great importance in the development of the profession and all should accept responsibility, where appropriate, in the training of colleagues. Members of the profession who in their official appointment have under their direction junior staff, trainees, students and assistants undertaking formal or informal professional training, should give these the benefit of their experience and knowledge, and should also treat them with the consideration and respect customary among members of the profession.

Members of the profession form working relationships in the course of their duties with numerous other people, both professional and otherwise, within and outside the museum in which they are employed. They are expected to conduct these relationships with courtesy and fair-mindedness and to render their professional services to others efficiently and at a high standard.

8.3. *Dealing*

No member of the museum profession should participate in any dealing (buying or selling for profit), in objects similar or related to the objects collected by the employing museum. Dealing by museum employees at any level of responsibility in objects that are collected by any other museum can also present serious problems even if there is no risk of direct conflict with the employing museum, and should be permitted only if, after full disclosure and review by the governing body of the employing museum or designated senior officer, explicit permission is granted, with or without conditions.

Article 14 of the ICOM *Statutes* provides that in no circumstance shall individual or institutional membership be accorded to anyone who, for reasons of commercial profit, buys or sells cultural property.

8.4. *Other Potential Conflicts of Interest*

Generally, members of the museum profession should refrain from all acts or activities which may be construed as a conflict of interest. Museum professionals by virtue of their knowledge, experience, and contacts are frequently offered opportunities, such as advisory and consultancy services, teaching, writing and broadcasting opportunities, or requests for valuations, in a personal capacity. Even where the national law and the individual's conditions of employment permit such activities, these may appear in the eyes of colleagues, the employing authority, or the general public, to create a conflict of interest. In such situations all legal and employment contract conditions must be scrupulously followed, and in the event of any potential conflict arising or being suggested, the matter should be reported immediately to an appropriate superior officer or the museum governing body, and steps must be taken to eliminate the potential conflict of interest.

Even where the conditions of employment permit any kind of outside activity, and there appears to be no risk of any conflict of interest, great care should be taken to ensure that such outside interests do not interfere in any way with the proper discharge of official duties and responsibilities.

8.5. *Authentication, Valuation and Illicit Material*

Members of the museum profession are encouraged to share their professional knowledge and expertise with both professional colleagues and the general public (see para. 7.2 above).

However, written certificates of authenticity or valuation (appraisals) should not be given, and opinions on the monetary value of objects should only be given on official request from other museums or competent legal, governmental or other responsible public authorities.

Members of the museum profession should not identify or otherwise authenticate objects where they have reason to believe or suspect that these have been illegally or illicitly acquired, transferred, imported or exported.

They should recognize that it is highly unethical for museums or the museum profession to support either directly or indirectly the illicit trade in cultural or natural objects (see para. 3.2 above), and under no circumstances should they act in a way that could be regarded as benefiting such illicit trade in any way, directly or indirectly. Where there is reason to believe or suspect illicit or illegal transfer, import or export, the competent authorities should be notified.

8.6. *Unprofessional Conduct*

Every member of the museum profession should be conversant with both any national or local laws, and any conditions of employment, concerning corrupt practices, and should at all times avoid situations which could rightly or wrongly be construed as corrupt or improper conduct of any kind. In particular no museum official should accept any gift, hospitality, or any form of reward from any dealer, auctioneer or other person as an improper inducement in respect of the purchase or disposal of museum items.

254

Also, in order to avoid any suspicion of corruption, a museum professional should not recommend any particular dealer, auctioneer or other person to a member of the public, nor should the official accept any "special price" or discount for personal purchases from any dealer with whom either the professional or employing museum has a professional relationship.

Question from the field: thirty-seven

Question: What are the ethical concerns about exhibiting objects as "original" if they are copies, but the originals no longer exist?

Response: A first response to this question is to state that copies of objects should not be exhibited as originals. If copies (reproductions) are included in an exhibition, they are labeled accordingly. Ethical practice dictates that the information provided the viewer be honest.

> "The museum should seek to ensure that information in displays and exhibitions is honest and objective and does not perpetuate myths or stereotypes."
>
> ICOM, *Code of Professional Ethics*, II. "Institutional Ethics," paragraph 2.8, p. 26.

However the idea of "copies" is being more closely scrutinized in recent times. The purists of a few years ago labeled everything not made by the right person or persons, at the right place and time, and under the right circumstances as a copy or forgery. The idea of the cultural continuum is being explored to determine the importance and meaning of objects made "in the style" of earlier works. Many objects related to social custom are constantly in change representing both the historic perspective and current influence. An example is found in the festival masks and costumes of the Americas. Traditional themes are still portrayed but new ideas and designs are intermingled with historic images. The resulting objects are not copies but the current manifestations of a tradition in transition.

In practice it is ethically correct to label a reproduction or representation of a particular object in a manner to note its origin. A reproduction or representation is still a copy even if the original is lost or destroyed.

Question from the field: thirty-eight

Question: The ICOM *Code of Professional Ethics* states that it is highly unethical for museums to acquire illicit material. What do you do when the primary sources for collection material are the workmen, farmers, and perhaps "grave robbers" who offer the object for sale to a museum? The fact that no national laws prevent activities of this sort further compounds this situation.

255

Response: The question is one that has an impact on many countries, and to respond to the issue ICOM provides a clear statement. However, almost every country has to address the circumstance of unauthorized archaeological field activity. In the United States, as in many parts of the world, it is legal for landowners to excavate and keep objects found on their property. Farmers or workmen often bring major archaeological finds to the attention of museums. The "opportunistic" or accidental find is a situation that will continue to exist and one for which a museum must establish policy. A purchase from this source is far less unethical than one that encourages and rewards intentional destruction of known sites or monuments.

The museum must question its role as a consumer of dubious material. Objects gained "over the counter" come with no indisputable title of ownership, no provenance, and no scientific data. The object has only minimal research value.

Museums recognize the negative impact of unrestricted excavation of archaeological sites and the destruction of ancient monuments. It is the museum community's responsibility to stimulate the passage of strict national laws to address these issues. Major national treasures and unknown amounts of vital information about preceding generations have already been lost to the market place. Unless the museum community works to prevent this looting, it will continue. The illicit trafficking in cultural materials compounds the difficulties of discovering and retrieving stolen property.

> "the museum should not acquire by purchase objects in any case where the governing body or responsible officer has reasonable cause to believe that their recovery involved the recent unscientific or intentional destruction or damage of ancient monuments or archaeological sites, or involved a failure to disclose the finds to the owner or occupier of the land, or to the proper legal or governmental authorities."
>
> ICOM, *Code of Professional Ethics*, section 3. "Acquisitions to Museum Collections," paragraph 3.2, p. 27.

□   □   □   □   □

Question from the field: thirty-nine

Question: The ICOM *Code of Professional Ethics* is a good document for institutions, but it fails to take into consideration a number of things most museum workers have to deal with every day. It is easy to say you should do something a certain way, but friends, social custom, and even job security can be a very strong force to allow things to happen in "different" ways. Under the right set of circumstances almost anything can be rationalized as being acceptable. What should be done to (1) establish a proper code of ethics for individual institutions, and (2) guide and protect the workers in museums?

Response: First, it is important to realize that no code of ethics can make anyone do anything. It must be an agreed course of action. Second, by its nature, the ICOM *Code of Professional Ethics* must be very broad to cover museums and museum-related activities worldwide. Each national committee should formulate a national code of ethics based on the policy defined by ICOM. Subsequently, each museum then establishes a code of ethics for their particular institution to reflect the ethical norms set forth by both ICOM and their national committee. In this way the institutional code of ethics becomes more personalized. It can be written in terms easily understood by the workers in a particular museum.

An institutional code of ethics should be workable, that is it should meet the needs of the institution. It should be flexible enough to be changed if the need arises, and inclusive enough to cover all the activities and workforce of the institution, including volunteers, board members, as well as staff. It must be simple enough to understand without interpretation.

The following is an example of some of the things you may wish to include in an institutional code of ethics to address personnel activities:

A guide to ethical practices for museum personnel

1. Museum personnel should act in a responsible manner, both legally and ethically, in all matters relating to the operation of the museum and fully endorse the responsibilities and duties incumbent upon a position of public trust.

2. Museum personnel should address, with equity, the social and cultural needs of all members of the museum's constituency, and endeavor to maintain a positive presence in the community.

3. Museum personnel should acquire, maintain, study, document, and provide public access through exhibitions of objects appropriate to the museum's defined mission and provide for all acquired objects equally.

4. Museum personnel should not derive personal benefit in any way from museum-related duties, activities, and/or information gained in the execution of museum work nor should any action be knowingly allowed that will give the appearance of impropriety in dealing with museum-related interests.

5. Museum personnel should exercise extreme care in the selection of objects to be added to the museum's collections including: ethical status, legality, relativity to mission, availability, needs, conditions, donor requirements, and the ability of the museum to properly preserve and utilize the objects.

6. Museum personnel should not covet or acquire objects significant to the cultural heritage of other lands or people, and should give extreme attention to those objects already in the museum's collection that may have religious or sacred meaning to others.

7. Museum personnel should not, excepting for special circumstances, deaccession objects and never in a manner that will bring question or discredit to the museum regarding the care and maintenance of the collections.

8. Museum personnel should place honesty, integrity, and social consciousness foremost in defining the education, exhibition, interpretation, and special program content of the museum, being certain that no intentionally hurtful or culturally demeaning attitudes or concepts are fostered.

257

9. Museum personnel should provide both opportunities and support for the intellectual growth and education of all members of the museum's staff including board members, curators, technical and support personnel, and volunteers.

10. Museum personnel should act in a supportive manner to the world community of museums by providing loans, information, technical assistance, or other aid as appropriate to the means and mission of the museum, and by endorsing and sustaining a comprehensive code of professional ethics.

Notes

1.   International Council of Museums (1986) "The Conservator–Restorer: A Definition of the Profession," *ICOM News*, Vol. 39, No. 1, pp. 5–6.

Suggested reading

Burcaw, G. E. (1975) *Introduction to Museum Work*, 2nd edn 1983, Nashville, Tenn.: American Association for State and Local History.

International Council of Museums (1990) *Statutes*, Paris: ICOM.

Kavanagh, G. (ed.) (1991) *The Museums Profession*, Leicester: Leicester University Press.

Malaro, M. (1985) *A Legal Primer on Managing Museum Collections*, 2nd edn 1987, Washington, DC: Smithsonian Institution Press.

Thompson, J. M. A. (ed.) (1984) *Manual of Curatorship, A Guide to Museum Practice*, 2nd edn 1992, London: Butterworth & Co.

Section V
Support material

18

Forms

Throughout the ICOM *Code of Professional Ethics* reference is made to establishing policies and procedure for museum-related activities. Records maintenance is a part of the procedural process and an integral element of collection care and utilization. Any object, work of art, scientific specimen, or historic artifact entering the museum must be identified, documented, and recorded in an accurate and permanent manner. The person doing the recording may vary from institution to institution or within a particular museum over a period of years. However, the implements of recording objects should remain as consistent as possible within the individual institution. Standardized forms are a reasonable and efficient means of maintaining records.

To aid in this process, forms should be developed to identify, document, and record information about objects. The forms should be inclusive enough to allow the necessary descriptive information for all elements of the collection. Forms should be designed to allow easy access to the information and a convenient method of entry.

Almost every museum has developed its own unique set of forms that address both real and anticipated needs. The following forms are for reference. They are drawn from a variety of sources and offered as examples of forms that have been developed to meet the needs of the institutions they represent.

Deed of Gift to SAMPLE FORM

MUSEO DE COMERCIO

_____
NAME OF DONOR

_____
ADDRESS

_____
CITY   STATE

hereafter referred to as the "Owner" of the property described below, hereby gives, transfers, assigns, and delivers all of the Owner's rights, titles, and interests in and to the property described below, including any reproduction right that the Owner may possess in and to said property to the Museo de Comercio as an unrestricted gift.

Dated this _____ day of _____ , 19 _____

_____   _____
(Signature of donor)   (Signature of donor)

Description of property:

The Museo de Comercio hereby accepts the above property under the conditions specified above.

Dated this _____ day of _____ , 19 _____

MUSEO DE COMERCIO

By _____

Please sign both copies of the Deed of Gift form and return to the Museo de Comercio in the enclosed envelope. You will receive a formal acknowledgment and your copy of the Deed of Gift signed by the Director of the Museum.

Revised 2/93

Figure 18.1 Deed of gift

```
┌─────────────────────────────────┐
│  MUSEO DEL CENTENARIO           │
│  1123 Loja, Ciudad, País        │
└─────────────────────────────────┘
```

Receipt No. _____

Date of Receipt _____

RECEIPT

The object(s) described below has (have) been received by the Museo del Centenario subject to the conditions printed on the back of this receipt.

From:

for

_____
                                        Registrar

Artist/ Maker	Description	Owner's Valuation

Remarks:

Revised 2/93

Figure 18.2 Object receipt form

SAMPLE FORM

Received from
MUSEO DEL CENTENARIO   RECEIPT
1123 Loja, Ciudad, País
in good condition unless otherwise noted

by: _____

on: _____ , the material itemized below:

Museum   Artist or
number   maker   Description

Remarks:

The Collection _____ Curator has been notified.

_____   _____
(date signed)   Registrar

_____   _____
(date signed)   Recipient (the person named above
Revised 12/92   or his/her authorized agent)

Figure 18.3 Object receipt form

OBJECT RECORD

MUSEO DE ARQUEOLOGIA

1. Artist/Maker

2. Name/title of work

3. Date: 4. Place of execution:

5. Medium/material

6. If a made/fabricated work list maker and location of duplicates:

7. Describe the process of making or locating this work/piece:

8. Note any special instructions for the installation, maintenance, or use of this object?

9. If appropriate, discuss/describe/define/explain the title/name of this object:

10. Describe documentation available on the source/social/symbolic/or popular reference of this object:

11. Note exceptional circumstances or incidents that relate to this object or its subsequent history:

REVISED 1/93

Figure 18.4 Object record form

SAMPLE FORM

MUSEO DE ARTE

Daily report of items received   Date: _____

       TO: Registrar

Received from	Number or mark	Title, name, artist, or maker Number of items or boxes	Remarks

Signed: _____

Revised 1/93

Figure 18.5 Object report form

SAMPLE FORM

MUSEO DE ORO
WORK SHEET

DATE: _____

ACCESSION NO.: _____ CATALOG NO.: _____

NATURE OF ACCESSION: _____

NAME AND ADDRESS OF SOURCE: _____

_____

DATE COLLECTED BY DONOR, ETC.: _____

_____

_____

DESCRIPTION: _____

_____

_____

_____

_____

_____

_____

_____

_____

_____

CONDITION: _____

_____

REFERENCE: _____

_____

DIMENSIONS: _____

REPAIR, FUMIGATION, ETC: _____

ACCOMPANYING MATERIALS: _____

_____

ESTIMATED VALUE & APPRAISER: _____

OBJECT CARD: __ DONOR CARD: __ LOCATION CARD: __ PHOTO: ___

MARKED: _____ NEGATIVE: _____ GIFT ACK.: _____ RECEIPT: _____

REVISED 4/92   REGISTRAR: _____

Figure 18.6 Accession worksheet

Catalog No. _____   Accession No. _____

MUSEUM OF CULTURAL HERITAGE   SAMPLE
FORM
ACCESSION INFORMATION SHEET

Received from:_____ Date: _____

Address: _____

_____

Description: _____

_____

_____

_____

_____

_____

_____

No. of Objects, Specimens , or Samples: _____

Estimated Value of Collection: _____

How Acquired:
- Gift ☐ _____
- Purchase ☐ _____
- Field Work ☐ _____
- Exchange ☐ _____
- Transfer ☐ _____

Condition:
- Good ☐ _____
- Fair ☐ _____
- Poor ☐ _____

History: _____

_____

_____

_____

_____

Photograph: ☐ Yes ☐ No   Negative Number: _____

Temporary Location: _____

Review: ☐ Registrar ☐ Curator ☐ Conservator ☐ Director

Signed: _____ Dated: _____

Figure 18.7 Accession information form

ACCESSION SHEET   SAMPLE FORM

Accession No. _____ Date _____ Previous No. (if any) _____

Catalog No. (to be added after cataloging)_____

Field catalog No._____ Date _____

Nature of accession (Gift, Purchase, Field Trip, Exchange, Other) _____
_____

Name and address of (Collector, Donor, Vendor, Other)_____
_____

Date of Acquisition (Collecting, Donation, Purchase, or Other)_____

Locality Collected or Purchased _____

Purchase Price _____ Estimated Value_____

Estimated Age_____

Brief Description and Identification (include: culture, country, linguistic group--technique of
manufacture, design, utility, etc.)   _____
_____
_____

Measurements (in cms.) _____

Location in Museum (on display, in the research collection, in laboratory, in collection storage,
etc.)_____

Condition on arrival_____ Date of repair, fumigation, etc. (directions of assembly
if dismantled) _____
_____

Identified by _____ Accessioned by _____

Cataloged by _____ Repaired by _____

History of Object _____
_____
_____

Accepted by _____

Documentary information and cross references

_____

_____

_____

_____   Photograph or drawing of object

Remarks _____

_____

_____

_____

Form Prepared by   _____

Figure 18.8 Accession form

DEPARTMENT
File or Accession No. ————————   Accession No. ————————

EL MUSEO DE COMERCIO
ACCESSION RECORD

SAMPLE FORM

————————
DATE OF RECEIPT

Received from ————————————————————————————

Address ————————————————————————————————

Description of Material ——————————————————————

————————————————————————————————————

————————————————————————————————————

————————————————————————————————————

————————————————————————————————————

Collector ———————————————————— No. of Objects ————

How Acquired	GIFT ☐ ————————		GOOD ☐
	PURCHASE ☐ Price $————————	Condition	FAIR ☐
	EXCHANGE ☐ ————————		POOR ☐
	TRANSFER ☐ ————————		

Loan received for:
EXAMINATION ☐
STUDY ☐
IDENTIFICATION ☐
EXHIBITION ☐
PURCHASE ☐
USE IN LECTURE ☐

Estimated value $ ————————
Source of funds for purchase

————————————————————

————————————————————

PLEASE SEND FORMAL
ACKNOWLEDGMENT ☐

Department Catalog No. ——————————————————————

Number and nature of object(s) given in exchange, or other information

————————————————————————————————————

————————————————————————————————————

————————————————————————————————————

————————————————————————————————————

Loan Returned on ———————————————— 19 ————

COPIES TO DONOR, CURATOR,
REGISTRAR, AND COLLECTIONS
MANAGER – IF FOR PURCHASE
ADDITIONAL COPY TO DIRECTOR
Revised 2/93

Signed ————————————————

Department of ————————————

————————————————————

Figure 18.9 Accession form

Musée du Patrimone
Rue de la Harpe   Accession No.

_____   _____   _____
    type of object   date   country of origin
description of object: _____

_____

vendor/donor: _____   received: _____

               _____   condition: _____

               _____   _____

price/value: _____

fund/source: _____   size: _____

authorization: _____   negative no. _____

               _____   photograph no. _____

Figure 18.10 Accession card

Note: The accession card identifies each object by the accession number and is filed numerically by the accession number. The information included on the accession card may vary according to the kind, type, and number of reference records used.

Catalog No.:	Object Type:	Sample **Catalog Card**	Object Common Name:
Origin:	Source:		Accession No.:
Date:	Description:		Photo No.:
Size:			Location:
Condition:			
	Notes:		
			Processed by:

Figure 18.11 Catalog card

Note: The catalog card is prepared by the curatorial department. A photograph of the object is dry mounted on the back of the card and the photograph number is recorded in the right column.

Object: _____ ID# | SAMPLE |

Country: _____ Material: _____

Date: _____ Artist/Maker: _____

Description: _____

_____

_____

_____

Dimensions: Tall: _____ Wide: _____ Deep: _____ Diameter: _____

Comments: _____

_____

_____

	Location
Source: _____	Room: _____
	Case: _____
_____	Shelf: _____

Form Revised 1/93

Figure 18.12 Object information card

	MUSEO DE ORO	Sample **Subject Card**

Object: Catalog No.:

Date: Photo.:   Neg.:   Accession No.:

Source:

Description: Dimensions:

Circa:

Cataloged By:

Reference:

Accompanying Materials:

Repair and Fumigation: Location:

Figure 18.13 Subject card

Note: One card is prepared for each accession from the information gathered on the worksheet. Location information is maintained in pencil so it can be changed if necessary.

MUSEO DE LA NACION

INGRESO DE BIENES CULTURALES

CODIGO

DE INGRESO:
DE ORIGEN:
OTROS:

POSEEDOR:

CODIGO: NOMBRE DEL POSEEDOR

APELLIDOS Y NOMBRE DEL REPRESENTANTE LEGAL

DIRECCION (Calle, No, Distrito, Provincia, Departamento, País)

OBSERVACIONES: TELEFONOS

SAMPLE FORM

BIEN CULTURAL:

CATEGORIA: MATERIAL:

CLASE: EPOCA:

CULTURA/ESTILO:

AUTOR:

TITULO:

TECNICA: FOTOS

REPRESENTACION:

ALTO: ANCHO: DIMETRO:

LARGO: PESO: ESPESOR:

ESTADO DE CONSERVACION:

ADQUISICION: NEGATIVOS:

SEGURO: Compañia: No. Póliza: Monto:

REGISTRO EN LUGAR DE ORIGEN	REGISTRO DE INGRESO AL MUSEO	REGISTRO CENTRO COMPUTO	DEVOLUCION
NOMBRE:	NOMBRE:	NOMBRE:	DEVOLUCION:
FECHA:	FECHA:	FECHA:	FECHA:

Figure 18.14 Receipt for cultural property form

MUSEUM OF FINE ARTS	SAMPLE
CONDITION REPORT	FORM

ACCESSION NUMBER _____ CATALOG NUMBER _____

ARTIST _____
           (LAST NAME,   FIRST NAME)

SIGNATURE/DATE ☐ YES ☐ NO WHERE _____

TITLE OF WORK _____

CLASS: ☐ PAINTING ☐ PRINT ☐ DRAWING ☐ SCULPTURE
                        (ED. ____)   (ED. ____)

MEDIUM: ☐ OIL   ☐ PENCIL   ☐ OTHER
        ☐ WATERCOLOR   ☐ INK   _____
        ☐ PASTEL   ☐ CHARCOAL   _____
        ☐ GOUACHE   ☐ BRONZE   _____

SUPPORT: ☐ CANVAS   ☐ PANEL
         ☐ BOARD   ☐ PAPER
         ☐ MASONITE ☐ OTHER _____

FRAMED: ☐ YES ☐ NO   BACKING _____

GLAZING: ☐ YES ☐ NO   TYPE: ☐ GLASS   ☐ PLEX

DIMENSIONS:

	FRAME	SCULPTURE
IMAGE		H _____
		W _____
H___	H___	L _____
		DIA. _____
W___		
	W ___	

COMMENTS: _____
_____
_____
_____

COMPILED BY: _____ DATE: _____ INSURANCE VALUE $ _____

Figure 18.15 Condition report form

MUSEUM OF FINE ARTS
Home Place, USA 00000

SAMPLE
FORM

attach photo here

**ARTIFACT ACTIVITY RECORD
DIVISION OF ART**

Accession Number: _____

Title: _____

Artist: _____

Date	Activity	Initialed by

Figure 18.16 Artifact activity record

INSTITUTO NACIONAL DE PATRIMONIO CULTURAL	DATE:		REGISTRATION NO.
	2-DIMENSIONAL		CODE NO.
	3-DIMENSIONAL		

PROJECT:

SAMPLE FORM

PHOTO

PHOTO

PHOTO DOCUMENTATION: _____ DATE:

Title: _____ Inscription: _____

Theme: _____ _____

_____ _____

Artist: _____ _____

Attributed to: _____ Material: _____

School: _____ _____

Studio: _____ Technique of Production: _____

Century or Date: _____ _____

Dimensions: Tall_____Wide _____ Thick_____ Diameter_____

State of Conservation: _____

_____

General Condition   Excellent ☐   Good ☐   Poor ☐

Figure 18.17 Object evaluation form

INSTITUTO NACIONAL DE PATRIMONIO CULTURAL	FECHA DE REGISTRO TECNICO	REGISTRO
DEPARTAMENTO NACIONAL DE INVENTARIO	INVENTARIO DE BIENES ARQUEOLOGICOS	CONTROL COLECCION

COLECCION	NOMBRE DEL PROPIETARIO	FIRMA Y.C.I.

REGIMEN DE PROPIEDAD:

PUBLICO		PRIVADA	
Estatal		Religioso	
Municipal		Particular	

LOCALIZACION:
Provincia: _____ Cantón: _____ Ciudad: _____
Parroquia: _____ Calle: _____ No: _____ Mz: _____
Sitio Geográfico:

BIEN CULTURAL:	MATERIA PRIMA:	FOTOGRAFIA:
FILIACION CULTURAL:	FASE:	
PERIODO HISTORICO:	CRONOLOGIA: RELATIVA:	

D I M E N S I O N E S					
Alto	Largo	Ancho	Diámetro	Espesor	Peso

MORFOLOGIA: Descripción

TECNICA DE MANUFACTURA:

ACABADOS:

DECORACION:

ESTADO DE CONSERVACION:	ESTADO DE INTEGRIDAD:

REGISTRADO POR: Fecha:	REVISADO POR: Fecha:

Figure 18.18 Inventory form

Infestation Report

MUSEUM OF HUMAN EXISTENCE
CITY, STATE 79409-3191

1. Date of Report: _____

2. Date Infestation Detected: _____ SAMPLE FORM

3. Person Investigating: _____

4. Collection/Division involved: _____

5. Specific location of infestation: _____

6. Identification of Infesting Organism: _____

      Life stage(s): _____

      Measurements: _____

7. Target material: _____

8. Description of Infestation: _____

_____

9. Action(s) taken: _____

_____

_____

_____

10. Chemical/Physical agent(s) used: _____

      Repellant: _____

      Fumigant: _____

      Freeze Chamber: ☐   Temp: _____ Duration: _____

11. Recommended follow-up procedures:

    1) _____
    _____

    2) _____
    _____

    3) _____
    _____

Report filed by: _____ Date: _____

Copies to: Director   Assistant Director   Registrar   Curator(s) of Collections

Figure 18.19 Infestation report form

El Museo de Comercio
San Francisco y Gran Columbia
Ciudad, País
Telephono 375 7 24 43 57

SAMPLE FORM

Loan Agreement
WORK OF ART

Please complete, sign, and return the original of this form. The copy is for your records.

EXHIBITION _____

DATE OF
EXHIBITION _____

DATES OF LOAN _____

LENDER _____

ADDRESS AND TELE-
PHONE NO. _____
Return shipment will be made to this address unless otherwise instructed.

CREDIT _____

ARTIST/MAKER _____

TITLE _____

MEDIUM _____ Dimensions in inches: H. _____ W. _____ D. _____
Painting, drawing, print: without frame or mat. Sculpture: no base.

DATE _____ Signature:_____
                                     How signed   Where

INSURANCE Valuation: _____
Coverage: Unless otherwise specified, the borrowing institution will insure
in the amount specified above throughout the period of the loan.

TRANSPORTATION To arrive no later than _____
                                       Shipping instructions will follow

PHOTOGRAPHS Are photographs available? Yes:_____ No:_____ If available, please send _____

Permission to reproduce in the catalog, for publicity and for education purposes, is
assumed unless otherwise stated by lender.

Is color reproduction material available?   Yes: _____ No: _____

If yes, please state type: _____
                            plates   color separations   transparencies

May this work be photographed for television broadcasts in connection with the
exhibition? Yes: _____ No: _____

CATALOG Previous collections, exhibitions, publications, bibliography. (Please indicate on
separate sheet.)

CONDITIONS **THIS LOAN IS SUBJECT TO THE CONDITIONS PRINTED ON THE**
GOVERNING LOAN **REVERSE SIDE OF THIS FORM.**

SIGNATURE OF LEGAL OWNER _____ DATE: _____

SIGNATURE OF AUTHORIZED BORROWER _____ DATE: _____
FORM REVISED 12/92

Figure 18.20 Loan form

EL MUSEO DE COMERCIO
San Francisco y Gran Colombia
Ciudad, País

SAMPLE
FORM

RECEIPT FOR LOANS

_____ 19 _____

Receipt from: _____

Address: _____

_____ Tel. _____

The following items, as a loan, to the Museo de Comercio for the period from

_____

to _____

Description	Value

It is my understanding that the above items loaned to the Museo de Comercio are subject to the conditions described on the reverse side of this receipt.

Received for the Museo de Comercio

By: _____

By: _____

_____

TO BE SIGNED UPON RETURN OF ITEMS

Received from the Museo de Comercio, the above items.

By: _____

Form Revised 4/4/92

Date: _____

Figure 18.21 Loan form

SAMPLE
FORM

CONDITIONS GOVERNING THE RECEIPT OF ITEMS LOANED TO THE MUSEO DE COMERCIO

1.   For the period of the loan the items may be exhibited, stored or otherwise used by the Museo, at our discretion, subject to our exercising the same care and decision in such exhibits, use, and storage as is customary in dealing with similar items owned by the Museo.

2.   The Museo will insure each item against fire, theft, and other casualty for the period of the loans in the amounts shown on this receipt as the value of each item. It is agreed that the liability of the Museo for loss or damage thereby ceases and is replaced by the liability of the insuring agency.

3.   It is further agreed that each item will, while on exhibit, be identified as the property of the lender.

4.   The Museo will return the items loaned to the lender on the date noted and upon presentation of this receipt.

5.   Items left with the Museo as a loan for a period of two years from the date hereof, without a request having been made for return, in consideration for its storage and safeguarding during said time, shall, after two years, be deemed an unrestricted gift to the Museo de Comercio and shall thereupon become the property of the Museo.

Figure 18.22 Reverse of loan form (Figures 18.20 and 18.21)

LOAN RECEIPT

SAMPLE
FORM

MUSEO DE ARTE
Calle Cuenca y Amazonas
Ciudad, País _____

Date Received: _____

The object(s) described below has (have) been received by El Museo de Arte as loan(s) under the conditions noted on the back of this receipt.

From:

For:

Registrar _____

Museum Number	Description	Insurance Value	

Revised 2/93

Figure 18.23 Loan receipt form

EXHIBITION REQUEST FORM

SAMPLE FORM

Send, mail or FAX the completed form to:

_____

_____

_____

For Administrative Use:

Exhibit Request No. _____

Date Received: _____

Date Reviewed: _____

Approved: ☐ Yes ☐ No

Section - Requestor Information:

_____   _____

Name   Telephone

_____ _____ _____ _____

Address   City   State   Zip

Section 2 - General Information:

Subject or title of proposed exhibition: _____

_____

Proposed duration of exhibition: ☐   6 to 8 weeks   short term

                                                   ☐   12 weeks to 1 year   temporary

                                                   ☐   1 year to 3 years   long term

Proposed beginning date: _____   _____   _____
                                                      day   month   year

Proposed ending date: _____   _____   _____
                                                      day   month   year

Provide one of the following measurements, if possible:

     Approximate number of Linear Feet required: _____

     Approximate number of Square Feet required: _____

Give an approximate number and/or description of objects/artifacts proposed to be included in the exhibition: _____

_____

_____

_____

_____

Briefly state why you think the Museum should present this exhibit: _____

_____

_____

_____

Figure 18.24.1 Exhibit request form (page 1)

Section 2 continued:
Exhibition source: (another institution or traveling service?) ☐ Yes ☐ No
   If Yes, list the source: _____

_____

Is the exhibition to be produced from within the Museum's collections? ☐ Yes ☐ No
   If Yes, list the collection area: _____
Will the exhibition include objects/artifacts from lending institutions? ☐ Yes ☐ No

   If Yes, list the institutions: _____

_____

Section 3 - Catalog Information:
Is a catalog proposed for the exhibition? ☐ Yes ☐ No
   If Yes, provide the following information:

      Number of pages: _____ Overall dimensions: _____

      Number of color photographs: _____

      Number of black and white photographs: _____

      Number of other graphics: _____

      Estimated cost of catalog production: $_____ Number printed:_____
Are other publications planned (gallery guides, posters, brochures)? ☐ Yes ☐ No
   Which? _____ Estimated cost: $ _____

Section 4 - Program Information:
What programs or special events are proposed in support of the exhibition?

   Opening reception   ☐ Yes ☐ No   Lecture(s)   ☐ Yes ☐ No

   Film(s)   ☐ Yes ☐ No   Workshop(s)   ☐ Yes ☐ No

   Outreach program(s)   ☐ Yes ☐ No   Seminar(s)   ☐ Yes ☐ No

   Gallery talk(s)   ☐ Yes ☐ No   Other: ☐ Yes ☐ No

Provide a brief statement concerning special audiences to be targeted: _____

_____

_____

_____

Are speakers, demonstrators, teachers, etc. to be invited for presentations?
   List name(s), title(s) and affiliation(s):

    1) _____

    2) _____

    3) _____

    4) _____

Figure 18.24.2 Exhibit request form (page 2)

Section 5 - Projected Budget Information
Provide an <u>estimated budget</u> for the proposed exhibition using the specified categories:

A) PRODUCTION (Supplies and materials needed to produce the exhibition).

Items	Amount

Total [   ]

B) PUBLICATIONS (Printed material to enhance, publicize and document the exhibit).

Items	Amount

Total [   ]

C) SHIPPING (List name of carrier and distance from port to port as basis for estimate).

Items	Amount

Total [   ]

D) FEES (Rental costs, consultant's, writer's, speaker's fees and/or honoraria).

Items	Amount

Total [   ]

E) INSURANCE (Include an approximate dollar valuation of object(s) as basis for the estimate).

Items	Amount

Total [   ]

GRAND TOTAL

Figure 18.24.3 Exhibit request form (page 3)

Exhibition Name		**EXHIBITION TIMELINE**	
Due Date	Requirement or Activity	Date Completed	Assignment To
_____ ( )	Timeline completed	_____	Planners
_____ ( )	Preliminary script completed	_____	Curator
_____ ( )	Object/artifact list finalized	_____	Curator
_____ ( )	Gallery/production plans due	_____	Designer
_____ ( )	Exhibition supplies ordered	_____	Designer
_____ ( )	Exhibition supplies received	_____	Designer
_____ ( )	Publicity plan formulated	_____	As Assigned
_____ ( )	Publications text/graphics due	_____	Curator
_____ ( )	Publications review completed	_____	Curator
_____ ( )	Publications items sent to printer	_____	Curator
_____ ( )	Educational plans completed	_____	Educator
_____ ( )	Exhibition label/text delivered	_____	Curator
_____ ( )	Exhibition graphics delivered	_____	Curator
_____ ( )	Shipping arrangements finalized	_____	Registrar
_____ ( )	Insurance arrangements finalized	_____	Registrar
_____ ( )	Objects/artifacts delivered	_____	Curator
_____ ( )	Condition report completed	_____	Registrar
_____ ( )	Pubs received and approved	_____	Curator
_____ ( )	Educational materials completed	_____	Educator
_____ ( )	Docent training completed	_____	Educator
_____ ( )	Reception planned/approved	_____	Team
_____ ( )	Space and services confirmed	_____	Team
_____ ( )	Exhibition installation completed	_____	Designer
_____ ( )	Director's walk-through	_____	Designer/ Curator
_____ ( )	Security walk-through	_____	Designer/ Curator

Exhibition Opening Date: _____

Comments: _____

_____

_____

_____

Form Revised 2/93

Figure 18.25 Exhibit timeline

19

Glossary of museum-related terms

Probably the greatest problem associated with any information exchange is semantics. In different regions of the same nation, words may convey different meanings and add confusion to an otherwise simple transfer of data. Communicating across national and linguistic boundaries compounds the issue. To relieve this situation and to establish a basic vocabulary, a number of museum-related terms require definition.

accession the process of transferring title or ownership from the providing source (fieldwork, purchase, gift, transfer, et cetera) to the museum.

acid-free a term generally referring to either paper or paper-board that has been treated (buffered) or made from fibers free of organic acids.

acquisition the act of gaining physical possession of an object, specimen, or sample.

adhesives glue or bonding material for joining two or more elements. There is no one adhesive that should be used on cultural or historical material. *Consult a conservation specialist* before using adhesives that cannot be reversed. Vegetable adhesives (starch paste) mixed in distilled water is considered safe for making hinges to mount works on paper. Rice starch is preferable to wheat starch as wheat is acidic.

affective learning learning based upon emotional response to stimuli; emotional learning.

alpha cellulose paper archival paper containing no sulfur – alkaline pH with 3 percent alkaline buffering. This paper should be used for applications where sulfur-free, alkaline buffered paper is required, particularly in the storage of photographic negatives and prints.

appraisal the assigning of a monetary value to an object.

artifact (artefact) an object, either two- or three-dimensional, that has been selected, altered, used, or made by human effort.

audio-visual devices machines that produce sound and/or images.

authentication to determine as genuine or the product of a particular person, region, or time.

blockbusters a term derived from the popular name of the huge bombs used in the Second World War to blast large sections of a city. In the museum sense, it refers to a revolutionary, powerful exhibition.

blue scales textile fading cards made of woolcloth dyed with blue dyes to different degrees of fastness. They show an indication of fading and are used to monitor objects on exhibit.

"box-in-a-box" configuration a frame of reference that views micro-environments as existing and dependent upon their surrounding macro-environments.

buffer a material or condition interposed between two other materials or conditions to reduce or slow the interaction between them.

canvas generally accepted as the most widely used painting surface since the fifteenth century, threads of cotton, linen, or hemp are woven to make canvas.

case a piece of exhibit furniture that encloses a space for collection object display, and that has internal lighting sources.

cataloging assigning an object to an established classification system and initiating a record of the nomenclature, provenance, number, and location of that object in the collection storage area.

clear title notes ownership without restrictions or conditions.

cleavage blisters that form between different layers of a painting that may later cause paint to come off.

cognitive learning knowledge based upon reasoned thought; rational learning.

collection an identifiable selection of objects having some significant commonality.

collection manager a person charged with care of a particular collection, normally working under the direction of a curator.

collective medium a particular means of expression used by more than one person in a collective effort, and for predetermined and agreed upon goals.

comfort freedom from stress or the fear of failure.

communication "the transfer of information and ideas with the deliberate intention to achieve certain changes, deemed desirable by the sender, in the knowledge, opinions, attitudes and/or behaviour of the reciever [*sic*]."[1]

concept-oriented exhibition a presentation that is focused upon the transmission of information and in which collection objects may or may not be used to support the story rather than being the main emphasis.

conflict of interest those acts or activities that may be construed to be contrary to ethical museum practices based on knowledge, experience, and contracts gained through conditions of employment.

conservation the processes for preserving and protecting objects from loss, decay, damage, or other forms of deterioration.

conservator a person with the appropriate scientific training to examine museum objects, works to prevent their deterioration, and provides the necessary treatment and repairs.

constituencies the various elements of the public served by a museum.

contract of gift a standard legal document used to transfer ownership of an object to a museum.

controlled environment surroundings in which temperature, relative humidity, direct sunlight, pollution, and other atmospheric conditions are regulated.

coordinating activities efforts aimed at keeping every task moving toward the same goal.

crack a crevice that goes through all layers of a picture.

crackle a series of tiny cracks that appear on a painting and look like a network of hair-like lines. These trap dirt.

cradling the addition of a series of wooden strips to the back of a panel painting applied at regular intervals both vertically and horizontally. This helps prevent the wood from separating.

cultural heritage a tradition, habit, skill, art form, or institution that is passed from one generation to the next.

cultural property the material manifestation of the concepts, habits, skills, art, or institutions of a specific people in a defined period of time.

cupping islands of varnish, paint, and possibly the ground layers which have their edges lifted. This may distort the canvas support.

curator a museum staff member or consultant who is a specialist in a particular field of study and who provides information, does research, and oversees the maintenance, use, and enhancement of collections.

deaccession the process for removing objects from a museum's collections.

deed of gift a document with the signature of the donor transferring title of an object to a museum.

designer a museum staff person or consultant who designs the exhibition, does working drawings, and coordinates fabrication and installation activities.

director the person providing conceptual leadership of the museum and charged with the responsibility for policy-making, funding, planning, organizing, staffing, supervising, and coordinating activities through the staff. The director is also responsible for the professional practices of the museum.

display the presentation of objects or information without special arrangement or interpretation based solely upon intrinsic merit. In the UK and Europe this word is used by choice instead of exhibition (q.v.).

docent a word derived from the Greek meaning a non-regular teacher. Used in the museum community to designate program or tour guides that provide informative lectures about exhibits.

educator a museum staff person or consultant who specializes in museum education and who produces instructional materials, advises about educational content for exhibitions, and oversees the implementation of educational programs.

electromagnetic radiation is the energy generated from and by light sources. The human eye is sensitive to the range of the electromagnetic spectrum from violet at the short-wavelength end through blue, green, yellow, and orange to red at the long-wavelength end.[2]

endowment a funding process in which a stated part of a money (corpus) is held to generate income and only that income may be spent.

ethafoam a polyethylene foam available in a range of densities. High-density sheets can be carved to create nests for object packing and storage. Foam shapes should be lined with acid-free tissue to avoid abrasion. Available through commercial distributors as Foamflex and Polyfoam (see: **polyfoams**).

ethics the process of establishing principles of right behavior that may serve as action guides for individuals or groups.

ethnic used in the museum community as a non-discriminatory term referring to a division or group of people distinguishable by language, custom, or some special characteristic.

evaluation report a document that sets down evaluation findings assessing an exhibition from the standpoints of meeting goals and successful development.

exhibit to present or expose to view, show, or display.

exhibit policy a written document that states a museum's philosophy and intent toward public exhibitions.

exhibition the act or fact of exhibiting collections, objects, or information to the public for the purpose of education, enlightenment, and enjoyment.

extermination the acts of either preventing the invasion of harmful organisms or of ridding a collection or collection items of an existing infestation through the use of chemical or mechanical means not considered particularly dangerous to humans in the dosages needed to kill the pests.

fabrication the work of creating the physical elements and pieces needed for the presentation of collection objects in an exhibition.

fair market value used to describe the monetary value of an object based on commercial demand rather than the perceived value established by the owner or producer.

field-generated specimens generally referring to biological material collected in the field (i.e., not in a laboratory).

field records all the data relating to material collected in the field. Should include information such as related permits, approvals, location, date, personnel, conditions, description of material collected (name, size, location, and condition), and all other pertinent and descriptive data to establish a "provenance" for the objects, samples, and/or specimens. This information may be called "field notes."

flaking total loss of the paint layers, usually associated with cleavage.

fluorescent lighting light sources in which electric current is passed through gases in a glass tube causing them to fluoresce and produce illumination.

foot-candle a unit for measuring illumination equal to the amount of light reaching a surface 1 foot square produced by a candle 1 foot away.

fumigation the use of a highly toxic chemical gas to kill any organisms existing in the target area or item. The chemicals used in fumigation are highly dangerous to humans and their use is controlled by law.

gallery a room specifically designated for exhibitions.

gallery guides written documents, usually brief and easy to carry, that are available for visitors to have and use to gain more information about an exhibition subject.

"gee whiz!" factor the tendency of humans to react positively or in awe to things that are large, colorful, famous, or in some other way out of the ordinary, hence the reaction, "gee whiz!"

gesso chalk and gelatin or casein glue painted on a surface to furnish a smooth painting ground.

graphic a two-dimensional depiction such as a photograph, painted design, drawing, silkscreen, et cetera, used to impart information, draw attention, or illustrate.

ground the white substance applied to a surface before painting is begun. Before the twentieth century, a mixture of gypsum, chalk, or marble with a glue medium, was used as a ground.

held-in-trust in some situations objects, samples, or specimens, such as those collected on governmentally controlled lands or endangered species, cannot be given with clear title; in those situations an institution/museum may choose to receive the material, give the same level of care and maintenance as the other objects in the collection, but designate it as "held-in-trust." This designation is restricted to carefully regulated situations and is not extended to collections owned or possessed by individuals. Held-in-trust collections should be carefully considered and allowed sparingly.

historic site a location with important historic connections usually relating to an important person or event.

HVAC Heating, Ventilation, and Air-Conditioning system.

hydrated salts chemicals that are hydrophilic and can be used to control relative humidity in enclosed spaces. Among these are sodium chloride, zinc sulfate, magnesium nitrate, magnesium chloride, and lithium chloride.

hydrophilic substances materials that readily absorb atmospheric water and are used as humidity buffers.

ICCROM the International Center for the Study of the Preservation and the Restoration of Cultural Property is an inter-governmental organization created by UNESCO in 1969. Its statutory functions are to collect and disseminate documentation of scientific problems of conservation, to promote research in this field, to provide advice on technical questions, and to assist in training technicians and raising the standard of restoration work. Address: ICCROM, Via di San Michele, 13, 00153 Rome, Italy.

ICOFOM International Committee for Museology – one of the standing committees of ICOM.

ICOM the International Council of Museums – the international non-governmental organization of museum and professional museum workers established to advance the interests of museology and other disciplines concerned with museum management and operations. Address: ICOM, Maison de l'Unesco, 1 rue Miollis, 75732 Paris Cedex 15, France.[3]

ICOM *Statutes* adopted by the 16th General Assembly of ICOM in The Hague, September 5, 1989, the ICOM *Statutes* describe and define ICOM organization, its role, membership, method, and objectives.

ICTOP International Committee for Training of Personnel – one of the standing committees of ICOM.

incandescent lighting light sources in which an electric current causes a filament to glow or incandesce producing illumination.

inert products made of non-reactive, chemically balanced materials with special attention given to acidic neutrality.

infestation a population of living organisms that exists in collections or collection items. The organisms may be as large as rats and mice, or as small as moths or fungi.

infrared radiation (IR) the part of the electromagnetic spectrum below visible light that humans interpret as heat.

inpainting areas that have been repaired by being filled in or "stopped" are covered with a thin layer of shellac, then tempera or oil paint is used to fill in the missing area. Inpainting is removable, yet masks defects.

insecticide any substance used to eliminate insects.

interactive a device that invites and accommodates interaction between the viewer and itself.

interpretation the act or process of explaining or clarifying, translating, or presenting a personal understanding about a subject or object.

inventory an itemized list of the objects included in a museum's collections.

left brain the left hemisphere of the human brain; the center for analytical thought, language, reasoning, reading, writing, and counting.

leisure activities activities that people engage in when they are not involved in a professional pursuit.

light meter electronic lux and foot-candle meters measure both low and high intensity levels in storage and exhibit areas. A photographic light meter is a relatively inexpensive device that can be used to measure light levels. These meters give approximate readings to as low as 5 foot-candles (50 lux).

lignin-free storage cases, boxes, and board containing no lignin, a complex organic acid that acts as a binding agent in woody plants.

lux a unit of illumination equal to the illumination of a 1 meter square surface uniformly 1 meter away from a candle equal to five foot-candles.

macro-environments the totality of the surrounding conditions and circumstances present in spaces generally room-size and larger.

management-oriented activities tasks that focus on providing the resources and personnel needed to realize a product.

Maslow's Hierarchy[4] a behavioral construction by Abraham H. Maslow that relates the sequential and consecutive nature of human needs to motivations.

mat, matte a border put around an image (picture) either as a frame or as a protective layer between the image and the frame.

micro-environments the totality of the surrounding conditions and circumstances present in small, often enclosed spaces.

mildew microscopic fungi that attack organic materials that are exposed to high humidity and dampness.

mission statement a written document that states a museum's institutional philosophy, scope, and responsibility.

mounting the attachment of an object/graphic to a supporting surface.

museology the branch of knowledge concerned with the study of the theories, procedures, concepts, and organization of museums.

museum "a museum is a non-profit-making, permanent institution in the service of society and of its development, and open to the public which acquires, conserves, researches, communicates and exhibits, for purposes of study, education and enjoyment, material evidence of people and their environment."[5]

"natural" buffering the interaction between collection objects and their surroundings in an enclosed space that reduces or slows fluctuations in relative humidity and temperature.

natural light the light produced by the sun that penetrates the Earth's atmosphere.

nomenclature a system of names used to describe museum objects.

object file a careful listing of all actions or activities impacting a particular object in the museum's collections including all conservation, restoration, exhibition, loan, or other uses of the object.

object-oriented exhibition a presentation of

collection objects with a primary goal of providing their exposure to public view with limited interpretation.

official repository in dealing with archaeological and scientific material collected on regulated land, it is not unusual for a particular institution/museum to be designated, by agreement, as the "official repository" for those materials. All objects taken from the particular location are deposited into the collections of the designated institution/museum.

100 percent rag a term referring to the material content of paper or board indicating a fiber composition other than wood – usually cotton or linen.

one-time only a common term in US jargon to mean a thing or situation may be done once but no more. Museums may allow "one-time only" use of photographic images of works of art in the collection, meaning permission is granted for one publication to include the image. In budgeting, "one-time only" requests are usually for special items that once purchased will not be requested again in the foreseeable future. In the UK the term would be "one-off."

open storage the practice of placing stored collections on public view without interpretation or planned educational content.

panel painting a painting support prepared, in the case of large works, by joining several wooden boards together. If heavy or thick enough, these boards may be pegged or reinforced with cross bars.

particulate matter any materials capable of being airborne: dust.

patrimony cultural property, both intellectual and real, passed from one generation to the next.

pattern recognition a visual–mental process that seeks and recognizes familiar things or patterns.

pH balanced a neutral balance of acid and alkaline.

pollutants gases and airborne particulate matter usually resulting from combustion or venting of chemicals associated with human, industrial, or other activities.

polyfoams polyethylene, polypropylene, polystyrene, and polyurethane foams are especially suited to packing for shipment. Polyethylene foams are the most chemically inert.

preparation arranging, attaching, supporting and other such activities that prepare an object/graphic for exhibit.

preventive conservation collection care to minimize conditions that may cause damage.

product-oriented activities exhibition development efforts concerned with collection objects and interpretive aims.

production the combined activities of fabrication, preparation, facilities renovation, and installation of exhibitions.

project manager a staff person who oversees the whole process of exhibition development by facilitating communication and assisting in providing resources, with the goal to see the project through to its predetermined objectives.

provenance from the French meaning derivation or origin of an object. The word is sometimes spelled "provenience" from the Latin, having substantially the same meaning. "Provenance" is used in this publication as it is the spelling used in the ICOM *Code of Professional Ethics*.

psychrometer a device for measuring relative humidity using the differences in the measurements from dry- and wet-bulb thermometers in moving air.

PVA polyvinyl acetate; a thermoplastic with good aging characteristics sometimes used as a fixative or sealing agent.

recording hygrothermograph a device for measuring and recording on a paper chart both temperature and humidity over time.

registrar the person charged with registering objects accessioned into a museum's collections, maintaining the registration records, and assigning the accession number.

registration assigning a permanent number to an object entering a museum's collections for the purpose of identification and collection management.

relative humidity the amount of water in a given volume of air compared to the amount of water vapor the same volume of air will hold at saturation (100 percent RH) at a given temperature.

relic a non-specific term used to describe things from the past, sometimes applied to ethnographic or historic objects.

relining when damage or decay of a painting is so bad that simple treatments will not slow the process, the entire picture, including the old canvas, is mounted on a new support. Usually new lined canvas is used, and a hot or cold setting adhesive joins the two canvases.

right brain the right hemisphere of the human brain; the center for intuitive thought, emotional or affective learning, and visualization.

security personnel those members of the museum staff assigned to the role and responsibility of maintaining security. Normally uniformed personnel with specific duties relating to security of visitors as well as objects exhibited and stored in the museum.

silica gel a commonly used hydrophilic substance

composed of a silicon + oxygen bond, neutral toward other substances, that can be used to control relative humidity within closed containers.

solander boxes conservation quality storage boxes of a particular type.

specimen an example of a particular class of objects normally used when referring to natural science collections.

sticky trap small paper traps treated with a sticky substance to catch and hold crawling insects. Sticky traps are useful in determining entry points and pathways of insects in and around the museum. Traps are numbered and located throughout the museum. With regular inspection, information can be gained about the type, number, entry, and direction of insects. From this data an insect control plan can be developed.

stopping after a painting has been cleaned, and in some cases relined, the damaged area is filled in or "stopped" to the level of the rest of the surface, then inpainted.

strategic planning sometimes called forward or long-range planning – the process integrates the physical, financial, philosophical, and educational goals of the museum or a particular collection area.

study collection objects collected and organized for research or instructional use not for exhibition.

subtitle an intermediate level of written information graphic, usually larger in typesize than a text block, and used to differentiate or emphasize subgroupings within an exhibition.

tactile exhibits exhibits that are designed to be touched.

target audience any sub-group within a population that can be identified by some common factor or factors, and that is specifically chosen as a group to be attracted.

tempera paint when referring to old painting, paint made of pigments mixed in an egg yolk or whole egg binding medium. Modern tempera paints are those containing an oil in emulsion, and used with water as a medium.

text or text block a written graphic that aids in the interpretation of groups of objects or exhibition sections.

thematic exhibitions exhibitions based upon a connecting theme that directs the choice of collection objects and information content.

thermohygrometer a device for measuring temperature and humidity levels.

title sign a graphic, often combining both text and pictorial design elements, usually placed at the entry to a gallery to attract attention and to announce the title of the exhibition.

tungsten–halogen bulbs (lamps) there are two types of bulbs (lamps) commonly used in museum exhibition illumination, PAR bulbs (parabolic aluminized reflector) and MR-16 (low-voltage, tungsten–halogen). MR-16 bulbs are smaller and more efficient than PAR bulbs; however, because they are low-voltage (12V), a transformer is required for use with standard electrical output.

type specimen the giving of names to identify biology specimens is taxonomy and central to this process is the type system. The word "type" in the name of the species indicates the earliest valid name used to describe that zoological specimen based on publication date. "A type specimen is the actual specimen that the taxonomist described as a new species and is the ultimate arbiter of the definition of that species."[6]

ultraviolet light (UV) the part of the electromagnetic spectrum immediately above the visible range: black light.

UNESCO United Nations Educational, Scientific, and Cultural Organization.

UNESCO Convention this Convention on the Means of Prohibiting and Preventing the Illicit Import, Export, and Transfer of Ownership of Cultural Property is to provide a process among nations for regulating international trade in cultural property.

Values-and-Lifestyles Segments (VALS)[7] a generalized socio-economic structure by Arnold Mitchell that helps identify population segments, interests, and motivations by their collective values and lifestyles.

varnish the removable outer protective layer that enhances the appearance of a painting. The varnish may be removed and replaced several times in the life of a painting.

visible light spectrum (VLS) those frequencies of the electromagnetic spectrum to which the human eye is visually sensitive; radiation that is perceived as light.

vitrine a piece of exhibit furniture, typically consisting of a base or pedestal with a clear enclosure on top for displaying objects, having no internal lighting sources.

wayfinders any visual, tactile, or auditory clues or devices that assist visitors in orienting themselves within a museum's facilities and surroundings, and help them locate destinations.

work of art an object of aesthetic importance created by a human being.

world-view an individual's rational model of reality; one's mental picture of the world consisting of facts, raw perceptual data, concepts, suppositions, theories, and generalizations.

Notes

1. Ferree, H. (ed.) (undated) *Groot praktijkboek voor effectieve communicatie*, Deventer, Antwerpen, pp. 13–15.
2. Thompson, J. M. A. (ed.) (1984) *Manual of Curatorship*, London: Butterworth.
3. International Council of Museums (1990) "Name and Legal Status," *Statutes*, Paris: ICOM, p. 1, article 1, paragraph 1.
4. Maslow, A. (1954) *Motivation and Personality*, New York: Harper & Row Publishers.
5. International Council of Museums (1990), "Definitions," *Statutes*, article 2, paragraph 1.
6. Thompson (ed.) *Manual of Curatorship*.
7. Mitchell, A. (1982) *The Nine American Lifestyles*, New York: Warner Books.

20
Bibliography

Adams, G. D. (1983) *Museum Public Relations*, Vol. 2, AASLH Management Series, Nashville, Tenn.: American Association for State and Local History. ISBN 0-910050-65-1.

Alderson, W. and S. Low (1987) *Interpretation of Historic Sites*, 2nd edn rev., Nashville, Tenn.: American Association for State and Local History. ISBN 0-910050-73-2.

Alexander, E. (1979) *Museums in Motion, An Introduction to the History and Functions of Museums*, 4th printing 1986, Nashville, Tenn.: American Association for State and Local History. ISBN 0-910050-35-X.

—— (1983) *Museum Masters, Their Museums and Their Influence*, Nashville, Tenn.: American Association for State and Local History. ISBN 0-910050-68-6.

Ambrose, T. and S. Runyard (1991) *Forward Planning*, London: Routledge. ISBN 0-415 06482-1 (cloth); ISBN 0-415-07026-0 (paper).

American Association of Museums (1969)*America's Museums: The Belmont Report*, Washington, DC: American Association of Museums. Library of Congress Catalog Card Number 74-80109.

Appelbaum, B. (1991) *Guide to Environmental Protection of Collections*, Madison, Conn.: Sound View Press. ISBN 0-932087-16-7.

Association of Art Museum Directors (1981) *Professional Practices in Art Museums, Report of the Ethics and Standards Committee*, Savannah, Ga.: Association of Art Museum Directors. Library of Congress Catalog Card Number 81-66765.

Bachmann, K. (ed.) (1992) *Conservation Concerns – A Guide for Collections and Curators*, Washington, DC: Smithsonian Institution Press. ISBN 1-56098-174-1.

Bandes, S. (project director) (1984) *Caring for Collections*, Washington, DC: American Association of Museums. ISBN (none listed).

Beibel, D. (1978) *Registration Methods for the Small Museum*, Nashville, Tenn.: American Association for State and Local History. ISBN 0-910050-37-6.

Belcher, M. (1991) *Exhibitions in Museums*, Leicester: Leicester University Press. ISBN 0-87474-913-1.

Blatti, J. (ed.) (1987) *Past Meets Present, Essays about Historic Interpretation and Public Audiences*, Washington, DC: Smithsonian Institution Press. ISBN 0-87474-272-2.

Bloom, J. and E. Powell (eds) (1984) *Museums for a New Century. A Report of the Commission on Museums for a New Century*, Washington, DC: American Association of Museums. ISBN 0-931201-08-X.

Brill, T. (1980) *Light – Its Interaction with Art and Antiquities*, New York and London: Plenum Press. ISBN 0-306-40416-8.

Burcaw, G. E. (1975) *Introduction to Museum Work*, 2nd edn 1983, Nashville, Tenn.: American Association for State and Local History. ISBN 0-910050-69-4.

Burstein, D. and F. Stasiowski (1982) *Project Management for the Design Professional*, London: Whitney Library of Design, an imprint of Watson-Guptill Publications. ISBN 0-8230-7434-X.

Dudley, D., I. Wilkinson, *et al.* (1981) *Museum Registration Methods*, 3rd edn rev., Washington, DC: American Association of Museums. ISBN (none listed); Library of Congress Catalog Number 79-52058.

Ellis, M. (1987) *The Care of Prints and Drawings*, Nashville, Tenn.: American Association of State and Local History. ISBN 0-910050-79-1.

Evelyn, H. (ed.) (1970) *Training of Museum Personnel*, London: ICOM. ISBN 0-238-78952-7.

Finlay, I. (1977) *Priceless Heritage: The Future of Museums*, London: Faber & Faber. ISBN 0-571-09107-5.

Finley, D. E. (1973) *A Standard of Excellence, Andrew W. Mellon Founds the National Gallery of Art at Washington, D.C.*, Washington, DC: Smithsonian Institution Press. ISBN 0-87474-132-7.

Finn, D. (1985) *How to Visit a Museum*, New York: Harry Abrams, Inc. ISBN 0-8109-2297-5.

Fondation de France/ICOM (1991) *Museums Without Barriers*, Paris: Fondation de France/ICOM in conjunction with Routledge. ISBN 0-415-05454-0 (cloth); ISBN 0-415-06994-7 (paper).

Genoways, H., C. Jones, and O. Rossolimo (eds) (1987) *Mammal Collection Management*, Lubbock, Tex.: Texas Tech University Press. ISBN 0-89672-157-5 (cloth); ISBN 0-89672-156-6 (paper).

George, G. and C. Sherrell-Leo (1989) *Starting Right, A Basic Guide to Museum Planning*, Nashville, Tenn.: American Association for State and Local History. ISBN 0-910050-78-3.

Guldbeck, P. (1972) *The Care of Historical Collections, A Conservation Handbook for the Nonspecialist*, 2nd edn 1976, Nashville, Tenn.: American Association for State and Local History. ISBN 0-910050-07-4.

—— (MacLeish, A. ed.) (1986) *The Care of Antiques and Historical Collections*, 2nd printing, Nashville, Tenn.: American Association for State and Local History. ISBN 0-910050-73-2.

Harley, R. D. (1970) *Artists' Pigments c. 1600–1835*, 2nd edn 1982, London: Butterworth Scientific. ISBN 0-408-70945-6.

Hooper-Greenhill, E. (1991) *Museum and Gallery Education*, Leicester: Leicester University Press. ISBN 0-7185-1306-1.

—— (1992) *Museums and the Shaping of Knowledge*, London: Routledge. ISBN 0-415-06145-8; ISBN 0-415-07031-7 (paper).

Horie, C. V. (1987) *Materials for Conservation*, London: Butterworth & Co. ISBN 0-40801-531-4.

Houle, C. (1990) *Governing Boards, Their Nature and Nurture*, San Francisco, Calif.: Jossey-Bass Publishers. ISBN 1-55542-157-1.

Howie, F. (ed.) (1987) *Safety in Museums and Galleries*, London: Butterworth & Co. (in association with the International Journal of Museum Management and Curatorship). ISBN 0-408-02362-7.

Hudson, K. (1977) *Museums for the 1980s*, New York: Holmes & Meier Publishers, Inc. ISBN 0-333-22031-5.

International Committee on Museum Security (1986) *A Manual of Basic Museum Security*, London: ICOM. ISBN 0-85022-209-5.

International Council of Museums (1986) *Public View, The ICOM Handbook of Museum Public Relations*, Paris: ICOM. ISBN 92-9012-107-6.

—— (1990) *Statutes*, Paris: ICOM.

Jones, B. (1986) *Protecting Historic Architecture and Museum Collections From Natural Disaster*, London: Butterworth & Co. ISBN 0-409-90035-4.

Kanikow, R. (1987) *Exhibit Design*, New York: PBC International. ISBN 0-86636-001-8.

Karp, I., C. Kreamer, and S. Lavine (eds) (1992) *Museums and Communities: The Politics of Public Culture*, Washington, DC: Smithsonian Institution Press. ISBN 1-56098-164-4 (cloth); ISBN 1-56098-189-X (paper).

Karp, I. and S. Lavine (eds) (1991) *Exhibiting Cultures: The Poetics and Politics of Museum Display*, Washington, DC: Smithsonian Institution Press. ISBN 1-56098-020-6 (cloth); ISBN 1-56098-021-4 (paper).

Katz, H. and M. Katz (1965) *Museums, U.S.A.*, Garden City, NY.: Doubleday & Co. Inc. ISBN (none listed); Library of Congress Catalog Card Number 65-12364.

Kavanagh, G. (ed.) (1991) *Museum Languages*, Leicester: Leicester University Press. ISBN 0-7185-1359-2.

—— (ed.) (1991) *The Museums Profession*, Leicester: Leicester University Press. ISBN 0-7185-1387-8.

Key, A. F. (1973) *Beyond Four Walls*, Toronto: McClelland & Stewart Ltd. ISBN 0-7710-4520-4.

Klein, L. (1986) *Exhibits: Planning and Design*, New York: Madison Square Press. ISBN 0-942604-18-0.

Kühn, H. (1986) *Conservation and Restoration of Works of Art and Antiquities*, Vol. 1, London: Butterworth & Co. ISBN 0-408-10851-7.

Lewis, R. (1976) *Manual for Museums*, Washington, DC: National Park Service, US Department of Interior. ISBN (none listed). US Goverment Printing Office Stock Number 024-005-00643-5.

Light, R., D. Roberts, and J. Stewart (eds) (1986) *Museum Documentation Systems*, London: Butterworth & Co. ISBN 0-408-10815-0.

Loomis, R. (1987) *Museum Visitor Evaluation: New Tool for Management*, Vol. 3, AASLH Management Series, Nashville, Tenn.: American Association for State and Local History. ISBN 0-910050-83-X.

Loor, L. (1987) *El museo como instrumento de aprendizaje*, Cuenca: Banco Central del Ecuador. ISBN (none listed).

Lord, B. and G. Lord (1983) *Planning Our Museum* (La Planification de nos musées), National Museums of Canada, Ottawa. Distributed by Nashville, Tenn.: American Association for State and Local History. ISBN 0-660-90275-3.

Lord, B., G. Lord and J. Nicks (1989) *The Cost of Collecting, Collection Management in UK Museums*, London: Her Majesty's Stationery Office. ISBN 0-11-290476-9.

Malaro, M. (1985) *A Legal Primer on Managing Museum Collections*, 2nd edn 1987, Washington, DC: Smithsonian Institution Press. ISBN 0-87474-656-6.

Mayo, E. (1984) *American Material Culture*, Bowling Green, OH: Bowling Green State University Popular Press. ISBN 0-87972-303-3.

Merriman, N. (1991) *Beyond the Glass Case*, Leicester: Leicester University Press. ISBN 0-7185-1349-5.

Messenger, P. (ed.) (1989) *The Ethics of Collecting Cultural Property*, Albuquerque, NM: University of New Mexico Press. ISBN 0-8263-1167-9.

Miller, R. (1980) *Personnel Policies for Museums: A Handbook for Management*, Washington, DC: American Association of Museums. ISBN (none listed); Library of Congress Catalog Card Number 80-80231.

Mills, J. and R. White (1987) *The Organic Chemistry of Museum Objects*, London: Butterworth & Co. ISBN 0-408-11810-5.

Mora, P., L. Mora and P. Philippot (1984) *Conservation of Wall Paintings*, London: Butterworth. ISBN 0-408-10812-6.

Museum Education Roundtable (1992) *Patterns in Practice*, Washington, DC: Museum Education Roundtable. ISBN 1-880437-00-7.

Neal, A. (1969) *HELP! for the Small Museum, Handbook of Exhibit Ideas and Methods*, Boulder, Colo.: Pruett Publishing. ISBN (none listed); Library of Congress Catalog Card Number 70-75438.

—— (1976) *Exhibits for the Small Museum*, Nashville, Tenn.: American Association for State and Local History. ISBN 0-910050-23-6.

Nichols, S. (ed.) (1984) *Museum Education Anthology 1973–1983*, Museum Education Roundtable, Washington, DC: American Association of Museums. ISBN (none listed).

O'Connell, B. (1985) *The Board Member's Book*, New York: The Foundation Center. ISBN 0-87954-133-4.

Olkowski, W., S. Doar, and H. Olkowski (1991) *Common-Sense Pest Control*, Newton, Conn.: The Taunton Press. ISBN 0-942391-63-2.

Pearce, S. (ed.) (1989) *Museum Studies in Material Culture*, Leicester: Leicester University Press. ISBN 0-7185-1288-X (cloth); ISBN 0-7185-1391-6 (paper).

—— (ed.) (1990) *Objects of Knowledge*, London: Athlone Press Ltd. ISBN 0-485-90001-7.

—— (ed.) (1991) *Museum Economics and the Community*, London: Athlone Press Ltd. ISBN 0-485-90002-5.

Pederson, A. (ed.) (1987) *Keeping Archives*, Sydney: Australian Society of Archivists. ISBN 0-9595565-9-1.

Phelan, M. (1982) *Museums and the Law*, Vol. 1, AASLH Management Series, Nashville, Tenn.: American Association for State and Local History. ISBN 0-910050-60-0.

Phillips, C. and P. Hogan (1984) *A Culture at Risk, Who Cares for America's Heritage?* Nashville, Tenn.: American Association for State and Local History. ISBN (none listed).

Plenderleith, H. and A. Werner (1956) *The Conservation of Antiquities and Works of Art*, 2nd edn 1974, London: Oxford University Press. ISBN 0-19-212960-0.

Quimby, M. (ed.) (1978) *Material Culture and the Study of American Life*, New York: W. W. Norton & Co. Inc. ISBN 0-393-05661-9 (cloth); ISBN 0-393-05665-1 (paper).

Reeve, J. (1986) *The Art of Showing Art*, Tulsa, Okla.: HCE Publications and Council Oak Books. ISBN 0-933031-04-1.

Reinwardt Academie (1983) *Exhibition Design as an Educational Tool*, Leiden: Reinwardt Academie. ISBN (none listed).

Research and Education Association (1982) *Handbook of Museum Technology*, New York: Research and Education Association. ISBN 0-87891-540-0.

Roberts, D. (1990) *Terminology for Museums*, Cambridge: Museum Documentation Association. ISBN 0-905963-62-8.

Schröder, H. (1981) *Museum Security Survey*, Paris: International Council of Museums. ISBN (none listed).

Sellers, C. (1980) *Mr. Peale's Museum*, New York: W. W. Norton & Co, Inc. ISBN 0-393-05700-3.

Serrell, B. (1985) *Making Exhibit Labels*, Nashville, Tenn.: American Association for State and Local History. ISBN 0-910050-64-3.

Shelley, M. (1987) *The Care and Handling of Art Objects*, New York: Metropolitan Museum of Art. ISBN 0-87099-318-6; (Abrams) ISBN 0-8109-1040-3.

Stolow, N. (1986) *Conservation and Exhibitions*, London: Butterworth & Co. ISBN 0-408-01434-2.

Taylor, L. (1987) *A Common Agenda for History Museums*, conference proceedings, Nashville, Tenn.: American Association for State and Local History, and Washington, DC: The Smithsonian Institution. ISBN (none listed).

Thompson, G. (1978) *The Museum Environment*, London: Butterworth & Co. Ltd. ISBN 0-408-70792-5.

Thompson, J. M. A. (ed.) (1984) *Manual of Curatorship, A Guide to Museum Practice*, 2nd edn 1992, London: Butterworth & Co. ISBN 0-7506-0351-8.

Tillotson, R. (D. Menkes ed.) (1977) *La Sécurité dans les musées*, (Museum Security), Paris: International Council of Museums. ISBN (none listed); Library of Congress Catalog Card Number 77-74644.

Ullberg, A. and P. Ullberg (1981) *Museum Trustee-ship*, Washington, DC: American Association of Museums. ISBN (none listed). Library of Congress Catalog Card Number: 81-68741.

van Mensch, P. (ed.) (1989) *Professionalising the Muses*, Amsterdam: AHA Books. ISBN 90-5246-013-2.

Verhaar, J. and H. Meeter (1989) *Project Model Exhibitions*, Leiden: Reinwardt Academie. ISBN (none listed).

Weil, S. E. (1983) *Beauty and the Beasts, On Museums, Art, The Law, and The Market*, Washington, DC: Smithsonian Institution Press. ISBN 0-87474-958-1 (cloth); ISBN 0-87474-957-3 (paper).

—— (1990) *Rethinking the Museum and Other Meditations*, Washington, DC: Smithsonian Institution Press. ISBN 0-87474-948-4 (cloth); ISBN 0-87474-953-0 (paper).

Witteborg, L. (1981) *Good Show! A Practical Guide for Temporary Exhibitions*, Washington, DC: Smithsonian Institution Traveling Exhibition Service. ISBN 0-86528-007-X.

Wittlin, A. S. (1970) *Museums: In Search of a Usable Future*, Cambridge, Mass.: MIT Press. ISBN 0-262-23039-9.

Zycherman, L. (ed.) (1988) *A Guide to Museum Pest Control*, Washington, DC: Association of Systematics Collections. ISBN 0-942924-14-2.

Index